TREES, SHRUBS AND FLOWERS TO KNOW

IN BRITISH COLUMBIA

TREES, SHRUBS AND FLOWERS

TO KNOW

IN BRITISH COLUMBIA

C. P. LYONS

ILLUSTRATIONS BY THE AUTHOR

J. M. DENT & SONS (CANADA) LIMITED
TORONTO   VANCOUVER

Published by
J. M. DENT & SONS (CANADA) LIMITED

Hardcover ISBN 0-460-95300-1

Paperback ISBN 0-460-95301-X

Printed and bound in Canada
by
THE ALGER PRESS LIMITED
Oshawa, Canada

TABLE OF CONTENTS

●

ABOUT THIS ILLUSTRATED GUIDE

PURPOSE:

To most people a string of words such as "radical leaves; short-petioled, obovate-flabelliform, crenately toothed; cauline sessile . . ." might well be a druggist's prescription or words to an ancient Greek war dance. But to the trained botanist they describe concisely and accurately part of the anatomy of one particular little buttercup. While not belittling the value of a special jargon to the scientist this book attempts a different treatment—one suitable for the non-specialist who wants guidance in terms of everyday language and observation opportunities.

You should realize that there is plenty of scope to record your own observations and thereby add to the start made here. As your interest grows you may well investigate more technical writings covering family relationships and the almost unbelievable intricacies of floral structure, adaption to environment, pollenization and seed dispersal. It is hoped this small book will provide the incentive.

SPECIAL FEATURES:

Illustrations are given for nearly every described tree, shrub, and flower. These not only show the conspicuous detail but depict the form and size of an average specimen. The complex arrangement of minute flower parts has not been attempted but rather the impression the eye receives of the outstanding aspect of flower, leaf, fruit, or cone.

On page 6 will be found a map of the Province with the different biotic or life zones shown. Each zone has its peculiarities of climate which reflect in the type of flora to be found. Lists of the more common plants for each zone are given. From this grouping persons travelling throughout British Columbia may be aware of the different zones they pass through and what is likely to be found.

Illustrated keys for the trees have been given which allow an easy and rapid breakdown to individual species. The shrubs have been grouped in various size classes and regrouped further to bring together those with a similarity of form or habitat. Flowers have been divided on the basis of broad color groups. An illustrated page makes it easy to recognize eight of the more common ferns in British Columbia. Edible plants are always interesting and knowledge of them may be vital in case of emergency. The more common ones have been listed in a special table.

The Flowering Timetables will be of special value to visitors unfamiliar with the native plants. A quick glance will show which shrubs and flowers will be in bloom at any particular time of the year. The chart also can prove of help by suggesting possibilities to the observer. Anyone climbing a mountain or crossing a high divide will find the Altitudinal Chart a handy guide to what may be expected at different elevation ranges.

BOOK ARRANGEMENT:

A departure is made from botanical tradition in arrangement whereby an arbutus tree, salal bush and clump of heather conceivably might follow one another because of their similarity in minute flower parts. Broad divisions have been made into trees, shrubs, flowers, and ferns. These are further arranged to bring together plants that frequent the same habitat or closely resemble one another. For example unarmed creepers form one group, plants growing in wet bogs another, and so on.

NAMES:

To lessen confusion, botanical and common names are correlated in large degree to those used in "Pocket Guide to the Trees and Shrubs of British Columbia" published in 1963 by the B.C. Forest Service. Scientific names for flowers, in most cases, follow those in "Vascular Plants of the Pacific Northwest" by Hitchcock, Cronquist, Ownbey, Thompson.

Common names do not always coincide with the above publications because an attempt has been made to retain familiar ones and use others with broad descriptive value. Where common names are not in general usage, a name accepted elsewhere has been taken. Redstem Ceanothus (*Ceanothus sanguineus*) and Mallow Ninebark (*Physocarpus malvaceus*) are two so designated. Where no common name reference could be found a simple descriptive name has been given as in the following: Pyramidal Spirea (*Spiraea pyramidata*) and Sub-alpine Blackberry (*Rubus nivalis*).

Scientific names are known throughout the world while common names are often a matter of local usage. The Latin name usually is in two parts like a person's. The following chart shows how a comparison might be made:

ANGLO-SAXONS	ERICACEAE
(A clan of peoples)	(A clan of plants)
JONES, SMITH, CLARK	VACCINIUM, RHODODENDRON, GAULTHERIA
(Families in the clan)	(Families in the clan)
JONES, WILLIAM	VACCINIUM OVALIFOLIUM
(A certain individual)	(A certain blueberry)

The last part of the Latin name is either a descriptive term or honors someone who discovered or described the plant. Often you will see such words as ovalifolium (oval—foliage or leaves) and tomentose (covered with matted hairs) which, if their Latin derivation is known, give leading clues. *Arbutus menziesii* and *Larix lyallii* show the significance of arbutus first being found by Archibald Menzies, surgeon and botanist with Captain Vancouver during his explorations from 1790-1795. Dr. David Lyall was also a surgeon and botanist who worked with the International Boundary Survey while the British Columbia-Washington Boundary was being marked. Significantly enough the only place in the Province where alpine larch is found other than the Rockies is along the International Boundary near the Hope-Princeton Highway.

ACKNOWLEDGMENT:

It is realized that many years of study and preparation properly could go into this book rather than the short time taken. Had it been necessary to puzzle over plant identifications in the usual way little progress could have been made. While not wishing to hold Mr. George Hardy, former Provincial Botanist, responsible for any discrepancies it can be said that his cheerful helpfulness throughout made this book possible. A number of persons have aided by collecting specimens and reporting on blooming times here and there. In any such book as this, constant revision, checking and re-arrangement become necessary. These and many other tasks have been undertaken by my wife. Without this extensive help and encouragement the book would have become a burdensome task instead of a project of sustained interest.

C. P. LYONS
876 Glengarry Place
Victoria, B.C. V9A 4N5

HOW TO USE THIS BOOK

I. IS IT A TREE, SHRUB OR FLOWER?

TREES have strong trunks covered with bark. They are usually over 20' high with trunks more than 2" in diameter. There may be a single trunk or a number of them.

SHRUBS have tough woody stems with a bark cover. Generally they are under 20' in height and 2" in diameter and have several stems.

FLOWERS have soft stems which die each year. Sometimes the root lives on producing a new flower each summer (perennials). Some flowers grow from seed and only live a year (annuals).

CONFUSING FORMS OF SHRUBS AND TREES AND HOW THEY ARE GROUPED IN THIS BOOK

AS TREES

Alders (mountain and Sitka)
Cherries
Dogwood
Junipers
Maples (vine and Douglas)
Western yew
Willows (Pacific and peachleaf)

AS SHRUBS

Elder (blue-berry)
Willows (all except two)
Mountain ashes
Scrub birch

II. MAKE SURE YOU HAVE A TYPICAL SAMPLE SPECIMEN!

Young shoots often have unnaturally large and misshapen leaves. Look carefully for flowers and fruit. Check a number of plants if necessary.

III. STUDY THE APPROPRIATE KEY!

See inside front and back cover for keys to the trees, and pages 54 - 55 for help with the shrubs. The Elevation Range Chart on page 14 and the Biotic Zone Lists on page 6 give the common flora of each region which helps in narrowing the field and suggesting possibilities.

IV. COMPARE LEAF, FLOWER AND FRUIT DETAILS WITH DRAWINGS AND NOTES!

All the native trees are illustrated and all the native shrubs except the less common and confusing species of willow, currant, gooseberry and wild rose. These usually have features in common with illustrated varieties which allow for a general grouping. Only the more common flowers and eye-catching plants and ferns are included.

V. COLOR THE DRAWINGS!

Use colored pencils, crayons or water colors to tone the drawings the correct color of living specimens. A touch of color will work wonders.

THE FLORA OF BRITISH COLUMBIA

There is always the tendency to think that something more attractive and interesting lies just beyond our reach. For example, how colorful the Eastern hardwoods are pictured, the exotic waving palms of California or the bristling cacti of New Mexico. But perhaps if we made a quick inventory of British Columbia we would appreciate what an outstanding variety of flora there is within a few miles of us. No less than seven out of the ten recognized forest regions of all Canada are found here. Few provinces can claim more than two types.

No other place in Canada has the parching desert climate of the South Okanagan and Similkameen Valleys. Here on the sun-baked slopes and benches grow the twisted antelope bush, the drab sagebrush and mats of spiny cactus. What a striking contrast with the sombre Coast forest with its forest giants, lush green ferns and thick ground cover of bracken and salal.

The floral changes experienced in a few miles of distance are amazing. Mountains rise from the shadowy forests of giants at sea level, through the twisted and stunted sub-alpine trees and shrubs, beyond the brilliant flower meadows of alpine terrain and continue bleak and bold until finally capped by ice or snow. Here in this land of solitude and silence, at elevations of from 7,500 to 10,000 feet, the conditions are similar to that of the arctic wastes. Tiny flowers and mosses pinch themselves into sheltered niches and smile briefly and brightly during the fleeting summer they know.

Over 3,000 different plants, which term includes trees and shrubs, have been collected in British Columbia. New ones are discovered each year and the list should grow for many years. Only the sketchiest of botanical information is available on the northern half of the Province.

A full appreciation of the trees, shrubs and flowers is often dulled because we are in such close association with them. Perhaps like old and valued friends they are taken too much for granted or possibly because they are strangers, the true worth of them isn't realized.

Our famous scenery, beautiful lakes and streams, watersheds, and commercial timber stands are only of value as long as the trees and plants are properly evaluated and managed. Learn first to recognize the flora as individuals. Then notice the special conditions each requires. See how the hardhack masses in wet road ditches or around ponds, the skunk cabbage in black muddy soil. Certain other plants will be discovered every time the hardhack or skunk cabbage is found. As more and more plants are identified there comes the realization that every one is part of an intricate living community; a community in very delicate balance, a friend if understood or a potential enemy in the form of floods, erosion or scenic scars if mishandled.

You will find these forest friends almost as close as your next door neighbor. Make their acquaintance and you can't help meeting more and more relations, each with some specially attractive feature to add pleasure to your every outing.

BIOTIC OR LIFE ZONE MAP

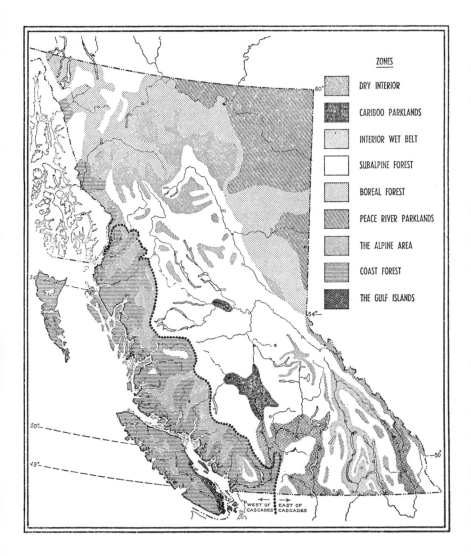

ZONES

DRY INTERIOR

CARIBOO PARKLANDS

INTERIOR WET BELT

SUBALPINE FOREST

BOREAL FOREST

PEACE RIVER PARKLANDS

THE ALPINE AREA

COAST FOREST

THE GULF ISLANDS

NOTE: The ranges employed here are adapted from the classification given by J. A. Munro and Dr. I. McT. Cowan in "A Review of the Bird Fauna of British Columbia" and published by the British Columbia Provincial Museum, Victoria, B.C.

BIOTIC OR LIFE ZONES

British Columbia can be divided into a number of biotic or life zones each resulting from particular climatic conditions. The series of mountain ranges running lengthwise through the southern half of the Province, and which intercept moisture-laden westerly winds, have formed a number of distinct paralleling wet and dry regions. Further major climatic influences which affect the flora in Central British Columbia are caused by the humidity associated with the extensive Skeena and Stikine River valleys.

Within each zone the flora has a characteristic association pattern. Certain species of trees grow together and with them particular shrubs and flowers. Various birds, animals, and insects thrive in this special condition of climate and forest because the things they depend on for feed and cover are found there. This dependency process of one life community existing because of another can be continued to the most minute forms of life.

A brief description is given of nine biotic zones but it should be noted that there are differences of opinion in boundaries and number of zones. Usually the Alpine Area is divided into Northern and Southern Zones. The Queen Charlotte Islands and the Fraser River Delta customarily are given distinct classifications but are grouped here with the Coast Forest Zone for simplification. The small section of desert country in the vicinity of Osoyoos has been included with the Dry Interior for the same reason.

It is impossible to give hard and fast lists of the flora of each zone. For example, western red cedar is found in isolated patches in the Dry Interior Zone and ponderosa pine crops up here and there in the Interior Wet Belt. Therefore only the more characteristic species are given.

DRY INTERIOR ZONE—Includes the lower slopes of the Okanagan and Similkameen Valleys. Extends northward to Clinton and west to Lytton. Small separate areas centre at Grand Forks and Creston. An extensive strip lies in the Kootenay Plains extending from the Border northward through Cranbrook and almost to Golden. Many of the shrubs found in the Okanagan Valley do not occur beyond the Grand Forks area.

Altitudinal range approximately 1,000' to 3,000'. Average rainfall is around 15". The summers are hot and the winters fairly mild with few zero temperatures. Rolling hills with scattered ponderosa pine and Douglas fir predominate. Ground cover is relatively sparse and never a hindrance to walking.

COMMON TREES	SHRUBS	FLOWERS
Ponderosa pine	Antelope bush	Bitterroot
Douglas fir	Sagebrush	Blue-eyed Mary
Dwarf juniper	Rabbitbush	Brown-eyed Susan
Rocky Mountain juniper	Saskatoon berry	Broom-rape, clustered
Aspen	Sumac	Cactus
Black cottonwood	Waxberry	Collomia
Columbian hawthorn	Mahonia, tall	Death camas
Douglas maple	Mahonia, creeping	Delphinium
Mountain alder	Poison-ivy	Evening primrose
Water (black) birch	Mock orange	Evening primrose, pallid
Western choke cherry	Elder, blue-berry	Fleabane, white
	Wild rose	Fringe cups
	Red-osier dogwood	Gumweed
	Soopolallie	Indian paintbrush
	Squaw currant	Large purple aster
	Silverberry	Locoweed
	Thimbleberry	Lupine
	Raspberry, black	Mariposa lily, elegant
	Raspberry, red	Mariposa lily, green-banded
	Clematis, blue	Mountain lady slipper
	Clematis, white	Mullein, great
	Willow spp.	Parsley, narrow leaved
		Pasque flower

FLOWERS—Continued

Peacock	Sagewort, dragon	St. Johnswort, common
Penstemon, Scouler's	Scarlet gilia	Wild flax
Phacelia	Sheep sorrel	Woolly thistle
Phacelia, white-leaved	Strawberry blite	Yarrow
Phlox	Spring sunflower	Yellow bell
Sagewort, cudweed		

CARIBOO PARKLANDS ZONE—Bounded in the east by the drainage line to the North Thompson River and on the west by the rising gradient of the Coast Range. The southern boundary is near Clinton and the northern about 15 miles south of Quesnel. A further small area is located west of Prince George. The vast rolling plateau with clumps of aspen and lodgepole pine doesn't vary appreciably in elevation. Many sloughs and small shallow lakes are to be found. Weather conditions are more severe than in the Dry Interior Zone.

COMMON TREES	SHRUBS	FLOWERS
Douglas fir	Black twinberry	Agoseris, orange-flowered
Lodgepole pine	Crowberry	Baneberry
Engelmann spruce	Dogbane, spreading	Bedstraw, northern
Alpine fir	Honeysuckle, red	Blue Jacob's ladder
Dwarf juniper	Huckleberry, black mtn.	Broom-rape, clustered
Rocky Mountain juniper	Kinnikinnick	Brown-eyed Susan
Aspen	Labrador tea	Bunchberry
Black cottonwood	Mahonia, tall	Columbine, blue
Western white birch	Pasture wormwood	Death camas
Douglas maple	Rabbitbush	False Solomon's seal
Mountain alder	Red-osier dogwood	False asphodel
Western choke cherry	Saskatoon berry	Goldenrod, thin
Bitter cherry	Scrub birch	Indian paintbrush
	Silverberry	Large purple aster
	Snowbrush	Large purple fleabane
	Soopolallie	Long-plumed purple avens
	Spirea, flat-top	Lupine
	Spirea, pyramidal	Mariposa lily, green-banded
	Squashberry	Meadow rue
	Swamp-laurel	Mullein, great
	Twin-flower	Orthocarpus yellow
	Waxberry	Penstemon, little-flowered
	Wild rose	Purple pea
		Raspberry, arctic

FLOWERS—Continued

Rattlesnake plantain	Star-flowered Solomon's seal	Tansy
Sagewort, dragon	Sticky geranium	White rein orchis
Sarsaparilla	Spring sunflower	Wild flax

INTERIOR WET BELT ZONE—A thick luxuriant forest including red cedar and hemlock somewhat like the Coastal forests and occupying valley bottoms along the Kootenay and Arrow Lakes, the "Big Bend" of the Columbia River, and Mabel and Shuswap Lakes adjoining the North Okanagan Valley. Altitudinal range approximately 1,800' to 3,500'. Winters are fairly cold and snowfall and rain are quite high averaging 40" to 50" per year.

COMMON TREES	SHRUBS	FLOWERS
Douglas fir	Black twinberry	Alumroot
Western red cedar	Devil's club	Arnica, heart-leaf
Western hemlock	Elder, red-berry	Bedstraw, northern
White pine	Elder, black-berry	Bleeding heart
Grand fir	False azalea	Blue-eyed Mary
Western larch	False box	Bunchberry

COMMON TREES	SHRUBS	FLOWERS
Lodgepole pine	Gooseberry, swamp	Cancer root, one-flowered
Engelmann spruce	Hardhack	Chocolate lily
Western yew	Hazel	Columbine
Dwarf juniper	Honeysuckle, orange	Coral root
Rocky Mountain juniper	Huckleberry, black mtn.	Cow parsnip
Aspen	Huckleberry, tall blue	Fairy bells, rough
Black cottonwood	Goats' beard	False asphodel
Water (black) birch	Indian hemp	False lady's slipper
Northwestern white birch	Kinnikinnick	False Solomon's seal
Bitter cherry	Labrador tea	Foam flower
Mountain alder	Mahonia, tall	Indian hellebore
Douglas maple	Mountain ash, Sitka	Indian paintbrush
	Ninebark	Large purple aster
	Raspberry, red	Lupine
	Red-osier dogwood	Meadow rue
	Red twinberry	Moccasin flower
	Redstem ceanothus	Monkshood
	Rhododendron, white	Mountain lily
	Salmonberry	Pearly everlasting
	Saskatoon berry	Pipsissewa
	Scrub birch	Pyrola
	Shrubby cinquefoil	Queen's cup
	Snowbrush	Raspberry, arctic
	Spirea, flat-top	Rattlesnake plantain
	Squashberry	Sarsaparilla
	Teaberry, western	Silver-green
	Thimbleberry	Skunk cabbage
	Trailing rubus	Star-flowered Solomon's seal
	Twin-flower	Snow lily
	Waxberry	Twisted stalk
		Western stenanthium
		Wild ginger
		Wild tiger lily
		Yarrow

SUB-ALPINE FOREST ZONE—The Engelmann spruce—alpine fir forest lying above the three zones previously described and below alpine slopes. Winters are cold, the summer moderately warm, and annual precipitation is over 50" per year.

COMMON TREES	SHRUBS	FLOWERS
Engelmann spruce	Alder buckthorn	Agoseris, orange-flowered
White Spruce	Black twinberry	Arnica, broad-leaf
Alpine fir	Red twinberry	Asphodel, northern
Lodgepole pine	Blackberry, sub-alpine	Bunchberry
Douglas fir	Blueberry, red alpine	Cinquefoil, mountain meadow
White pine	Copper bush	Columbine spp.
White-bark pine	Crowberry	Cotton grass
Alpine larch	Currant, sticky	Elephant head
Dwarf juniper	Elder, black-berry	Eriogonum, sulphur
Aspen	False box	Eriogonum, cushion
Alder, mountain	Gooseberry, swamp	False asphodel
Alder, Sitka	Heather, red	False forget-me-not
	Heather, white moss	False lady's slipper
	Heather, yellow	False Solomon's seal
	Huckleberry, black mtn.	Fireweed, alpine
	Kinnikinnick	Foam flower
	Labrador tea	Gentian

SUB-ALPINE FOREST ZONE —Continued

COMMON TREES	SHRUBS	FLOWERS
	Mahonia, creeping	Grass of Parnassus
	Mountain ash, Sitka	Green lily
	Mountain ash, western	Harebell, alpine
	Red-osier dogwood	Indian hellebore
	Redstem ceanothus	Indian paintbrush
	Rhododendron, white	Ladies' tresses
	Scrub birch	Leptarrhena
	Shrubby cinquefoil	Longstem greencaps
	Soopolallie	Lupine
	Spirea, flat-top	Moss campion
	Squashberry	Mountain bluebells
	Teaberry, mountain	Mountain daisy
	Thimbleberry	Mountain forget-me-not
	Trailing rubus	Mountain valerian
	Twin-flower	Penstemon, Menzie's

FLOWERS—Continued

Pipsissewa	Red monkey flower	White rein orchis
Pyrola	Snow lily	Wood betony
Queen's cup	Spreading phlox	Yellow monkey flower
Ragwort, western golden	Western anemone	Yellow willow herb

BOREAL FOREST ZONE—The boreal forest is beyond reach of the average resident or visitor because it lies in the northern regions of the Province. It occupies the lower elevations along the Stikine and Dean Rivers Plateau, the Liard River and Atlin-Teslin Lakes Region in the far northwest corner of B.C. A fairly dense forest is formed below timberline at approximately 4,000'. Weather conditions are severe and rainfall is low being 12.5".

COMMON TREES	*SHRUBS	*FLOWERS
White spruce	Black twinberry	Asphodel, northern
Black spruce	Crowberry	Baneberry
Tamarack	False azalea	Buckbean
Alpine fir	Kinnikinnick	Bunchberry
Lodgepole pine	Labrador tea	Butterwort, common
Aspen	Moorwort	False Solomon's seal
Black cottonwood	Scrub birch	Green lily
Balsam poplar	Shrubby cinquefoil	Indian hellebore
Alaska white birch	Saskatoon berry	Indian paintbrush
Sitka alder	Soopolallie	Ladies' tresses
Mountain alder	Spirea, flat-top	Meadow spirea
Dwarf juniper	Squashberry	Monkshood
	Thimbleberry	Moss campion
	Twin-flower	Pipsissewa
	Waxberry	Raspberry, arctic
		Sandwort, mountain
		Star flower
*These lists are largely speculative.		Strawberry blite
		Twisted stalk
		Veronica
		White dryas
		White fleabane
		White rein orchis
		Wood betony
		Yellow dryas
		Yellow monkey flower
		Yellow willow herb

PEACE RIVER PARKLANDS ZONE—The Peace River Region is comparatively small and lies in the far north-eastern corner of the Province. Large aspens in open stands are mixed here and there with more dense groups of white spruce, white birches and willow. Winters are very cold with average temperature below 0°. Summers are moderately warm and precipitation is about 18".

COMMON TREES	SHRUBS	FLOWERS
White spruce	Bilberry, mountain	Agoseris, smooth
Engelmann spruce	Black twinberry	Asphodel, northern
Black spruce	Blueberry, Canada	Avens, large-leaved
Lodgepole pine	Clematis, blue	Baneberry
Tamarack	Crowberry	Blue-eyed grass
Alpine fir	Dogbane, spreading	Broom-rape, clustered
Dwarf juniper	Goats' beard	Bunchberry
Rocky Mountain juniper	Gooseberry, smooth	Cactus
Aspen	Gooseberry, swamp	Columbine spp.
Balsam poplar	Hazel	Coral root
Black cottonwood	Huckleberry, dwarf	Cow parsnip
Alaska white birch	Kinnikinnick	False asphodel
Northwestern white birch	Labrador tea	False Solomon's seal
Sitka alder	Mountain ash, Sitka	Foam flower
Western choke cherry	Pasture wormwood	Fringe cups
	Raspberry, red	Grass of Parnassus
	Red-osier dogwood	Gentian
	Saskatoon berry	Goldenrod
	Scrub birch	Indian hellebore
	Silverberry	Indian paintbrush
	Soopolallie	Ladies' tresses
	Spirea, flat-top	Large purple aster
	Squashberry	Locoweed
	Thimbleberry	Long-plumed purple avens
	Trailing rubus	Meadow rue
	Twin-flower	Monkshood
	Waxberry	Purple pea
		Pussytoes, rosy and white
		Rough fairy bells
		Sarsaparilla
		Silverweed
		Star-flowered Solomon's seal
		Stinging nettle
		Strawberry blite
		Twisted stalk
		Yellow dryas
		Yellow monkey flower

THE ALPINE AREA ZONE—This zone includes all the terrain lying above timberline. Timberline varies in elevation from 4,500' at the Coast to 6,000' in the Interior and 7,500' at the Rocky Mountains. As may be expected weather conditions are severe with long winters and short summers.

COMMON TREES	SHRUBS	FLOWERS
Above timberline, but possibly stunted alpine fir and dwarf juniper.	Dwarf willow	Agoseris, orange-flowered
	Cascade willow	Alpine bistort
	Alpine willow	Alpine coltsfoot
	Rocky Mtn. willow	Alpine fireweed
	Dwarf huckleberry	Alpine harebell
	Red alpine blueberry	Aplopappus, Lyall's
	White moss heather	Broad-leaf arnica
	Red heather	Cinquefoil, fan-leaf
	Yellow heather	Columbine
	Mountain teaberry	Douglas campion

COMMON TREES	SHRUBS	FLOWERS
	Black-berry elder	Dryas, white
	Labrador tea	Dryas, yellow
	Trailing azalea	Elephant head
	Black mtn. huckleberry	Eriogonum, cushion

	FLOWERS—Continued	
Eriogonum, sulphur	Indian thistle	Red monkey flower
False forget-me-not	Ladies' tresses	Saxifrage, Lyall's
Gentian spp.	Longstem greencaps	Saxifrage, spotted
Giant ragwort	Lupine spp.	Saxifrage, Tolmie
Globe flower	Meadow spirea	Snow lily
Golden fleabane	Moss campion	Western anemone
Grass of Parnassus	Mountain daisy	White rein orchis
Green lily	Mountain forget-me-not	Wood betony
Indian hellebore	Mountain valerian	Yellow monkey flower
Indian paintbrush	Penstemon, Menzie's	Yellow willow herb

COAST FOREST ZONE—The forests on the western slopes of the Cascades and Coast Ranges, the Queen Charlotte Islands, and over most of Vancouver Island are included here although the Fraser River Delta and Queen Charlotte Islands are usually listed as separate zones. The heavy forest of Douglas fir, red cedar, western hemlock, broadleaf maple and red alder at lower elevations, gives way at higher elevations to mountain hemlock, yellow cedar and alpine fir. Salal and a heavy growth of ferns are other characteristics. Winters are mild, summers moderate and rainfall high being over 100″ a year on most of the Coast range.

COMMON TREES	SHRUBS	FLOWERS
Douglas fir	Blackberry, trailing	Alumroot
Western hemlock	Black twinberry	Aster, Douglas
Western red cedar	Copper bush	Baneberry
Grand fir	Cranberry	Bedstraw, northern
Amabilis fir	Currant, red flower	Avens, large-leaved
Western white pine	Currant, stink	Bleeding heart
Mountain hemlock	Devil's club	Blue-eyed Mary
Western yew	Elder, blue-berry	Blue sailors
Lodgepole (shore) pine	Elder, red-berry	Brodiaea, harvest
Sitka spruce	False azalea	Bunchberry
Yellow cedar	False box	Cancer root, one-flowered
Dwarf juniper	Goats' beard	Catchfly, night-flowering
White-bark pine	Gooseberry, gummy	Cat's ear, hairy
Red alder	Gooseberry, wild	Cat's ear, smooth
Broadleaf maple	Hardhack	Chocolate lily
Black cottonwood	Hazel	Coltsfoot
Northwestern white birch	Honeysuckle, orange	Columbine
Western white birch	Huckleberry, black mtn.	Coral root
Bitter cherry	Huckleberry, tall blue	Cow parsnip
Mountain alder	Kinnikinnick	Curled dock
Sitka alder	Mahonia, tall	False bugbane
Dogwood	Mock orange	False Solomon's seal
Vine maple	Mountain ash, Sitka	Field chamomile
Cascara	Ninebark	Field chickweed
Pacific willow	Ocean spray	Goldenrod
Peachleaf willow	Oregon grape	Ground cone
Pacific crabapple	Raspberry, black	Hedge nettle
Black hawthorn	Red-osier dogwood	Indian hellebore
	Rhododendron, white	Indian hellebore
	Salal	Indian pipe

COMMON TREES	SHRUBS	FLOWERS
	Salmonberry	Lady slipper, mountain
	Saskatoon berry	Lupine spp.
	Snowbrush	Miner's lettuce spp.
	Sweet gale	Montia
	Swamp laurel	Mullein, great
	Thimbleberry	Oregon fairy bells
	Twin-flower	Oxeye daisy
	Waxberry	Peacock
	Western teaberry	Pearly everlasting
	Wild rose spp.	Pipsissewa

FLOWERS—Continued

COMMON TREES	SHRUBS	FLOWERS
Phacelia, varied-leaved	Silver-green	Vanilla leaf
Purple pea	Silverweed	Violets, blue and yellow
Pussytoes, white and rosy	Spring gold	Wild ginger
Pyrola	Star flower	Wild lily-of-the-valley
Queen's cup	Star-flowered Solomon's seal	Wild tiger lily
Rattlesnake plantain	Stonecrop	Woolly sunflower
Saxifrage	Sundew spp.	Yarrow
Sea blush	Trillium	Yellow monkey flower
Self-heal	Twisted stalk	Youth-on-age

GULF ISLANDS ZONE—The rocky islands in Georgia Strait south of Texada Island and a strip south from Comox on Vancouver Island where garry oak and the flaunting arbutus are characteristic, make up this limited zone. Both the oak and arbutus are low altitude trees not usually growing above 800'. In contrast to the high precipitation over the adjacent Coast forest is the average figure of 30" per year. Open, grassy or rocky knolls are common.

The flora is probably the most varied in the Province. All the species listed for the Coast Forest are found with the exception of white-bark pine, the two white birches and vine maple. The latter two are present but quite rare. In addition to the Coast Forest list is the following characteristic flora.

COMMON TREES	SHRUBS	FLOWERS
Garry oak	* Broom	Bluebell
Arbutus	* Gorse	Blue-eyed grass
	Hairy manzanita	Brodiaea, large-flowered
	Honeysuckle, purple	Broom-rape
	Huckleberry, evergreen	Camas
	Indian-plum	Cactus (very localized)
	Poison oak	Collomia
	Soopolallie	Death camas
	* Not native shrubs.	Easter lily
		Easter lily, pink
		Fringe cups
		Indian consumption plant
		Owl's clover, pink
		Phacelia
		Satin flower
		Saxifrage, rusty
		St. Johnswort, common
		Whitlow grass, vernal
		Wild carrot
		Wild carrot, little

ELEVATION RANGES
OF
COMMON TREES, SHRUBS AND FLOWERS

TREES	SHRUBS	FLOWERS	
ABOVE TIMBERLINE. STUNTED ALPINE FIR AND DWARF JUNIPER.	WHITE MOSS HEATHER, RED HEATHER, BLACK MTN. HUCKLEBERRY.	MOUNTAIN DAISY, ARNICA, GENTIAN, INDIAN HELLEBORE, RED AND YELLOW MONKEY FLOWER, COLUMBINE, MTN. VALERIAN, LUPINE.	7000'+ ↑ ↓ 4500'
MOUNTAIN HEMLOCK. ALPINE AND AMABILIS FIR, YELLOW CEDAR, WHITE-BARK AND WHITE PINE, DWARF JUNIPER, SITKA ALDER.	FALSE AZALEA, COPPER BUSH, WHITE RHODODENDRON, CROWBERRY, MTN. ASH, BLACK MTN. HUCKLEBERRY, TRAILING RUBUS, MTN. SPIREA.	DOUGLAS ASTER, QUEEN'S CUP, FALSE SOLOMON'S SEAL, TWISTED STALK, MEADOW SPIREA, COTTON GRASS.	4500' ↑ ↓ 2800'
DOUGLAS FIR, HEMLOCK, RED CEDAR, AMABILIS FIR, GRAND FIR, RED ALDER, BROADLEAF AND VINE MAPLE, DOGWOOD, CASCARA, BLACK COTTONWOOD, PACIFIC WILLOW, PACIFIC CRAB-APPLE, BLACK HAWTHORN.	FALSE BOX, SALAL, GOAT'S BEARD, DEVIL'S CLUB, BLACK TWINBERRY, SALMONBERRY, THIMBLEBERRY, MOCK ORANGE, OCEAN SPRAY, RED-BERRY ELDER, HARDHACK, RED HUCKLEBERRY, TWIN-FLOWER, ORANGE HONEYSUCKLE, HAZEL.	BUNCHBERRY, VANILLA LEAF, WILD LILY-OF-THE-VALLEY, STAR FLOWER, PURPLE PEA, RATTLESNAKE PLANTAIN, TRILLIUM, BLEEDING HEART, FAIRY BELLS, PIPISSEWA, BLUE-EYED MARY, PEACOCK, MINER'S LETTUCE, VIOLETS.	2800' ↑ ↓ 0'
ABOVE TIMBERLINE.	WHITE MOSS HEATHER, RED HEATHER, DWARF WILLOWS, BLACK MTN. HUCKLEBERRY, MOUNTAIN TEABERRY, DWARF HUCKLEBERRY, BLACK-BERRY ELDER.	BROAD-LEAF ARNICA, COLUMBINE, WHITE AND YELLOW DRYAS, CUSHION ERIOGONUM, FALSE FORGET-ME-NOT, GENTIAN, INDIAN HELLEBORE, INDIAN PAINTBRUSH.	8000' ↑ ↓ 6000'
ENGELMANN SPRUCE, ALPINE FIR, LODGEPOLE PINE, DOUGLAS FIR, LARCH, DWARF JUNIPER, ASPEN, MOUNTAIN AND SITKA ALDER.	BLACK AND RED TWINBERRY, RED ALPINE BLUEBERRY, BLACK MTN. HUCKLEBERRY, KINNIKINNICK, LABRADOR TEA, SITKA MTN. ASH, SOOPOLALLIE, FLAT-TOP SPIREA, TWIN-FLOWER, SWAMP GOOSEBERRY.	BROAD-LEAF ARNICA, BUNCHBERRY, COLUMBINE, FALSE LADY'S SLIPPER, FALSE SOLOMON'S SEAL, INDIAN PAINTBRUSH, LUPINE, MEADOW RUE, MOUNTAIN DAISY, MOUNTAIN VALERIAN, PIPISSEWA.	6000' ↑ ↓ 2900'
PONDEROSA PINE, DOUGLAS FIR, ASPEN, BLACK COTTONWOOD, DOUGLAS MAPLE, WATER BIRCH, MTN. ALDER, CHOKECHERRY, HAWTHORN, JUNIPERS.	ANTELOPE BUSH, SAGEBRUSH, RABBITBUSH, SASK. BERRY, SUMAC, TALL MAHONIA, BLUE-BERRY ELDER, POISON IVY, SQUAW CURRANT, SOOPOLALLIE, WHITE CLEMATIS.	BITTERROOT, YELLOW BELLS, PEACOCK, DELPHINIUM, PHLOX, PHACELIA, SCARLET GILIA, SPRING SUNFLOWERS, FRINGE CUPS, MARIPOSA LILY, CACTUS.	2900' ↑ ↓ 1100'
ABOVE TIMBERLINE. DWARF JUNIPER.	HUCKLEBERRY, DWARF HUCKLEBERRY, WHITE MOSS HEATHER, RED HEATHER, DWARF AND ALPINE WILLOWS, CROWBERRY.	GRASS OF PARNASSUS, GENTIAN, LADY'S TRESSES, MOSS CAMPION, MOUNTAIN DAISY, MOUNTAIN VALERIAN, WESTERN ANEMONE, WOOD BETONY, LUPINE, INDIAN PAINTBRUSH, ELEPHANT HEAD, WHITE REIN ORCHIS.	9000'+ ↑ ↓ 5500'
ENGLEMANN SPRUCE, ALPINE FIR, MOUNTAIN HEMLOCK, WHITE SPRUCE, WHITE-BARK PINE.	BLACK-BERRY ELDER, FALSE AZALEA, BLACK MTN. HUCKLEBERRY, SITKA MTN. ASH, WHITE RHODODENDRON.	INDIAN HELLEBORE, WILD TIGER LILY, GRASS OF PARNASSUS, BROAD-LEAF ARNICA.	5500' ↑ ↓ 4500'
DOUGLAS FIR, WESTERN HEMLOCK, RED CEDAR, WHITE PINE, GRAND FIR, LODGEPOLE PINE, YEW, ASPEN, BLACK COTTONWOOD, N. W. WHITE BIRCH, BITTER CHERRY, MOUNTAIN ALDER, DOUGLAS MAPLE.	BLACK TWINBERRY, DEVIL'S CLUB, RED-BERRY ELDER, FALSE BOX, HARDHACK, HAZEL, GOAT'S BEARD, KINNIKINNICK, RED TWINBERRY, SALMONBERRY, THIMBLEBERRY, SQUASHBERRY, SOOPOLALLIE, RED-STEM CEANOTHUS, TWIN-FLOWER.	HEART-LEAF ARNICA, BLEEDING HEART, BUNCHBERRY, LUPINE, COLUMBINE, COW PARSNIP, FOAM FLOWER, MOUNTAIN LILY, SNOW LILY, QUEEN'S CUP, PIPISSEWA, SARSAPARILLA, MOCCASIN FLOWER, INDIAN PAINTBRUSH.	4500' ↑ ↓ 2000'
ABOVE TIMBERLINE.	DWARF WILLOWS, WHITE MOSS HEATHER, RED HEATHER, YELLOW HEATHER, BLACK MTN. HUCKLEBERRY MOUNTAIN BILBERRY	MOSS CAMPION, ALPINE HAREBELL, ELEPHANT HEAD, GENTIAN, GREEN LILY, MOUNTAIN DAISY, CUSHION ERIOGONIUM, LUPINE, GRASS OF PARNASSUS, COLUMBINE SPP., RED MONKEY FLOWER, FALSE FORGET-ME-NOT, WHITE REIN ORCHIS, YELLOW MONKEY FLOWER.	10,000' ↑ ↓ 7500'
ALPINE FIR, LODGEPOLE PINE, WHITE-BARK AND LIMBER PINE, ENGELMANN SPRUCE, JUNIPERS, ALPINE LARCH, DOUGLAS FIR, SITKA ALDER.	BLUE CLEMATIS, RED-BERRY ELDER, LABRADOR TEA, SHRUBBY CINQUEFOIL, RED AND BLACK TWINBERRY, WHITE RHODODENDRON, SITKA MTN. ASH, CROWBERRY, SPREADING DOGBANE, SOOPOLALLIE, SCRUB BIRCH, RED ALPINE, BLUE BERRY, BLACK MTN. HUCKLEBERRY, TWIN-FLOWER, SNOWBRUSH, RED-OSIER DOGWOOD.	COW PARSNIP, GENTIAN, FIREWEED, MTN. VALERIAN, BUNCHBERRY, BEARD TONGUE, PEACOCK, BLUE-EYED MARY, FALSE LADY'S SLIPPER, PYROLA, YELLOW DRYAS, VIOLETS, LONGSTEM GREENCAPS, LADY'S TRESSES, LARGE PURPLE ASTER, GIANT RAGWORT.	7500' ↑ ↓ 4000'
ENG. SPRUCE, WHITE SPRUCE, JUNIPERS, ASPEN, COTTONWOOD, DOUG. MAPLE, N.W. WHITE BIRCH, MTN. ALDER.	SQUASHBERRY, FLAT-TOP SPIREA, KINNIKINNICK, TWIN-FLOWER, FALSE AZALEA, SASK. BERRY, SNOWBRUSH.	MOCCASIN FLOWER, WESTERN GOLDEN RAGWORT, BUNCHBERRY, YELLOW COLUMBINE, PYROLA.	4000' ↑ ↓ 3500'

ELEVATION RANGES
of
COMMON TREES, SHRUBS & FLOWERS

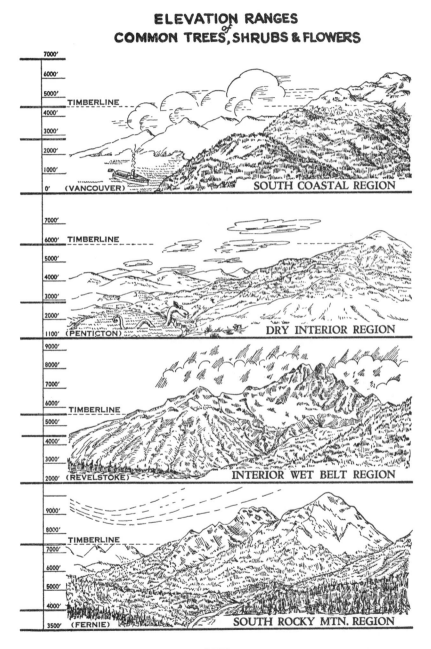

7000'
6000'
5000'
TIMBERLINE
4000'
3000'
2000'
1000'
0' (VANCOUVER)   SOUTH COASTAL REGION

7000'
6000' TIMBERLINE
5000'
4000'
3000'
2000'
1100' (PENTICTON)   DRY INTERIOR REGION

9000'
8000'
7000'
6000' TIMBERLINE
5000'
4000'
3000'
2000' (REVELSTOKE)   INTERIOR WET BELT REGION

9000'
8000'
TIMBERLINE
7000'
6000'
5000'
4000'
3500' (FERNIE)   SOUTH ROCKY MTN. REGION

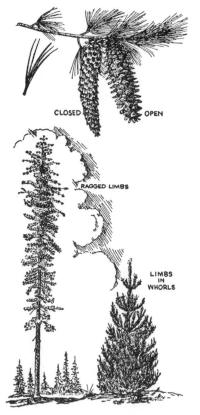

CLOSED   OPEN

RAGGED LIMBS

LIMBS IN WHORLS

WESTERN WHITE PINE
(Pinus monticola)

White Pine - Silver Pine

RANGE: Vancouver Island and an adjacent Mainland strip lying west of the Cascades; Common in the Interior Wet Belt i.e., Kootenays, Arrow Lakes, Big Bend Highway, Shuswap and north to Quesnel Lake. On Coast often growing to near sub-alpine elevations. In Interior it drops out near 3,500'.

FORM: When growing under fair conditions it has a remarkable straight trunk like a sturdy flagpole. Trees 1'-3' in diameter and to 120' high are most common. Regular whorls of horizontal limbs are characteristic and these form a narrow crown on the top two-thirds of the tree. Here and there an overly long limb protrudes making a recognizable design from afar.

BARK: Silvery grey on trees up to 6" in diameter. Then becoming dark and deeply fissured to form a regular pattern of small, thick plates that is quite distinctive from any other native tree.

LEAVES: Bundles of 5 needles to a sheath. Needles 2"-5" long and bluish-green in color. Other 5-needle pines have needles about 2" long.

FRUIT: An unusual cone 5"-9" long, slightly curved and with the tips of the scales a darker brown. The cones are so large that the clusters can be seen plainly on the topmost limbs during summer and fall months.

WOOD: A light, fine-grained wood, easily worked and a high proportion free from defects. Prized for special construction purposes, also match blocks. An ideal wood for carving.

DID YOU KNOW that there is usually a thick carpet of brown needles under this pine. In heavy timber its presence is often noticed this way.

QUICK CHECK: From afar, a few protruding limbs and clusters of large cones in upper crown. 5-needle pine with needles 2"-9" long. Curved cones 5"-9" long.

WHITEBARK AND *LIMBER PINE
(Pinus albicaulis; Pinus flexilus)

*LIMBER PINE closely resembles whitebark pine in twisted, irregular form and high mountain habitat. However the cones are 3" - 8" long whereas those of whitebark pine don't exceed 3" in length. In general the range is limited to high slopes of the southern Rockies. Numerous trees can be seen at an elevation of 3,300' along the highway between Golden and Field.

RANGE: A tree of sub-alpine and timberline elevations where it grows on rocky exposed places. Mountains above 3,500' elevation on Vancouver Island and Coast. Cacades and eastward into Rockies at elevations of 5,000' and more. Occurs only in southern half of B.C.

FORM: A crooked, lop-sided tree seldom over 30' high and 20" diameter. Long, limber branches drooping to ground on old trees. Sometimes shrub-like from severe exposure.

BARK: Thin, smooth and light-colored on young trees but becoming grey and brown with reddish tones and loosely scaly on old trees.

LEAVES: 5 needles to a sheaf. Needles are stout, slightly curved and from 1½" - 3" long. They tend to cluster thickly at twig ends and thus give a view of whitish-barked limbs throughout the tree.

FRUIT: A heavy purplish cone to 3" long. Often very pitchy.

WOOD: A soft, light wood only used in cases of necessity.

DID YOU KNOW that the limbs of this tree are quite rubbery giving them the resilience to withstand severe ice and snow loads. The cones drop to the ground unopened and the seed is released as the cone falls apart.

QUICK CHECK: High mountain habitat, 5 needles and thick cones.

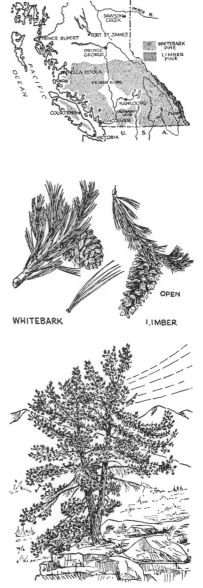

WHITEBARK   LIMBER   OPEN

PONDEROSA PINE
(Pinus ponderosa)

Western Yellow Pine

RANGE: Common tree of valley bottoms and mountain slopes up to 3,000' in Okanagan and Similkameen Valleys. Extends in the Cariboo to 2 miles north of Clinton. Also at Lower Arrow Lake, Kootenay Lake and Kootenay River Valley north to Columbia Lake. Lower Skagit Valley.

FORM: A distinctive tree of straight trunk topped by a loose mass of heavy branches with tufts of brushy foliage. The large twisted branches stick out here and there without plan but nevertheless produce a towsled narrow cone outline. Few trees over 3' thick are to be seen but fine specimens around 2' through and 80'-90' high are quite common. Young trees have a distinct whorl to their branches and a characteristic voluptuousness to their glossy green foliage.

BARK: The flaky terra-cotta red bark of this stately pine stands out in bold color on distant hillsides making tree recognition possible from afar. Young trees have a very dark bark but as they age, reddish furrows begin to show. Trunks over 12" thick produce thin flaking scales much like pieces of a jig-saw puzzle.

LEAF: The yellow pine has the longest needles of any evergreen in B.C. The brushy tufts are made up of needles about 6"-9" long with 3 needles to the sheaf. Sometimes 4 or 5 to the bundle are found here and there on young trees.

FRUIT: A roundish, shiny, light-brown cone that ripens on the tree and falls during September and later months. It is usually 3"-4" long and 2"-3" thick. The seed is plump and heavy but the stout wing whirls it through the air.

WOOD: A light yellow color with contrasting dark brown knots when freshly cut. Soft and light. Used for interior finishing (knotty pine), boxes.

DID YOU KNOW that Indian braves used the bark scales to make small hot fires which gave off no smoke and cooled rapidly leaving enemies no clue as to their time of movements. Pine cones too, are excellent for a quick hot fire.

QUICK CHECK: From afar, orange-red bark. Watch for possible confusion with larch if in its range. Three long needles to a sheaf is positive proof.

(18)

LODGEPOLE PINE
(Pinus contorta latifolia)

Jack Pine - Black Pine

NOTE: the most commonly used name for this tree is jack pine. However this name is correctly used for *Pinus banksiana,* a close relative east of the Rockies and probably not extending into B.C.

SHORE PINE (*P. contorta contorta*) is recognized by some authorities as a closely related tree growing in poor soil or swampy ground close to the sea coast. Generally it is twisted and crooked in form with bushy, irregular limbs. In other features it very closely resembles lodgepole pine.

RANGE: A tree likely to be found almost any place in B.C. from middle mountain to sub-alpine elevations.

FORM: Under normal conditions a tall, slender tree to 18" in diameter and 100' high. The crown is narrow and rounded with the thin limbs often occurring only on the top third of the tree. Young trees are narrowly conical with regular whorls of bushy, up-pointing limbs.

BARK: Mottled, dark grey with some trees showing light brown areas. Light covering of small, loose scales.

LEAVES: 2 needles to a bundle. $1\frac{1}{2}$" - $2\frac{1}{2}$" long and often with yellowish-green tinge.

FRUIT: A hard oval cone, spiny, and up to 2" long. Usually clustered and often hanging unopened on tree for several years.

WOOD: A straight grained, light wood, pale in color. Generally regarded as a weed species in B.C. but gradually assuming importance because of abundance and accessibility. Used largely for railway ties, mine props and fuel.

DID YOU KNOW that most burned-over forests east of the Cascades grow up in a very dense stand of lodgepole pine. This is because the cones withstand fires and later open to release their seed.

QUICK CHECK: A two-needle pine, the only one in B.C.

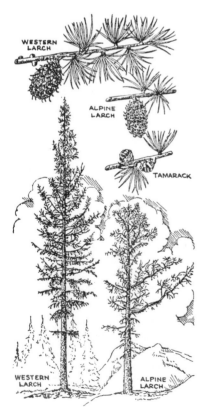

WESTERN LARCH
(Larix occidentalis)

Larch - Tamarack

TAMARACK (*L. laricina*) is a smaller edition of the above being up to 80' high and 20" in diameter. It differs principally in seeking a bog habitat and having small cones about ½" long. Northeastern B.C. to Cassiar Mtns. Spotty at Clucluz and Aleza L., Chilako R., Liard R.

ALPINE LARCH (*L. lyallii*) is confined to high mountains and only enters B.C. in and near Manning Park on the Hope-Princeton Highway. It tends to develop a craggy, windswept form with irregular, heavy branches. Other features are quite similar to western larch.

RANGE: Eastward from Okanagan Lake to flank of Rockies. Northward to Shuswap Lake and Columbia Lake. Altitudinal range approximately 2,000' to 4,000'

FORM: A straight, tapering trunk possibly 3' thick and 160' high. Most trees 1' - 2' in diameter. In the narrow, open crown every one of the short horizontal limbs can be seen. Limbs near the top of the tree have a distinctive up-curve to their tips and the lower ends a downward twist.

BARK: Changing from thin, scaly, light brown bark on trees up to 10" in diameter to a deeply furrowed, orange-red and loosely scaly bark on old trees. Resembles ponderosa pine from a distance.

LEAVES: Needle-like, in clusters of 1 - 2 dozen arising from knobs on the twigs. About 1" long and yellow-green. Turning light golden yellow in fall and dropping to the ground.

FRUIT: A light cone 1" - 1½" long with protruding bracts. Old cones often failing to drop from some limbs.

WOOD: Heavy, reddish wood, very durable in contact with ground. Used for ties, pit props and general construction. Important commercial species.

DID YOU KNOW that in the fall larches can be seen on distant mountains by their yellow-gold color? Grouse often eat the fallen needles.

QUICK CHECK: Loose, open crown displaying all limbs with ends twisting up or down. Needles in bunches.

WHITE SPRUCE
(Picea glauca ssp. glauca)

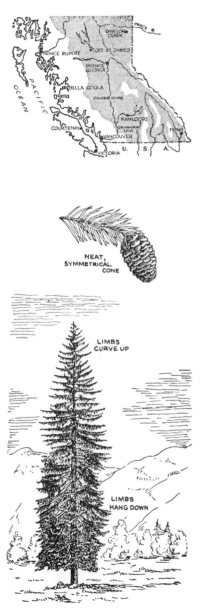

RANGE: Sometimes listed as not occurring in south half of B.C. Greatly confused in range and appearance with Engelmann spruce. Found in more arid valley bottoms of southern Interior but occasionally interspersed with Engelmann. Replaced by Engelmann at elevations of 3,500' and greater but is almost sole spruce in north half of Province. (See black spruce).

FORM: No clear distinction from the many variations of Englemann spruce. Limbs have a tendency to be more wide-spreading and bushy with a triangular effect from tassel-like side branchlets. Limbs often extend to the ground.

BARK: Greyish and scaly with reddish brown tinges showing between and underneath the thin scales.

LEAVES: 4-sided, sharp-pointed leaves to 1" long. Tendency to twist to upper side of limb. Pungent smell when bruised.

FRUIT: When ripe, a brown cone from 1¼" - 2" long. Scales are very smooth and neatly rounded on their margins. Trim and symmetrical in appearance as compared to Engelmann spruce.

WOOD: Generally not distinguishable from Engèlmann spruce being soft, light, clear-grained and light-colored. Important tree in the north where it is the main commercial specie.

DID YOU KNOW that squirrels often gather hundreds of spruce cones into a single hiding place? Piles of scales left after the cones are broken apart may be several feet deep.

NEAT, SYMMETRICAL CONE

LIMBS CURVE UP

LIMBS HANG DOWN

QUICK CHECK: A spruce by squarish or stalked needles. A neat, symmetrical cone to 2" long.

(21)

ENGELMANN SPRUCE
(Picea glauca ssp. engelmannii)

RAGGED CONE

Mountain Spruce

Beside this spruce some authorities list white spruce (*P. glauca ssp. glauca*) as occurring in B.C. Few persons profess to tell them apart with certainty. Widely divergent opinions are found in range descriptions. This book chooses to recognize white spruce and to give its range as extending into South Central B.C. and being the common spruce of the more arid valley bottoms. Differentiation from Engelmann spruce has been based solely on a marked variation in cones—a means that is thought to be unreliable by many people.

RANGE: One of the more widespread trees in south half of the Province. Appears on the westerly flank of the Cascades at an elevation of 3,800'. Extends across the Province to the Rockies. Sometimes mixed with white spruce in the wetter valley bottoms but sole spruce of higher elevations, 3,800' to near timberline. Replaced by white spruce in north half of Province.

FORM: Impossible to make clear distinction from white spruce. When in thick stands, narrowly conical with straight clean trunk. Topmost branches twist upwards, middle ones point out and lower drop strongly. Branchlets hang like tassels from main boughs particularly in trees in the open or at lower elevations. Ordinarily a tree 1' - 3' in diameter and 100' - 140' high.

BARK: Trunk covered by loose greyish scales between which show a brownish or rusty red tinge.

LEAVES: 4-sided, dull-pointed needles about 1" long and blue-green in color. Tendency to curve towards topside of twig. Pungent smell when crushed but this characteristic also found in white spruce.

FRUIT: A light brown cone 1" - 2½" long. Scales thin, finely ridged on back and tip slightly ragged. Hasn't the neat symmetrical look of white spruce cones. Purplish when immature.

WOOD: Soft, straight-grained and creamy white in color. Very important tree to Interior forest industry. Cut extensively for general construction and pulp.

DID YOU KNOW a quick way to tell spruce needles is to roll them between the fingers? The 4 edges allow them to roll easily whereas a flat needle won't turn.

QUICK CHECK: A spruce by stalked needles. Cones with flexible ridged scales and finely-waved margin. Untidy look.

SITKA SPRUCE
(Picea sitchensis)

Tideland Spruce - Coast Spruce

RANGE: A narrow strip along the Coast of B.C. and on adjacent islands. A tree confined to an elevation of less than 1,000' and seldom found more than 50 miles from tidewater. Most common along immediate coastline. Scattered trees in Fraser Valley as far east as Hope. North in Cheakamus R. Valley to Garibaldi Station.

FORM: Varies considerably depending on whether a forest tree or one growing in the open. In humid Coast forests it produces a long, clean trunk 3' - 6' thick topped by a thin crown of short branches reaching 150' in height. In the open, limbs are strongly out-thrust and carry a triangular fringe of drooping branchlets. Limbs extend almost to the ground. This latter form is easily distinguishable from a considerable distance.

BARK: Covered with thin, loose, crisp scales of rusty-brown hue.

LEAVES: Flattish rather than 4-angled and bristle out in all directions from twig. Very sharp to the touch.

FRUIT: An easily recognized cone by reason of its disorderly array of thin, irregular, wavy-edged scales. Most cones about 2" long.

WOOD: Fairly light and soft and varying from creamish to pale buff in color. Forest trees have a large proportion of clear, straight-grained wood making it excellent for fine construction. Also very important as a pulp tree.

DID YOU KNOW that Sitka spruce from the Queen Charlotte Islands was chosen during the last war as the most desirable wood for aircraft construction?

QUICK CHECK: Coast habitat, needles bristling out all around twig and light, disorderly cone.

(23)

BLACK SPRUCE
(*Picea mariana*)

RANGE: In broad terms, the north half of the Province lying east of the Cascades. Lack of information exists about the southerly limit. It extends to 20 miles south of Jasper in the Rockies and occurs along the C.N.R. near Mt. Robson. One report records it in the Chilcotin. Black spruce is characteristically found in swamps or bogs although in more northerly regions it is less limited to this habitat. It is very common along the Alaska Highway.

FORM: Usually quite distinctive by its narrow, irregular crown which has a tendency to **form** thick clumps and bulges. The straight trunk **has** very little taper. Most trees are from 5" - 10" in diameter and up to 50' high. In northern limits it tends to become twisted and shrublike. Most limbs are short and horizontal.

BARK: A dirty grey, scaly bark quite similar to lodgepole pine. Twigs blackish and hairy.

LEAVES: Stiff, shortish needles about ½" long.

FRUIT Almost round, grey-brown cone ½" - 1" long—the smallest of all the spruces. Usually several in a cluster. They often remain on the tree for several years.

WOOD: Light, soft and very fine-grained. Pale in color. Important for pulp in the East but not used appreciably in B.C.

THICK, KNOBBY TOP

DID YOU KNOW that black spruce grows almost to the Arctic Ocean and ranges completely across the northern regions of Canada.

QUICK CHECK: From afar, knobby spire tree top in swamp habitat. Small cones with many old ones remaining on tree.

HEMLOCK (WESTERN AND *MOUNTAIN)
(*Tsuga heterophylla* and *Tsuga mertensiana*)

Alaska Pine

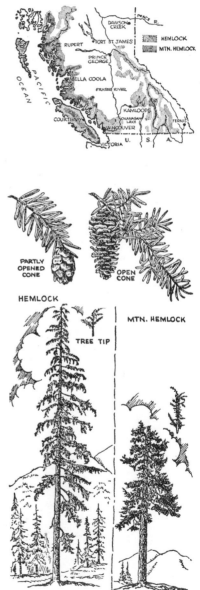

*MOUNTAIN HEMLOCK (*Tsuga mertensiana*) is a common tree on the Coast in proximity to western hemlock but is found at the higher elevations of 2,600' and up to timberline. In its scattered occurrence in the Interior it ranges from 4,000' to 5,500'. The dark green needles grow in disorderly array around the twigs giving a thick tufted appearance to the foliage. Branches tend to have an upward sweep at their tips. The stout leader has the characteristic "hemlock" droop. Cones are 1" - 2" long, twice the length of those of western hemlock.

RANGE: Coast forests up to 2,800' and Interior wet belt up to 5,000'.

FORM: A large tree thriving in dense shade. From 2' - 4' in diameter and 120' - 160' high. Limbs long and irregularly spaced on trunk. The top-most twig (leader) droops in graceful fashion. Foliage on young trees is drooping, feathery, and very attractive.

BARK: About 1" thick with flat scaly ridges and deep furrows on mature trees. Dark rich brown in color. Young trees have thin, fine-scaled bark of lighter color.

LEAF: About ½" long, flat and blunt. More or less two-ranked. Two fine white lines on under surface. Each leaf with short stalk and twist at base of needle.

FRUIT: A light cone not over 1" long which ripens in fall and drops during winter.

WOOD: A tree that 20 years ago was considered of low value now ranks high in importance as a pulpwood species. Finds wide use in lumber industry and bark is high in tannin content.

DID YOU KNOW that hemlock is a prized ornamental in Great Britain? It can grow and reproduce in dense shade. Young trees often start on top of stumps or fallen logs. It usually grows with Douglas fir, red cedar, and Sitka spruce.

QUICK CHECK: The drooping tree tip identifies hemlock from afar. Leaves and cones are good points, too.

(25)

DOUGLAS FIR
(Pseudotsuga menziesii)

Fir - Douglas Spruce - Oregon Pine

The Coast Douglas Fir is recognized by some authorities as a different variety from the Interior or Dry Belt Tree. The differing features are so slight that only the one tree is considered here.

RANGE: Over most of south half of B.C. Reaches its best growth on Pacific Coast where it grows on a variety of soils. Its upper altitudinal range on the Coast is approximately 2,800' and, in the southern Interior 3,500'. It may reach 6000' in the Rockies. North to Stuart and McLeod Lakes.

FORM: Trees over 200' high and 6' in diameter are seldom seen now. Most mature trees on Pacific Coast, 3' - 4' in diameter, 200' high, and in Interior seldom over 30" in diameter. Young trees form broad sloping pyramid. Lower branches straight or drooping and higher curve upward. Old trees lose this form and develop heavy crooked limbs and have a flattened or irregular top. In shade, lower limbs drop off leaving a long clear trunk.

BARK: Smooth grey-brown with resin blisters on young trees up to 6" in diameter. Then as tree increases in age bark becomes thick and deeply fissured into reddish-brown ridges. Sometimes reaches over I' thick. This prevents damage from fires but makes an excellent fuel.

LEAF: Flat, sharp-pointed needles about I" in length. Not prickly to the touch like spruce.

FRUIT: A cone ripening in the fall and dropping to the ground. Cones hang downward and are 2" - 3" long. The bracts between the cone scales are triple-pronged and protrude so as to be easily visible and thus make an unmistakable identifying feature.

WOOD: Generally reddish but sometimes yellowish in color with prominent annual rings. Splits cleanly and is very strong. Important for heavy construction and interior and exterior finishing.

DID YOU KNOW that Douglas fir is the tree seen most often by people in B.C.? It grows in dense stands on the Coast or associated with hemlock, cedar and amabilis fir. In the Interior it is found with ponderosa pine at the lower elevation and lodgepole pine, white pine and larch at higher levels. Discovered by David Douglas, famed Scottish botanist, in 1829. Favorite Christmas tree—mostly cut in Interior because of thicker form. Largest tree in B.C. and Canada and only exceeded by redwoods on Pacific Coast.

QUICK CHECK: "Pitchfork" bracts on cone.

ALPINE FIR
(*Abies lasiocarpa*)

Mountain Fir

RANGE: A tree of sub-alpine and near elevations, it is found throughout B.C. except for the Queen Charlotte Islands. Contrary to some reports it grows at higher elevations on Vancouver Island. It is most common east of the Cascades where it appears near 3,500' elevation and continues to timberline.

FORM: Distinguished by its symmetrical, narrow, spire-like form. The branches are in whorls and very short and stiff toward the top. Most slope downward. Trees may reach 4' in diameter and 150' high but usually are 10" - 16" in diameter and 50' - 75' high. At timberline it becomes stunted and sprawls with limbs to the ground.

BARK: On young trees thin, smooth, and grey with conspicuous resin blisters. On old trees, 12" or more in diameter, irregular, shallow furrows and reddish scales but still smooth on upper section.

LEAF: Flat, blunt needles about 1" long twisting upward from underside of twigs to bush densely around twig. Sharp-pointed on cone limbs. Blue-green in color with pungent smell. Silvery tinge to new growth. Twig ends orange brown and older growth hairy.

FRUIT: A group of heavy, hard, wooden cones 2" - 4" long, purple in color and standing erect near the top of the tree. Often blotched with sticky pitch.

WOOD: A light-colored soft wood of little commercial importance.

DID YOU KNOW that most sub-alpine and timberline pictures in B.C. show the alpine fir as the picturesque symmetrical trees in the scene? The short stiff branches usually slope downward and are constructed to withstand heavy loads of ice and snow that may completely encase them in midwinter.

QUICK CHECK: Flat needles, circular scars on twigs. Spire form. Locality and altitude ranges.

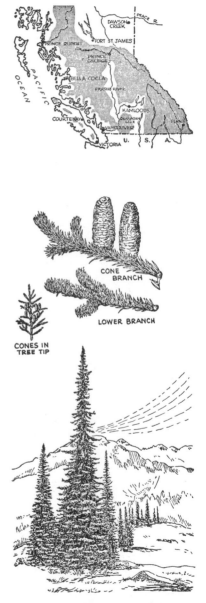

CONE BRANCH

LOWER BRANCH

CONES IN TREE TIP

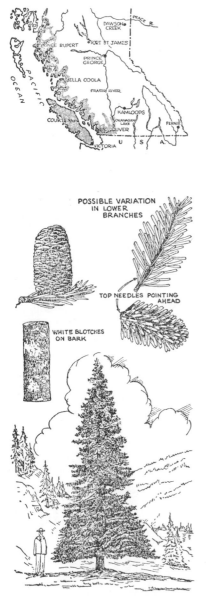

POSSIBLE VARIATION
IN LOWER
BRANCHES

TOP NEEDLES POINTING
AHEAD

WHITE BLOTCHES
ON BARK

AMABILIS FIR
(*Abies amabilis*)

Balsam Fir - Silver Fir - White Fir - Lovely Fir

RANGE: West slopes of the Coast Range and on Vancouver Island. Varies from sea level to 4,500'. Usually on moist, shady bottomlands above general level of Douglas fir—hemlock type. Prominent at 2,800' to 4,000' on Coast Mountains.

FORM: A straight tree up to 100' and 2½' in diameter, spire-pointed, rounded cone on older trees, thickly foliated and very symmetrical. Branches except those on top third, curving down and away from trunk and often extending to the ground. A remarkably beautiful tree in form and color. At high elevations it resembles alpine fir in general shape.

BARK: Smooth ash-grey unbroken bark splotched with chalky-white patches. Old trees usually seamed and much like mountain hemlock bark.

LEAF: Flat needle leaf about 1¼" long, grooved on upper side and has two white lines on under surface. Needles blunt pointed and most with small notch on end. Notice how they point forward along the top of the twigs and those near the underside twist up to produce a flattish effect when a bough is seen from beneath. These characteristics should limit any confusion with grand fir which has two-ranked needles. Twigs tend to be hairy.

FRUIT: An erect cone 4" - 5" long, dark purple in color. Falls apart in early fall leaving spike core standing on bough for several months.

WOOD: Soft, light, and yellowish brown. Generally cut for pulp.

DID YOU KNOW that the silvery color is given by two white lines on the lower side of the needles? Trees likely to be associated with it at lower levels are Douglas fir, hemlock and white pine. At higher elevation mountain hemlock and alpine fir are common companions. Many woodsmen prefer the springy boughs of amabilis fir to any other tree for making a "bough" bed.

QUICK CHECK: Circular leaf scars on twigs identify true firs. Needles point forward along top sides of twigs. Young trees and those in good growing sites have smooth bark with white patches.

GRAND FIR
(Abies grandis)

Lowland Fir - Western Balsam

RANGE: Lower slopes and valleys of southern Coastal region and Vancouver Island. Probably not general above 3,000' elevation. Also lower valleys of Kootenay and Arrow Lakes region.

FORM: A tall straight tree averaging 2'-3' in diameter and up to 125' high. A broad pyramidal shape when young with distinct horizontal pattern to branch ends. Older trees with rounded top and conical form when open grown but free of lower branches and irregular of crown in shade. All branches except tip have graceful downward swing.

BARK: Young trees up to 8" in diameter have thin smooth bark with numerous resin blisters. White mottlings may lead to confusion with the bark of amabilis fir or young Douglas fir. Older trees have hard irregular furrows and ridges.

LEAF: Flat needle leaves 1¼" - 2" long. They are blunt or slightly notched and grow in a flat rank from either side of the twig. The upper surface is dark green and has a central groove while the underside is silvery from two whitish stripes.

FRUIT: An erect cone 2" - 4" long and about 1" thick. They are very noticeable on the tips of trees in late August. As the cones ripen and the scales and seeds start to fall an untidy brown mass marks the tree top. Most of the cones have broken up by October.

WOOD: A soft light wood with a faint brownish color. Grand fir is usually cut as part of a logging operation and sees utilization for pulp or lumber for cheap wood products.

DID YOU KNOW that woodsmen place great faith in the healing properties of the gum from the resin blisters? It makes a handy glue too. Grand fir is usually found in valley bottoms growing as part of the Douglas fir - hemlock - red cedar forest.

QUICK CHECK: From afar the heavy conical crown tip is quite reliable. If close make sure it is a true fir either by leaf scars on the twigs or from the erect cones. Two-ranked needles make it grand fir.

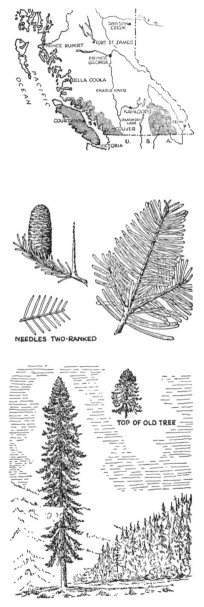

NEEDLES TWO-RANKED

TOP OF OLD TREE

WESTERN RED CEDAR
(Thuja plicata)

RANGE: A common forest tree west of the Cascades where it grows up to 2,800' elevation. Also abundant in the Wet Interior Zone with an upper altitudinal limit of 4,200'. Scattered pockets and riverside fringes occur in the Similkameen and Okanagan Valleys.

FORM: A giant tree on the Coast often over 150' high and 6' in diameter. The trunk tapers from a fluted base to a long spike-like top which is often dead. On mature trees the branches are long and irregular and usually point downward very distinctly. The frond-like branchlets impart a feathery or lacy appearance to the form. Young trees have a conical outline from regular spreading branches. A yellowish green color marks this tree from other dark green conifers.

BARK: Thin and stringy and can be pulled off in long strips. No other native B.C. tree except yellow cedar has bark resembling this. Indians valued it highly for making baskets, clothes and mats.

LEAF: Scaly, blunt leaves pressed in pairs tightly to the twig. Branchlets hang like fronds or sprays from main boughs.

FRUIT: A small cone 1/2" long which hangs on over winter.

WOOD: A reddish fragrant wood splitting with remarkable ease into thin boards. It Is very light and free from pitch or resin. Used at one time by Indians for massive war canoes and lodges. Now valuable for shingles, siding and posts because of its resistance to decay. Fallen trees remain sound after 100 years.

DID YOU KNOW that the largest red cedars grow on Vancouver Island? One 13'6" in diameter and 875 years old was cut in 1948 near Comox. Indians hollowed canoes 60' long from a single trunk.

QUICK CHECK: Stringy dark bark and fluted trunk at base. Twigs are smooth and, when stroked against the grain, are not prickly to the touch like yellow cedar.

YELLOW CEDAR
(Chamaecyparis nootkatensis)

RANGE: On Coastal slopes and islands from Alaska to Oregon. Spotty occurrence in northern half of range with altitudinal range from sea level to alpine. Common on upland plateaus and mountains of Vancouver Island. Mingles with mountain hemlock and balsam fir on North Shore Mountains above 2,600' elevation. Patch in Slocan Valley.

FORM: A shaggy tree usually less than 80' high. The trunk is often slightly twisted and tapers quickly toward the top. Well formed trees up to 2' in diameter are common but growth appears slow and breakage heavy with increased age. The limbs sweep out and down with fern-like fronds hanging from them. The tip of the tree is slender and droops very much like hemlock. Young trees are shrubby and warped but gradually straighten as they grow taller.

BARK: On trees over 8" in diameter, the bark appears a distinctive dirty white from a distance. It is stringy and brittle and hangs in loose rough pieces. Unlike red cedar it won't pull off in long strips but breaks in stiff sections. Young trees have a fairly smooth, reddish bark.

PRICKLY SCALES

LEAF: Scaly overlapping leaves very similar to red cedar but prickly to the touch when stroked "against the grain."

FRUIT A knobby rounded berry, greenish white in color until ripening in late September or October to a reddish brown cone which falls during the winter.

WOOD: Soft, light yellow in color with a very noticeable sharp fragrance when freshly cut. It resists rot and insects and, being easily worked, is a favorite of boat builders. It is one of the most popular woods in B.C. for arrow making and carving.

DID YOU KNOW that some gnarled monarchs 5' and 6' in diameter may be the oldest trees in Canada with ages of over 1,000 years?

QUICK CHECK: Prickly cedar-like foliage and stringy white bark. Limited range and elevation.

DWARF JUNIPER
(*Juniperus communis var. saxatilis*)

Common Juniper

CRAWLING JUNIPER (*J. horizontalis*) is a recent discovery in B.C. It closely resembles the above in its low, crawling appearance. Differences are in the blue berries not having a noticeable bloom and being on short, bent stalks. Berry seeds number from 1 - 4, while dwarf juniper has 1 to 3. The reported range is in the dry Windermere Valley. Specimens have also been taken in Central B.C., the Yukon, and northern Rockies.

Dwarf juniper is included as a tree in botanical descriptions because it reaches tree proportions in one or two places in its widely distributed range embracing the northern half of the world.

RANGE: Throughout B.C. Most frequent at sub-alpine and alpine elevations on Vancouver Island and Coastal area. Common on rockslides and arid places in the Interior and with wide altitudinal range. Scattered along Alaska Highway.

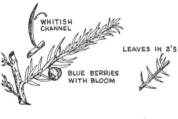

FORM: A sprawling shrub holding close to the rock at higher elevations but in valley bottoms often a bushy, upright mat several feet high and 4' - 10' across.

BARK: A thin, reddish-grey bark rough with scales.

LEAVES: Narrow, sharp-pointed needles with shallow, whitish channel on underside. Close examination shows that the needles are arranged in whorls of three.

FRUIT: Dark blue, knobby berries covered with whitish bloom.

WOOD: Shrubs are too small to produce wood of any value.

DID YOU KNOW that dwarf juniper is the most widely distributed tree or shrub in the northern half of the world?

QUICK CHECK: "Juniper" shrub with all needles, short, channelled and mostly in groups of three.

ROCKY MOUNTAIN JUNIPER
(Juniperus scopulorum)

Rocky Mountain Red Cedar - Western Juniper

RANGE: South half of Province east of Cascades. Possible sporadic occurrence in North Central B.C. Sparsely scattered in Gulf Island Zone. Very abundant in Dry Interior and Cariboo Parklands Zones. Found mostly in dry places at low to middle mountain elevation. Sometimes seen on edges of swamps. Spotty occurrence in Peace River area. Babine Lake.

FORM: Generally a bushy, shrublike tree with one or several short, stout, trunks to 8" thickness. Commonly 6'- 15' high. Varies from neat symmetrical shape to extremely ragged. Sometimes even crawling in habit.

BARK: Thin, stringy bark with reddish-brown tinges.

LEAVES: Often two distinct kinds on same tree. Young shoots with sharp, needle-like leaves about ½" long. Older branches with smooth, scaly leaves like western red cedar. Foliage variable in color and exceedingly attractive in many cases.

KNOBBY BLUE BERRIES

FRUIT: Lumpy blue berries requiring two years to ripen. They contain one or two large, grooved seeds.

WOOD: A reddish heart wood with a wide ring of white sapwood. Light and soft. Used occassionally for small ornamental work. In the East, a near species is much sought for pencil wood.

DID YOU KNOW that the berries of juniper are used in the flavoring of gin?

QUICK CHECK: "Juniper" look, scaly leaves on older branches, bluish berries.

WESTERN YEW
(Taxus brevifolia)

Pacific Yew

RANGE: A low altitude tree from sea-level to 1,000' elevation on Vancouver Island and Coast Forest Zone but growing up to elevations of 4,000' in Wet Interior Zone. Generally a tree of river banks and damp canyons and seeking the shade of other trees. One small grove near Kelowna.

FORM: A small bushy, untidy tree averaging 15' - 30' high. The seamed twisting trunk seldom is over 12" in diameter. Because the yew prefers deep shade and grows under larger trees it develops an ungainly limb pattern with long branches of uneven length. Sometimes the limbs grow almost to the ground. Spiny shoots from the trunk add to the ragged appearance. In extreme shade a sprawling shrub may be formed.

BARK: The rich red tints of the rough scaly bark usually draw attention to this hide-away tree. Often the thin bark is fluted and seamed as if the tree had suffered agonies in its slow growth.

LEAF: Flat, sharp-pointed needles with a short stem. Most needles are between 1/2" and 3/4" long but some twigs have shorter ones. Dull green in color on top they show stripes of two-tone light green below. Although new shoots have a brushy needle effect, older limbs have a rough, two-ranked appearance much like hemlock.

FRUIT: Single greenish berries turning reddish in September. The horny seed uses this eye-catching dress to attract birds and so be carried to new fields.

WOOD: Perhaps the most attractively colored native wood because of the yellow sapwood contrasting with the rich red heartwood. Extremely hard and durable but of neglible commercial importance because of its small size and rarity.

DID YOU KNOW that the tough and springy yew supplied the fighting bows for most of the ancient armies and today is still prized by archers?

QUICK CHECK: Scaly red trunk. Sharp-pointed needles with two-tone color beneath.

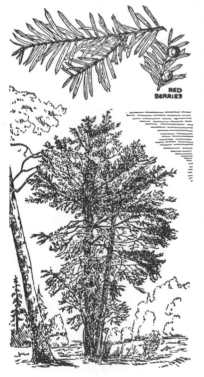

RED BERRIES

(34)

TREMBLING ASPEN
(Populus tremuloides)

Quaking Aspen

RANGE: An abundant tree throughout that part of the Province east of the Cascades. Extends from valley bottom to 4,000' in elevation. Occasional clumps on Vancouver Island but even sparser in Coastal Forest Zone.

FORM: In the Dry Interior it gathers in low spreading groves 20' - 30' high where there is evidence of moisture. In wetter regions graceful trees to 80' high are common. These have straight trunks to 16" in diameter and carry on their top halves a loose, rounded crown of brittle branches. The characteristic groves of aspen result from spreading roots which send up shoots.

BARK: Mostly smooth and white with black "horseshoe" markings here and there. Chalklike substance can be rubbed off. Older trees with fissured and blackened bark near base. Young cottonwood trees with which it might be confused have smooth, green-white bark without black patches.

LEAVES: An abruptly tipped, rounded or heart-shaped leaf to 3" long. Leaf stems flattened at right angles to leaf blade. Foliage is an attractive fresh green color.

FRUIT: Appears with the first leaves as catkins of small, greenish capsules. Generally unnoticed.

WOOD: A weak, soft wood almost white in color. Brittle and fast rotting. Although used for pulp and crating in the East and favored in the United States for excelsior and match stock it is seldom used in B.C. except for firewood.

DID YOU KNOW that the leaves tremble with the slightest breeze because of the flattened leaf stems. The chalky substance on the bark is supposed to be heaviest on the south side of the tree. Thus aspen can act as a direction finder.

QUICK CHECK: Whitish bark marked with black splotches. Flat leaf stem.

NORTHERN BLACK COTTONWOOD
(*Populus trichocarpa*)

YOUNG LEAVES

OLD LEAVES

BALSAM POPLAR

OLD TREE

YOUNG TREE

BALSAM POPLAR (*P. balsamifera*) is almost identical in appearance with the above and few persons will be able to tell them apart. Balsam poplar leaves are thinner, and greenish beneath often spotted with rust, instead of the silvery sheen of the northern black cottonwood. Note the range limitations.

RANGE: Possibly the most widespread of the larger broadleaf trees. Found at low and middle elevations throughout B.C. except east of the Rockies in the northeastern part of the Province. A tree invariably seeking river banks, gravel bars or low-lying land.

FORM: The great change in form between young and old trees confuses many people into thinking there are two distinct species. Young trees up to 40' or 50' high assume a symmetrical conical form with stout, up-pointing branches. With increased age, the limbs become very thick, irregular, and crooked, and point outward or twist downward. The top tends to flatten from breakage of the higher limbs.

BARK: On young trees up to 6" in diameter the bark is smooth and green. Don't be confused with aspen which has white bark marked with black blotchings. Bark furrowing increases with age until mature trees show a series of hard, dark grey ridges several inches thick.

LEAVES: In general, widely triangular and from 2½" - 5" long. Yellowish-green in color but much lighter beneath. Some leaves on young trees or sprouts may be to 8" long and have a more narrow tapering leaf. Teeth on new leaves are quite regular but ragged and wavy on old leaves.

FRUIT: In spring, a long string of rough greenish beads. These ripen and split open in a cottony mass which blows far and wide.

WOOD: A soft light wood of drab color used largely for veneer and the making of boxes. Its suitability for these varied purposes including pulpwood and the wide distribution make it the most important broadleaf tree in B.C. Rots quickly when in contact with the ground.

DID YOU KNOW that the thick sticky buds have a fragrant odor in springtime? The sticky substance can be used as an ointment on small cuts or as a makeshift glue. The hard, unripe seeds have been adapted for pea-shooter ammunition.

QUICK CHECK: Yellowish-green foliage among other trees. Smooth, whitish-green bark on young trees; thick, furrowed bark on older trees. River and bottomland habitat.

PACIFIC WILLOW
(Salix lasiandra)

Western Black Willow - Black Willow

"EARS" ON YOUNG LEAVES

TWIST TO
LEAF END

PEACHLEAF WILLOW (*S. amygdaloides*) is listed in various works as a tree ranging along streams in southeastern B.C. However the writer doubts that it occurs in B.C. except in very limited localities. Its main characteristics are thin drooping branchlets and "peachlike" leaves. It can be confused easily with Pacific willow. Osoyoos Lake is one place where it is found.

RANGE: At lower elevations along stream banks and near other water sources. Extends eastward from Vancouver Island to the Kootenays but is confined to a southerly strip. Common in lower Similkameen Valley.

FORM: A crooked trunk branching into a number of upright limbs which produce a ragged, rounded outline to the crown. Seldom more than 30' high and 16" in diameter. The thin leaves and long slender twigs impart a graceful appearance.

BARK: Blackish in color and channelled into irregular, rough plates from many furrows and cross seams. The rather thick branchlets are smooth and orange to brown in color, while new twigs are light green.

LEAVES: Quite distinctive because of a long thin point with a sideways twist. From 2" - 5" long and very finely toothed. A shiny, dark green above but with a whitish pallor beneath. Leaf stems are thickish and less than $\frac{1}{2}$" long.

FRUIT: Thick catkins about 2" long and appearing with the leaves. A bright yellow color is characteristic at maturity followed by a fuzzy white cotton often showing on the trees until July.

WOOD: Pale brown and brittle. Very soft and not used for any specific purpose.

DID YOU KNOW that the liking for water often results in long rows of these trees outlining the margins of sloughs and streams. Sections of limbs stuck in wet ground will root easily and quickly. Most willows have two small "ears" or wings at the base of their leaf stems when the leaves are young. The two willows mentioned here are regarded as the only two "tree" willows in the Province.

QUICK CHECK: A black-barked, ragged tree growing near water. Shiny, dark green leaves with a long thin point usually twisted to the side

THE WHITE BIRCHES
(Betula papyrifera varieties)

These birches are most confusing as to name, identification and range. For many years *Betula occidentalis*, variously called Western White Birch or Western Birch, was regarded as the white-barked birch extending from the Coast to the Rockies. The botanical name *occidentalis* is now used for water birch while the white birches in B.C. have been divided into 3 varieties. The writer's experience suggests that few persons will be able to separate the first two varieties listed below with any certainty or describe features that aren't so subject to variation as to render them unworkable. Most experts attempt identification by catkin scales and seeds.

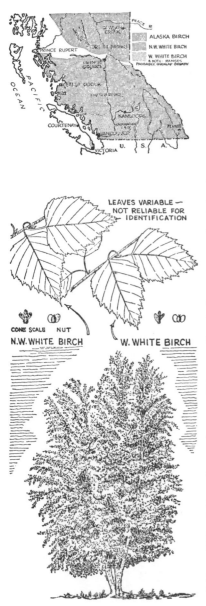

LEAVES VARIABLE — NOT RELIABLE FOR IDENTIFICATION

CONE SCALE   NUT
N.W. WHITE BIRCH

W. WHITE BIRCH

NORTHWESTERN WHITE BIRCH (*B. papyrifera subcordata*): Relatively small birch tree to 60' high. Leaves to 3" long, squarish or slightly heart-shaped to base. A suggestion of double teeth on some leaves. Bark in thin layers, creamish-white to light orange on old trees. Often reddish-brown on young trees.

RANGE: Across the south and central part of the Province. Common in the Kootenays at low and high elevations.

WESTERN WHITE BIRCH (*B. papyrifera commutata*): Often a tall tree reaching 100' or more in height and 16" in diameter. Leaves to 3" long, many wedge-shaped at base. Most doubly-serrate. Peeling, white to orange bark.

RANGE: Sporadic on Saanich Peninsula, Vancouver Island. Common on Coast and Fraser Valley. Extends eastward in low valley bottoms.

ALASKA PAPER BIRCH (*B. papyrifera humilis*): A small tree to 30' high with smallish, triangular leaves. Bark varies from white to red.

RANGE: From Alaska into the northern part of the Province.

SWAMP BIRCH (*B. pumila glandulifera*): A brushy shrub of bogs. Limited occurrence to Lost Lake near Victoria. Probably on Lower Mainland. Leaves mostly 1" long, rounded. Bark, chestnut brown.

SCRUB BIRCH (*B. glandulosa*) is described under the shrub section of this book.

WATER BIRCH
(Betula occidentalis)

Black Birch - Red Birch - Mountain Birch

RANGE: East of the Cascades to the Rockies. Most abundant in drier regions and generally absent in Interior Wet Belt Zone. Northern boundary not determined but possibly extending to Yukon.

FORM: Most commonly a wide spreading, graceful shrub to 20' high with stems arisng from one main clump. In rich soils beside creeks or in meadows it occassionally becomes a tree to 50' high and 12" in diameter. Branches very slender and willowy.

BARK: Rich reddish-brown with prominent light-colored markings. Not peeling except on larger trees where there is some curling. Greenish young twigs very warty. Mature twigs shiny red.

LEAVES: A roundish leaf with an abrupt, sharp point. Mostly 1" - 2" long. Light green undersurface often finely dotted.

FRUIT: Catkins showing up prominently by summer. Thickish, about 1" long.

WOOD: Fine-grained, soft and light, splitting easily. Larger trees used for firewood and farm use.

DID YOU KNOW that all birch bark is very durable? The wood of fallen trees will rot away leaving a shell of bark. The attractive, richly colored bark was once used by the Indians in their basket weaving to give a decorative pattern.

QUICK CHECK: Wet places along creeks and meadows in drier regions. Copper-brown bark and new twigs heavily warty.

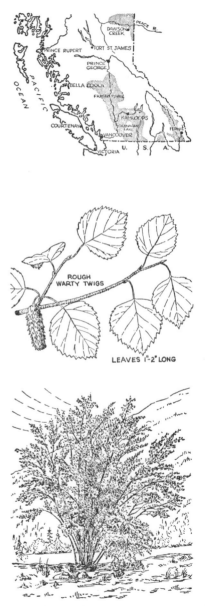

ROUGH WARTY TWIGS

LEAVES 1"-2" LONG

RED ALDER
(*Alnus rubra*)

Oregon Alder

There are three alders in B.C., red, Sitka and mountain alder. White alder is not known to occur. Alders produce naked buds in the summer, each on a short stalk. Tassel-like catkins several inches long appear in early spring, Small woody cones form in the fall and hang until the following spring. Leaves have straight veins running to the margin.

RANGE: Very common west of the Cascades but also appearing infrequently at low elevations here and there in the Okanagan Valley, the Cariboo and Central Interior.

FORM: This varies a good deal with age and density of stand. Young trees to 30' high and growing in the open are broadly conical from irregularly spaced, long, straight limbs pointing out and upward. With increased age the lower limbs disappear leaving a long clear trunk with a narrow conical crown. The common size for older trees is from 8" - 14" in diameter and up to 80' high. Much larger trees do occur.

BARK: Slightly roughened bark, dirty grey in color. Older trees with clear trunks are blotched with white markings. Their base is sometimes seamed and thickly scaly.

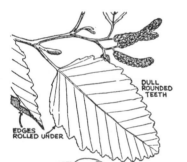

LEAVES: Most leaves 3" - 5" long, dull green above and sometimes rusty-tinged below. The dull teeth form rounded lobes quite unlike the other two native alders. The extreme outer leaf edge curls under on most leaves.

FRUIT: A cluster of brownish cones each slightly more than ½" long and remaining on the tree until late spring. The nut is bordered by very narrow wings. Very attractive catkins, several inches long, appear in early spring before the leaves and show up vividly as they change in color from yellow to brown.

WOOD: Light, fine grained and easily worked without splintering. Does not check or warp and is valuable in furniture construction. Serves as a base for expensive veneers but finishes well itself. The dry wood makes excellent fuel and burns leaving very little ash.

DID YOU KNOW that freshly peeled alder bark turns bright orange on the undersurface? The Indians used this inner bark to make a dye.

QUICK CHECK: Round-lobed leaves with edges rolled under.

MOUNTAIN ALDER
(Alnus tenuifolia)

Thinleaf Alder

RANGE: East of the Cascades and in the south half of the Province, extending to and beyond the Rocky Mountains. Reaches as far as the Rockies in the north half. Occurs from valley bottom to high mountain elevations. Often growing with Sitka alder at higher elevations. Seeks wet ground, creek edges, and usually found in pure clumps and borders where there is good exposure. This is the common alder of the Interior.

FORM: At higher elevations, much like Sitka alder, sprawling and shrublike. In valleys it is a small tree to 40' high and 12" in diameter. The branches are fairly straight and point upward to form a loose conical crown.

BARK: Thin, smooth, dirty green-grey with lighter horizontal markings especially prominent on younger trees. Older trees tend to flake and scale near their base. In the wetter parts of its range it is often partially covered by a scaly, whitish-green lichen.

LEAVES: Distinctly double-toothed with definite sharp teeth unlike red alder which has shallow, rounded teeth. Leaves, 2" - 4" long, are dark green with a yellow central vein.

FRUIT: A cluster of 3 - 9 hard, brown cones about ½" long. These hang on the trees until the following summer and are very prominent in the spring. The nut is bordered by very narrow wings.

WOOD: A soft light wood similar to Sitka alder but, because of the tree size, sees some use as fuel. Rots quickly in contact with the earth.

DID YOU KNOW that the leaves of alder trees do not turn brown in the fall but remain green until they drop? A decoction of alder bark was used by Indians in the treatment of rheumatic fever. Quite recently the bark has been found to contain salicin, a standard medicinal prescription for this disease.

QUICK CHECK: Check for alder by small, woody cones, naked buds, or straight-veined leaves. Distinct, double-toothed leaves identify it. Red alder leaves are rolled inward on their margins and its general range is west of the Cascades.

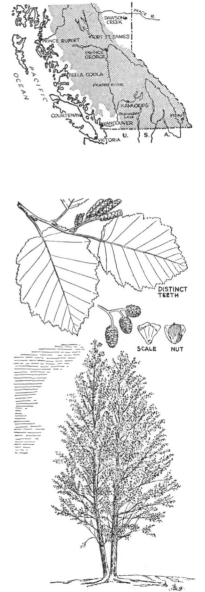

DISTINCT TEETH

SCALE   NUT

(41)

SITKA ALDER
(Alnus sinuata)

Green Alder - Mountain Alder

RANGE: Westward from the Rocky Mountains throughout B.C. on mountain slopes of 3,000' and upward. Occasionally extends to low levels. Almost always in damp places such as along streams or bordering swampy meadows. Will stand partial shade.

FORM: Usually a sprawling shrub to 10' high with crooked, upward curving limbs. Sometimes it grows as a small twisted tree to 30' high. Branches stick outward to form a loose, ragged outline.

BARK: Smooth, greyish-green in color and marked with light-colored, warty lenticels. In the wetter parts of its range it is often mottled by a scaly, greenish-white lichen.

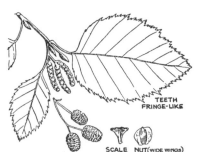

TEETH FRINGE-LIKE

SCALE   NUT(WIDE WINGS)

LEAVES: Readily distinguished from the other alders by the fine sharp teeth which give a fringe-like appearance to the margin. Leaves are from 2" - 4" long, ovalish in shape and glossy green in color.

FRUIT: A cluster of 3 - 6 hard, brownish cones about ½" long. The small nuts which can be shaken from the cones have wide wings on either side.

WOOD: A soft wood with little strength and not used for anything unless of necessity.

DID YOU KNOW that the crooked sprawling limbs are protection against the deep snows of winter? They bend to the ground when weighted and rise back as they are released.

QUICK CHECK: An alder by reason of cones, naked buds or leaves with straight veins running to margin. Fringe-like margins make it Sitka alder.

GARRY OAK
(Quercus garryana)

White Oak - Oregon Oak

RANGE: The only oak in B.C. and greatly limited in range. On Vancouver Island near southern tip and extending northward in patches along east Coast on open, rocky locations as far north as Comox. Common on Gulf Islands. One small grove is located on the south side of the Fraser River, 1½ miles above Yale. Another occurs on Sumas Mountain. A tree of low elevations and often mixed with arbutus.

FORM: A most picturesque tree when mature because of its huge, gnarled limbs and massive, shaggy crown. The heavy trunk may be up to 3' thick and shortly branches into stout limbs. Its form is unmistakable with that of any other native tree.

BARK: Soon fissuring to produce narrow, horny ridges with occassional stout scales. Light grey in color.

LEAVES: Typical lobed oak leaf, 3" - 6" long, thick, and dark green.

FRUIT: A smooth, brown acorn ½" - 1" long dropping in the fall with a knurled or roughened cup often attached to its base. Although the acorns are purported to be sweet and edible they see little or no use for this purpose.

WOOD: Typical hard, strong and heavy as in other oaks. Wood checks and warps with drying which, together with the short trunks, gives garry oak little commercial value. It makes excellent fuel when thoroughly dry. Rots quickly in contact with the ground.

DID YOU KNOW that the shiny acorns are used in making novelty items and costume jewelry?

QUICK CHECK: A massive, shaggy tree of limited range. Oak leaves and acorns.

PACIFIC CRAB-APPLE
(Malus diversifolia)
(Malus fusca)

Oregon Crab-Apple

LEAVES VERY VARIABLE IN SHAPE

SHARP SPURS

RANGE: Coastal strip of entire Province including adjacent islands. Seeks low, damp places such as stream and swamp edges where it often forms an impenetrable thicket. Common on low ocean frontage.

FORM: A small, scraggly tree to 30' high and 12" in diameter or often shrublike with a number of straight, smooth stems an inch or two thick. Very bushy when growing in the open. It doesn't carry true thorns but numerous, stout and sharp spurs an inch or two long give a realistic imitation.

BARK: Very fissured, scaly and patchy on old trunks and branches.

LEAVES: Much like those of apple trees except for tendency to produce irregular lobes and a variety of shapes. Thick, sharply toothed and with prominent veins. Mostly 2" - 3½" long.

FRUIT: Clusters of white, fragrant, "apple blossoms" appear from April 15 to May 15. Followed by bunches of little, oblong apples about ½" long. These are first greenish in color but turn yellowish or blushed with red. They are edible but rather acid in flavor.

WOOD: Very compact and fine-grained. Sometimes used in small ornamental turnery because of toughness and brownish hue of wood.

DID YOU KNOW that beautiful autumn colors are produced from yellow and russet colored leaves?

QUICK CHECK: Wet land habitat, some lobed "apple" leaves, fragrant flowers, or clusters of small apples.

(44)

BLACK HAWTHORN
(Crataegus douglasii)

Black Haw

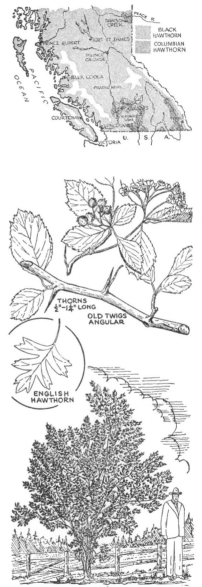

COLUMBIAN HAWTHORN (*C. columbiana*) is found also in B.C. It has slender thorns from 1" - 2" long and dark scarlet berries. The range is throughout the Dry Interior Zone but its occurrence there is by no means as frequent as black hawthorn.

ENGLISH HAWTHORN (*C. Oxyacantha*) is a widespread escape in the southern portion of Vancouver Island. Its spiny limbs carry deeply lobed leaves and colorful bunches of scarlet berries that persist over winter.

RANGE: Wettish places like edges of streams and meadows. Common along roadsides and fields. Wide range throughout southern two-thirds of Province. Low to middle mountain elevations.

FORM: Either a small, bushy tree to 20' high or a tangle of lower shrublike growth making an impenetrable thicket. Twigs have alternating crooks. Spines are from ½" - 1¼" long and needle-sharp.

BARK: Dirty grey in color, very rough and scaly. Often mottled with patches of lichen. Young shoots smooth and shiny. Very similar to Pacific crab-apple.

LEAVES: Thickish, oval leaves to 3" long with 5-9 small lobes at top end.

FRUIT: Showy clusters of smelly white blossoms during April to May, followed by bunches of small, black-purple "apples"—ripe by late July. Though quite edible, rough seeds make them unpopular for eating. The apples wither quickly once ripe.

WOOD: Tough, close-grained but seldom utilized.

DID YOU KNOW that Paul Bunyan always used a big hawthorn tree as a back-scratcher?

QUICK CHECK: A bushy tree with sharp spines ½" - 1¼" long. Zig-zag twigs.

(45)

BITTER CHERRY
(*Prunus emarginata*)

The tree form of this cherry sometimes is distinguished as a variety, *Prunus emarginata mollis*. It is found in the wetter parts of the range and has leaves to 4" long. This book treats them as one species. Be on the watch around towns and farms for hybrid forms resulting from cross pollenization with domestic trees.

WILD RED CHERRY (*P. pensylvanica*) is supposed to range westward from the Rockies to the Kootenays. However the writer doubts that this tree is found in B.C. except for a slight intrusion along the Rockies. The leaves are much longer-pointed than the above and the berries each have a stem about 1" long.

RANGE: Lower elevations on Vancouver Island, southern Coastal Zone, to 3,000' through the Wet Interior extending to sub-alpine forest zone. Common on east slopes of mountains between Grand Forks and Nelson. Ootsa Lake.

FORM: Presents a wide variation depending on type of soil and climatic factors. At the Coast it is a slender tree up to 10" in diameter and 60' high. The branches are straight and point upwards. On drier sites and at higher elevations a low crooked shrub up to 10' high may be expected. Leaves grow along the branches rather than on side twigs, thus the tree framework is quite accurately outlined.

BARK: Dirty, lightly roughened and grayish-brown in color. Marked with grayish lenticels up to 2" long.

LEAVES: On shrubby trees, they vary from 1½" - 3" long but in tall trees they may be 4" long. Blunt leaf points on older leaves, sharp on new growth; fine, rounded teeth and two small knobs or glands on the stem are other features.

FRUIT: The fragrant white flowers may be seen during April and May. They form rounded clusters toward limb ends and are replaced by pea-size bright red berries of extremely bitter taste. Each berry is on a short stem about ½" long. These stems branch from a stouter central stem from ½" - 1" in length.

WOOD: A brittle, quick-rotting wood sometimes cut for fuel.

DID YOU KNOW that the cherry bark can be peeled from the tree and polished to a rich red? Indians used strips of this bark in their basket weaving to give color to their work.

QUICK CHECK: From a distance the small narrow leaves outline the limb framework. Glands on dull-pointed leaf make it the bitter cherry. Rounded clusters of white flowers (5 - 10) or bright red berries on stems about ½" long.

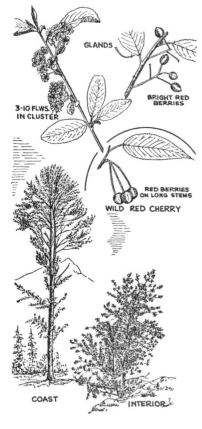

GLANDS

3-10 FLWS. IN CLUSTER

BRIGHT RED BERRIES

RED BERRIES ON LONG STEMS

WILD RED CHERRY

COAST

INTERIOR

WESTERN CHOKE CHERRY
(Prunus virginiana demissa)

This is the cherry listed in many writings as *Prunus demissa*. A variety of this, black choke cherry, *Prunus virginiana melanocarpa* is now recognized by some authorities. It is described as the choke cherry of the most southerly part of the Dry Interior. The fruit is almost black, and the stems do not have glands. However, the writer has never been able to find specimens without these glands. For simplification the above are treated as one similar to past practice in most botanical writings.

RANGE: East of the Coast Range except for sparse occurrence near south end of Vancouver Island. Common in Dry Interior regions across the Province. Although often found on exposed locations it prefers damp ground of fair richness. White clematis and poison ivy are likely to be growing in the vicinity. Peace River area.

FORM: Varying from heavy crooked shrubs less than 10' high to small trees 20' in height. Often forming a sprawling irregular mass from several bushes grouped together. A noticeable feature is the abundance of dark green leaves.

BARK: Greyish brown in color and roughened from numerous small fissures.

LEAVES: Dark green and wider above the middle. Sharp-pointed and finely saw-toothed. Leaf stems above ½" - ¾" long. Two small knobs or glands are located on the upper part of the stem but supposedly not on those of black choke cherry.

FRUIT: The flowers preceding the fruit are very noticeable in May. They are white, about ½" across and form in dense, cylindrical clusters near the ends of the limbs. Berries are a dark purple and between ¼" and ½" in diameter. Although very puckery to taste they make fine jams and jellies.

WOOD: Brittle, fine-grained and of no importance.

DID YOU KNOW that the bruised bark gives off a pungent smell. It has a very bitter taste as has the bark of all cherries.

QUICK CHECK: From a distance the crooked form and heavy, dark green foliage. In spring, long clusters of white flowers; in fall, masses of dark purplish berries. Glands on the leaf stems.

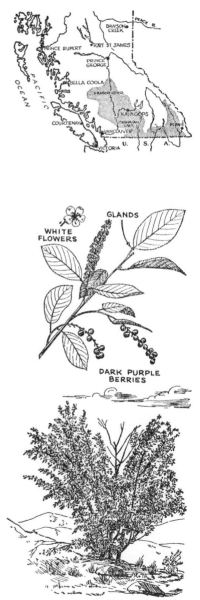

WHITE FLOWERS

GLANDS

DARK PURPLE BERRIES

BROADLEAF MAPLE
(*Acer macrophyllum*)

Bigleaf Maple - Oregon Maple

RANGE: West of Cascades at elevations under 1,000'. Extending northward to beyond Prince Rupert. On Vancouver and Queen Charlotte Islands. In Fraser Canyon to near Siska Lodge. To 10 miles east of Hope along Hope-Princeton Highway.

FORM: A massive, bushy tree. In the open, it grows to 80' high with a trunk to 2' thick, which soon branches into numerous upright limbs. Among forest trees it grows straight with a loose crown of up-pointing branches surmounting a clear trunk. Often forked or several trunks close together.

BARK: Finely roughened on trees to 6" in diameter. Then becoming furrowed into narrow, horny ridges. Drab, grey-brown in color.

LEAVES: The largest tree leaf in B.C. being on occasion to 16" long. More commonly 6" - 10" long and divided into 5 prominent lobes. The brilliant fall coloring of the other two maples isn't shared—the leaves only turning a pale yellow.

FRUIT: Flowers appear with, or soon after, the leaves in April. They are quite prominent as pale yellow hanging clusters. Paired maple wings about 2" long and at 45° to 60° to one another are seen from late summer to early winter.

WOOD: Fine-grained and fairly dense. Very valuable in B.C. for furniture, interior finish and other specialty uses.

DID YOU KNOW that thick moss and ferns often make their home on rough maple trunks and lower limbs?

QUICK CHECK: Large, 5 - lobed maple leaves.

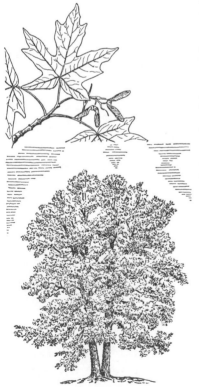

(48)

DOUGLAS MAPLE
(Acer glabrum var. douglasii)

Dwarf Maple - Rocky Mountain Maple

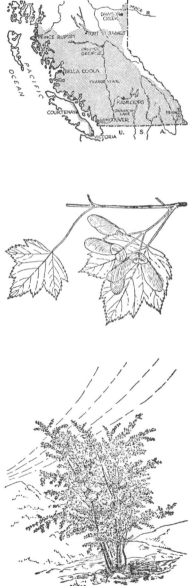

RANGE: Spotty occurrence along Coast southward from Alaska. Usually shrubby and occurring at middle mountain elevations. Scattered near southern tip of Vancouver Island and found along east coast here and there. Very abundant and widespread east of Cascades and in southern half of Province. Grows to over 4,000' in elevation and extends considerably northward of the Canadian National Railway.

FORM: Sometimes a number of spreading stems up to 25' high and forming a loose, wide-spreading crown. Very often shrublike and under 10' high.

BARK: Smooth and grey-brown on main trunks. New twigs bright red.

LEAVES: A relatively small leaf 1" - 3" across and with 3 - 5 toothed lobes. Dark green in color but often blotched with vivid red dabs. The leaf stem is grooved and usually bright red. Produces very colorful red and crimson autumn foliage.

FRUIT: Pairs of maple "wings" about 1" long and almost forming a right angle to one another. Pinkish tinged during late summer.

WOOD: Not used because of small size of tree.

DID YOU KNOW that this maple leaf is very much like the "Maple Leaf of Canada"? The forked limbs provide very fine sling-shot crutches. None of the maple in B.C. produce usable maple syrup.

QUICK CHECK: Small "maple" leaf with 3 - 5 toothed lobes.

(49)

VINE MAPLE
(Acer circinatum)

RANGE: Lower and middle elevations of Coastal Forest from Knight Inlet southward. Very rare on Vancouver Island except for valleys of Robertson and Salmon Rivers. Probably sporadic occurrence in wetter places in Interior, since found in Wells Gray Park, 150 miles north of Kamloops. A tree of damp places along creeks or meadows where soils are fairly good. Very tolerant of shade and usually found growing under another tree.

FORM: Seldom found with a single trunk. More characteristically a bushy mass to 20' high from a number of stems 2" - 5" in diameter. If in the open it becomes a compact symmetrical shrub. Otherwise, as the name suggests, a straggly, crooked form is most common.

BARK: A smooth, pale green bark on trunk and limbs but occassionally becoming dull brown.

LEAF: A circular leaf with 7 - 9 short lobes like spread, blunt fingers. Lobes are sharply toothed. Leaves vary from 2" - 6" across.

FRUIT: Maple "wings" so widely spread as to be almost in a straight line. They vary from ¾" - 1½" long and are quite red when ripe.

WOOD: A surprisingly heavy wood of fine grain. Rots quickly when in contact with earth. Seldom used because of its small size, crooked form and weakness.

DID YOU KNOW that woodsmen use green vine maple for pot hooks and reflectors around camp-fires because it is almost impossible to burn? Vine maple has the most vividly colored autumn foliage of any Coastal tree or shrub.

QUICK CHECK: Leaf with 7 - 9 blunt, spreading fingers or lobes. Wide-spreading wings and limited range.

IN SHADE   OPEN GROWN

CASCARA
(Rhamnus purshiana)

RANGE: At low elevations on Vancouver Island and Gulf Islands. Coastal strip of Mainland to Bella Coola. Southern part of Interior Wet Belt i.e. Arrow and Kootenay Lakes. Also 10 miles east of Creston to Yahk.

FORM: Older trees to 30' high and 10" in diameter seldom seen now. Often twisted and irregularly limbed if fighting for light. Young trees straight. Limbs relatively few and upright.

BARK: Smooth, slightly mottled grey bark resembling young red alder. Older trees tend to be scaly near their base.

LEAVES: Large, "cherry-like" leaves, quite distinctive by their shape and tendency to cluster. 2½" - 6" long, finely toothed and with prominent parallel veins. Paler green beneath. Leaf buds and uncurling leaves coppery in early spring.

FRUIT: Clusters of small, greenish flowers usually go unnoticed in late spring. The plump, blue-black berries about ⅜" across are most prominent and seen in late summer. Several cluster together on short stems which branch from a longer main stem. The seedy berries are edible but not rated very highly.

WOOD: Light, brittle and of no value although during the last war tests were made on its drug content. The bark was harvested in great quantity during the war. Prices rose from 4c to 20c a pound. A permit is required to cut trees on Crown land.

DID YOU KNOW that the drug Cascara Sagrada is made from the bark? This laxative has been held in high regard by the medical profession for many decades.

QUICK CHECK: Large, ovalish, strongly veined leaves in loose whorls. Clusters of blue-black berries. Alderleaf buckthorn, a closely related shrub overlaps the range of cascara in the Kootenays. It has single, black berries.

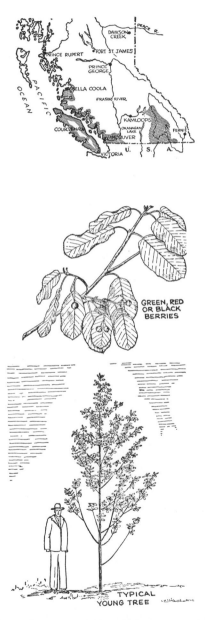

GREEN, RED OR BLACK BERRIES

TYPICAL YOUNG TREE

PACIFIC DOGWOOD
(Cornus nuttallii)

Flowering Dogwood - Western Dogwood

RANGE: Common along the east Coast of Vancouver Island and Alberni region. Along Mainland Coast area adjacent to Vancouver Island. Extends into Fraser Canyon for 30 miles north of Hope. Upper elevation range approximately 1,000'. Reported occurrence along Seymour Arm of Shuswap Lake.

FORM: Sometimes a bushy lop-sided tree to 12" in diameter and 30' high. Often has several trunks which are soon divided into heavy, upward-pointing limbs. Quite common as a very bushy shrub less than 10' high. Twigs are symmetrically branched opposite to one another and at right angles to the preceding pair.

BARK: Blackish-brown and smooth except on older trees which are finely ridged.

LEAVES: Glossy dark green above and much lighter below. Opposite, 3" - 4" long and with characteristic "dogwood veins" curving parallel to the leaf edge. In the fall, leaves generally are tinged with red.

FRUIT: Dogwood blossoms appear from April to June and sometimes again in September. The bloom is from 2½" - 5" across and may have from 4 - 6 white, showy bracts surrounding a rounded knob of greenish flowers. This central cluster turns into a compact group of red, bead-like berries thus adding gay color to the tree during August and September.

WOOD: A hard, fine-grained wood that has no particular use.

DID YOU KNOW that the dogwood is the unofficial floral emblem of the Province? The limited range prevents general acceptance. It and the cascara are the only trees protected by law. Skewers or "dags" once were made from its wood, hence the name "dagwood" later popularized as "dogwood."

QUICK CHECK: Unmistakable "dogwood" leaves, flowers and fruit. In winter the symmetrical branching is sufficient.

4-6 SHOWY BRACTS

RED BERRIES

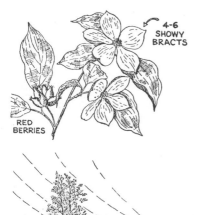

SHRUB FORM

ARBUTUS
(Arbutus menziesii)

Madrone

RANGE: A prominent tree of the Gulf Islands Zone and usually associated with garry oak. Very sparse west of Alberni summit but scattered trees at Great Central Lake. Northward limit between Qualicum and Courtenay. Scattered trees along Coast of Mainland from Bute Inlet southward.

FORM: A tree seldom more than 16″ in diameter with twisting trunk and heavy irregular branches. When open-grown it assumes an irregular rounded outline but in shady surroundings there is a wide variation in shape.

BARK: An unusual and quite distinctive mottled, reddish-orange effect is produced by large, loose scales which curl raggedly and then drop. Sometimes the trunk is quite smooth if scales have fallen. Only native tree with this type and color of bark.

LEAF: Alternate, evergreen leaves from 3″ - 6″ long. They have a thick leathery texture and are glossy dark green above and whitish green beneath.

FRUIT: The clusters of creamy-white, bell-shaped flowers of May are followed in late summer by irregular masses of small, orange-red berries each about ⅜″ across. They are seedy and not edible but much sought after by birds.

WOOD: Although soft and easily worked when green it becomes extremely hard when dry. Its tendency to warp and check limits use to a few novelty items. The bright color of the bark is not retained to any degree by the brownish wood.

DID YOU KNOW that arbutus is the only native broadleaf evergreen in Canada? On most of its range in B.C. it is a good indicator of rock or a hard subsoil lying not far beneath the surface. The glossy leaves prevent water from remaining on them and thus, in winter, protect themselves from a damaging ice coating.

QUICK CHECK: A tree of limited range with exfoliating orange-red bark and thick, glossy, evergreen leaves.

ORANGE-RED BERRIES

CREAMY "BELL" FLOWERS

KEY TO THE SHRUBS

Most keys are based on minute differences in flower or seed structure and may require in their use a fair knowledge of structural botany as well as several specimens showing these phases. Very often, a person finds shrubs without flower or seed and is at a loss for a clue. A simple method given here is the breaking of the shrubs into groupings by their general size and habitat. Besides the listings that follow a good deal of help can be obtained from "Nature's Calendar for Flowering Shrubs" page 172; the lists of the more common shrubs for each biotic zone, pages 7 - 13; and the altitudinal groupings, page 14.

ARMED SHRUBS

CREEPERS AND CLIMBERS

SHRUBS WITH EYE-CATCHING FEATURES

SHOWY FLOWERS

Broom (yellow)
Elder (white)
Goats' Beard (white)
Hardhack (pink)
Mahonia (yellow)
Mock Orange (white)
Ninebark (white)
Ocean Spray (white)
Rabbitbrush (yellow)
Rhododendron (red)
Rhododendron (white)
Salmonberry (red)
Saskatoon Berry (white)
Shrubby Cinquefoil
  (yellow)
Snowbrush (white)
Thimbleberry (white)
Twin-flower (pink)
Gorse (yellow)

SHOWY BERRIES

Cranberry, high-bush (red)
Currant, Squaw (red)
Devil's Club (red)
Elder (red, blue, black)
Kinnikinnick (red)
Mahonia (blue-black)
Mountain Ash (red)
Red-osier Dogwood
  (dull white)
Rose, Wild (red)
Salmonberry
  (yellow to red)
Saskatoon Berry
  (blue to black)
Soopolallie (red)
Squashberry (red)
Thimbleberry (red)
Twinberry (red)
Waxberry (white)

UNUSUAL LEAVES

Azalea, False
  (white hairs)
Birch, Scrub
  (small, round)
Cinquefoil, Shrubby
  (3-7 fingers)
Labrador Tea
  (brown wool)
Mahonia (holly-like)
Ninebark (3-lobed)
Rhododendron, white
  (coppery hairs)
Silverberry (silvery)
Soopolallie (brown rust)
Snowbrush (sticky)
Squashberry (3-lobed)

KEY TO THE SHRUBS

The following doesn't include the shrubs listed on page 54 as CREEPERS, CLIMBERS and ARMED SHRUBS. The groupings combine shrubs related in general form or growing together under similar conditions. The order of arrangement of the shrubs in this book follows as close as possible the divisions outlined on these facing pages.

UNDER 2' HIGH

EDIBLE BERRIES
	Page
Huckleberry, Dwarf	58
Blueberry, Canada	58
Blueberry, Red Alpine	58
*Huckleberry, Black Mountain	88

SUB-ALPINE AND ALPINE
Heather, White, Moss	59
Heather, Red	59
Heather, Yellow	59
Crowberry	59

"SPIRAEA" LEAF
*Spirea, Flat-top	60
*Spirea, Mountain	60
*Spirea, Pyramidal	60

BOGS OR WET SLOPES
*Labrador Tea	73
*Labrador Tea, Mtn.	73
*Swamp-laurel	74
*Moorwort	74

HAIRY RED BERRY
Teaberry, Mountain	67
Teaberry, Western	67

DRY INTERIOR ZONE
*Rabbitbrush	92
*Tetradymia	92
*Pasture Wormwood	92
*Poison Ivy	91

MISCELLANEOUS
*Dogbane, Spreading	71
*Cinquefoil, Shrubby	71
*Waxberry	72
*False Box	72

"HOLLY" LEAVES
*Mahonia (Oregon Grape)	70

*Usually over 1' high. Sometimes over 2'.

2' - 6' HIGH

LEAF WHORLS
	Page
Azalea, False	94
Copper Bush	94
Rhododendron, White	95
Rhododendron, Red	95

DRY INTERIOR ZONE
†Antelope Bush	93
Sagebrush	93
Snowbrush	83
Ceanothus, Red-stem	83
Soopolallie	84
†Silverberry	84
Currant, Squaw	85
Sumac	85

SWAMPY GROUND
Hardhack	64
Sweet Gale	64
†Buckthorn, Alderleaf	65
†Birch, Scrub	65
†Dogwood, Red-osier	66

SOUTH VANCOUVER ISLAND
Gorse	96
Manzanita, Hairy	96
Broom	96

EDIBLE BERRIES
Huckleberry, Black Mtn.	88
Huckleberry, Tall Blue	88
Huckleberry, Red	89
Huckleberry, Evergreen	89

† Often over 6' high.

2' - 6' HIGH

SHOWY FLOWERS
	Page
†Ocean Spray	86
†Mock Orange	86

COAST OR WET INTERIOR
†Salal	78
†Indian-plum	78
†Hazel	79
Goats' Beard	79
†Thimbleberry	87
†Salmonberry	87
†Twinberry, Black	77
Currant, Red-flower	99
Currant, Sticky	99

MOUNTAIN SLOPES
Twinberry, Red	81
Honeysuckle, Blue Fly	81
Ninebark, Mallow	81
†Mountain Ash, Sitka	68
†Mountain Ash, Western	68
Squashberry	80
Cranberry, High-bush	80
Currant, Stink	98
Currant, Hudson Bay	98

† Often over 6' high.

OVER 6' HIGH

LARGE COMPOUND LEAF
Elder, Black-berry	69
Elder, Red-berry	69
Elder, Blue-berry	69

3-LOBED LEAF
Ninebark	66

HALF LEAF NOTCHED
Saskatoon Berry	82

DAMP GROUND
Dogwood, Red-osier	66
Dogwood, Western	66

EVERGREEN LEAF
Wax-myrtle	64

Note: The following plants may be shrubby but usually are classed under Trees. Junipers, Dogwood, Sitka Alder, Hawthorn, Crab-apple and Cherries.

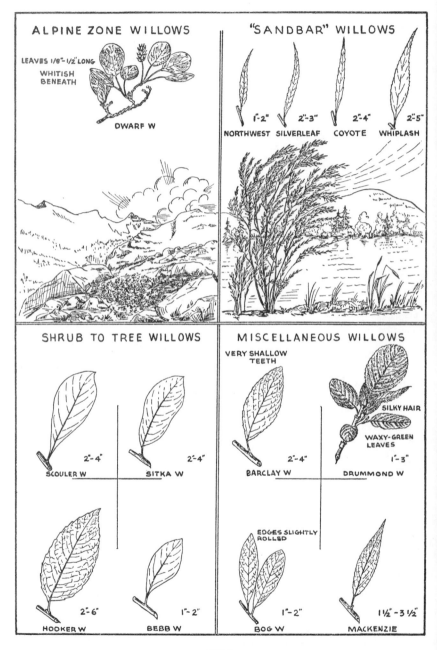

ALPINE ZONE WILLOWS

LEAVES 1/8"-1/2" LONG
WHITISH BENEATH

DWARF W

"SANDBAR" WILLOWS

1"-2" NORTHWEST
2"-3" SILVERLEAF
2"-4" COYOTE
2"-5" WHIPLASH

SHRUB TO TREE WILLOWS

2"-4" SCOULER W
2"-4" SITKA W
2"-6" HOOKER W
1"-2" BEBB W

MISCELLANEOUS WILLOWS

VERY SHALLOW TEETH

2"-4" BARCLAY W

SILKY HAIR
WAXY-GREEN LEAVES
1"-3" DRUMMOND W

EDGES SLIGHTLY ROLLED

1"-2" BOG W

1½"-3½" MACKENZIE

(56)

WILLOWS
(Salix spp.)

Willows are one of the most familiar and widespread groups of shrubs in the Province. Although most grow along creeks or rivers certain species are found high upon mountain slopes, where they form a shrubby mat only a few inches high.

All willows like sunlight and seek open places. Their bark is exceptionally bitter. In spring and early summer each leaf stem has two shiny, false leaves growing at the base. Most willow leaves are long and graceful with smooth or slightly toothed edges. Winter buds have a single, hood-like scale. "Pussy willows" and white, fluffy catkins are very noticeable in the spring.

With thirty or more willows in B.C. only a trained botanist can cope with their identification. This is because many species flower before the leaves appear; male and female flowers are on different shrubs; leaf and twig characteristics often vary greatly with age; and hybridization is common.

Two willows likely to reach tree size are Peachleaf Willow and Pacific Willow. They are described under TREES. The following is a selection of the more common and recognizable willows:

ALPINE WILLOWS
To 6" High, Shrubby, Mat-like

CASCADE W. (*S. cascadensis*)
Leaves 1/4"-3/4", glossy green. Interior Mountains.

DWARF W. (*S. nivalis*)
Leaves 1/8"-1/2", silvery beneath. Widespread.

ALPINE W. (*S. arctica*)
Leaves 1/2"-1 1/2", yellow stems. Selkirk and Rocky Moutains.

SHRUBS TO SMALL TREES
Leaves Wide, Roundish

SCOULER W. (*S. scouleriana*)
Leaves 2"-4", 1/3 as wide, rounded or broad tip. Smooth on both sides. Widespread in B.C. First to bloom.

SITKA W. (*S. sitchensis*)
Leaves 2"-4" long, 1/3 as wide, rounded tip. Velvety with fine hairs beneath. Watercourses through B.C.

HOOKER W. (*S. hookeriana*)
Leaves 2"-6" long, 1/2 as wide, dull-pointed. Woolly hairs beneath. Wet or dry land, southern Vancouver Island.

BEBB W. (*S. bebbiana*)
Leaves to 2" long, 1/2 as wide, round-pointed. Rocky Mountains.

"SAND BAR" WILLOWS
To 15' High, Slender Limbs, Narrow Leaves

NORTHWEST W. (*S. sessilifolia*)
Leaves 1"-2", pea-green, pointed both ends, hairy beneath. Coast to Cascades.

SILVERLEAF W. (*S. argophylla*)
Leaves 2"-3", silvery with white hairs. River banks Dry Interior Zone.

COYOTE W. (*S. exigua*)
Leaves 2"-4", long, 1/8"-1/4" wide. Silvery green. East of Cascade Mountains.

WHIPLASH W. (*S. caudata*)
Narrow leaves 2"-5" long, long tapering point. Green both sides. Fine teeth. Long brown "whips". Dry Interior Zone.

MISCELLANEOUS WILLOWS

BARCLAY W. (*S. barclayi*)
Variable leaves, 2"-4" long, ovalish, sharp-pointed, hairy above, bloom beneath. Common willow of sub-alpine.

DRUMMOND W. (*S. drummondiana*)
Leaves 1"-3" long, ovalish, white velvety beneath with mat of hairs. Common in Rockies to 7,000'.

BOG W. (*S. pedicellaris*)
Low shrubs to 5'. Leaves to 2", edges rolled, short stems. Bogs and wet places.

MACKENZIE W. (*S. mackenziana*)
Shrub or small tree. Leaves 1 1/2" - 3 1/2" long, sharp-pointed, rounded at base, "powdery" beneath. Stems hairy. Low to high elevations. Widespread.

DWARF HUCKLEBERRY
(Vaccinium caespitosum)

Dwarf Bilberry — Dwarf Blueberry

Imagine a huckleberry bush only an inch high! Sometimes this dwarf bush is only this high but more often it is 4" - 8". The many thin round twigs carry a heavy mass of finely toothed leaves less than 1" long. The flowers are pinkish while the smallish solitary abundant berries are blue.

QUICK CHECK: A bushy shrub to 8" high. Leaves ¼" - 1" long, widest above centre.

RANGE: Widespread throughout B.C. from sea level to alpine heights. Common on edges of swamps or in mountain meadows. Also on rocky ridges at high elevation. Alaska Highway.

CANADA BLUEBERRY
(Vaccinium myrtilloides)

Canada blueberry is distinguished easily by the clusters of flowers or berries. Abundant in its northern range, it carpets acre upon acre of forest floor. The leaves are sharp-pointed and without teeth. End twigs are round, green and finely hairy. The black berries with blue bloom are very sweet and quickly picked. They ripen by August.

QUICK CHECK: Clusters of flowers or berries.

RANGE: Common through Central B.C. Bogs or swamps in Southern B.C.

BOG BILBERRY *(V. occidentale)* to 2' high. Flower drooping, 1-4, berry black with bloom. Swamps in north B.C. Mountain swamps in west.

GROUSEBERRY
(Vaccinium scoparium)

Grouse Huckleberry

This, the smallest of the blueberries, may form a lacey green carpet 3" - 6" high over the dry gravelly forest soil. Very often it is the most abundant shrub over acres of ground. For some reason it is almost always found under lodgepole pine stands growing at elevations of 3,500' and up. There is a characteristic sour odor to these massed shrubs.

Each little bush is a network of kinky green twigs with oval leaves up to ½" long. The berries are from ⅛" - ¼" in diameter, red and very pleasant to taste.

QUICK CHECK: Bushy little shrubs with green angled twigs and oval leaves less than ½" long. Small red berries. Grows under lodgepole pine.

RANGE: Generally above 3,500' elevations on mountains east of the Cascades.

WHITE MOSS HEATHER
(Cassiope mertensiana)

Once moss heather and heather are given a close look they never need be confused. Ordinary moss hasn't leaves and moss heather, for remembering purposes, hasn't them either. Actually the ridges of small scales are leaves but are pressed so closely that the twigs look like green pipe cleaners.

A common plant of sub-alpine and alpine areas it may grow in neat clumps several feet across and a foot high or in ragged sprawling masses over extensive areas of rock and ground. The small white flowers are bell-shaped and closely resemble those of yellow heather.

QUICK CHECK: A low matted plant with scales pressed to twigs. Small white bell flower.

RANGE: Sub-alpine and alpine mountains.

C. tetragona and *C. stelleriana* closely resemble the above except that the first has grooves on the leaves. The latter has leaves that spread out from the stem. Both range widely through the Province.

RED HEATHER
(Phyllodoce empetriformis)

A common low matted plant of the high mountains, sometimes almost the sole carpet for extensive alpine slopes. When in bloom it is topped with hundreds of rose-red "bell" blossoms —an ample reward in floral beauty for the mountain climber. The leaves are short and needle-like.

QUICK CHECK: A "heather" plant with short needle leaves. Rose-red flowers.

RANGE: Sub-alpine and alpine slopes.

YELLOW HEATHER *(P. glanduliflora)* is very similar to the above except for the creamy flowers. Often the two mingle in a spreading mat with the contrast being shown in vivid fashion by the different blooms. The range is the same.

CROWBERRY
(Empetrum nigrum)

Crowberry differs from heather in having a number of small purplish flowers or round berries as black as a crow. Whereas the heathers usually grow in dry exposed places near timberline or above it, crowberry seeks shady places beneath the trees. Its leaves are about 1/4" long, thick and needle-like.

QUICK CHECK: Thick short "needle" leaves. Flowers, small, purple. Berries smooth and black.

RANGE: Moist shaded forests above 3,000' at Coast and 4,000' in Interior and extending to timberline. Widespread throughout B.C. Alaska Hwy.

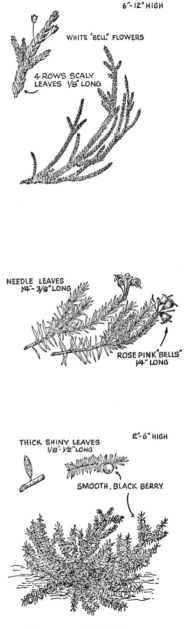

6"-12" HIGH

WHITE "BELL" FLOWERS

4-ROWS SCALY LEAVES 1/8" LONG

NEEDLE LEAVES 1/4"-3/8" LONG

ROSE PINK "BELLS" 1/4" LONG

THICK SHINY LEAVES 1/8"-1/2" LONG

2"-6" HIGH

SMOOTH, BLACK BERRY

SHRUBS

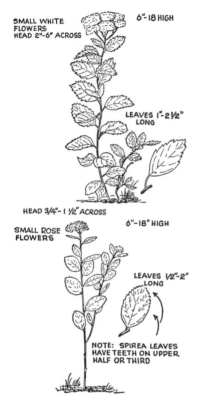

5 SMALL WHITE FLOWERS HEAD 2"-6" ACROSS

6"-18 HIGH

LEAVES 1"-2½" LONG

HEAD ¾"-1½" ACROSS

6"-18" HIGH

SMALL ROSE FLOWERS

LEAVES ½"-2" LONG

NOTE: SPIREA LEAVES HAVE TEETH ON UPPER HALF OR THIRD

SMALL WHITE OR PINK FLOWERS HEAD 1"-4" HIGH

12"-30" HIGH

LEAVES 1"-3" LONG

FLAT-TOP SPIREA
(Spiraea lucida)

White Meadow Sweet — Birch-Leaf Spirea

This is a low spirea not over 2' high and very common throughout the drier, more open forests. The stem is slender and often has several branches. The leaves are rounded like a birch leaf and coarsely toothed along the upper two-thirds. Not all the shrubs bloom but those that do are capped with a dense flat-topped crown of small white flowers. Common associates are Douglas fir, larch, lodgepole pine, soopolallie and kinnikinnick.

QUICK CHECK: A low shrub with rounded spirea leaf. Flat white flower head on some. Don't confuse with scrubby Saskatoon berry.

RANGE: East of the Cascades in dry open mountain forests. Cariboo Parklands and upper limit of Dry Interior Zone. Quesnel, Stuart Lake, Vanderhoof.

MOUNTAIN SPIREA
(Spiraea densiflora)

Pink Meadow Sweet — Sub-alpine Spirea

As the various names suggest this species is one of high mountain slopes. It is a typical spirea with a slender stem rarely over 2' high, very leafy with oval leaves to 2" long. The tiny pink flowers are massed in small heads ¾" - 1½" across. Sub-alpine meadows throughout B.C. are home to this trim little shrub.

PYRAMIDAL SPIREA
(Spiraea pyramidata)

The 1" - 4" long pyramidal head of white or pinkish flowers and large leaves irregularly toothed on the top two-thirds will identify this shrub. Although not of common occurrence it is widely distributed from middle Coastal elevations to 4,500' elevations in the Interior. It has been collected in the Cariboo Parklands Zone and as far north as Stuart Lake. Also at Yale and Manning Park.

KINNIKINNICK
(Arctostaphylos Uva-ursi)

Bearberry

Kinnikinnick is one of the more common and widely distributed evergreen shrubs in the Province. Although small of leaf and trailing in habit it has a number of characteristics that bring it to the attention. Most compelling are the bright red berries dotted among the glossy green leaves. These are very prominent from August to late winter and favored by grouse and bear.

Wherever there is a coarse gravel soil kinnikinnick will form a low green mat or extend exploring arms over rotten logs, rocks, or down the face of road cuts. The small evergreen leaves are leathery and grow alternately. The larger stems have reddish bark and the roots pursue an unbelievably twisting course through rocky soil. Flowers are small, pinkish and bell-shaped.

The popular name kinnikinnick is an Indian word meaning a smoking mixture. Although the leaves of this plant were only one of the ingredients, the shrub has taken on this name.

QUICK CHECK: A trailing plant with ½" - 1" long, alternate, evergreen leaves. Bell-shaped pink flowers or mealy red berries.

RANGE: On exposed, well-drained soils throughout B.C. from sea-level to near timberline.

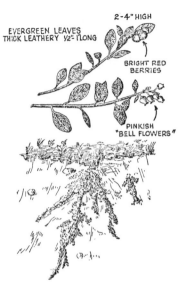

2 - 4" HIGH

EVERGREEN LEAVES THICK LEATHERY ½" - 1" LONG

BRIGHT RED BERRIES

PINKISH "BELL FLOWERS"

TWIN-FLOWER
(Linnaea borealis)

Twin-flower is so dainty and gay with flowers during summer months that it may be thought of as a flower although the woody vine brings it within the shrub grouping. A person won't go far into shady cool woods without seeing the thin spreading vines, perhaps 3' - 4' long, crawling over the forest floor. The little evergreen leaves are less than ½" long and almost round. Although shiny dark green above, a much paler tint is found on the underside. Notice the several well-separated nicks or teeth along the upper half of the leaves. This feature will clear up any identification trouble.

In June and July numerous slender flower stems shoot up 2" - 4" from the vine. Each stem carries a pair of pink "twin" flowers so delicately scented their fragrance won't soon be forgotten. Linnaeus, the famous Swedish botanist and founder of the present system of botanical classification chose the twin-flower as his favorite plant.

QUICK CHECK: Slender vine with alternate, oval to round, evergreen leaves with few minute teeth on upper half. Pink "twin" flowers.

RANGE: Cool moist woods throughout B.C. From sea-level to timberline.

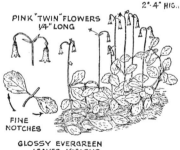

2" - 4" HIGH

PINK "TWIN" FLOWERS ¼" LONG

FINE NOTCHES

GLOSSY EVERGREEN LEAVES ½" LONG

CRANBERRY
Vaccinium oxvcoccus)

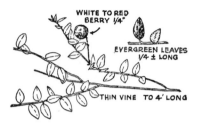

WHITE TO RED BERRY 1/4"

EVERGREEN LEAVES 1/4 ± LONG

THIN VINE TO 4' LONG

Although belonging to the blueberry family, this cranberry bears little resemblance to any of them. It is found in peaty, mossy bogs and consists of a very thin vine perhaps 4' long and almost hidden in the moss. From the slender stem tiny evergreen leaves branch out. Often a hunt must be made to find one of its pink flowers or a berry which changes in color from white to red. Labrador tea and swamp laurel often hide this dainty cranberry from view.

Cranberries were much sought after by the first pioneers in America. They called them crane berries because of the fanciful resemblance of the flower to the head and neck of a crane.

QUICK CHECK: Very slender vine growing in bogs. Leaves alternate, sharp-pointed, evergreen and almost stemless. Flowers pink and berry white or red. Cloudberry which also grows in damp places has bristly hairs on the leaf.

RANGE: Commonly given as "bogs throughout B.C.", but many bogs over relatively large areas fail to show it. Probably quite common in low Coastal forest bogs. Mile 12 Hope-Princeton Highway. Fairly common along Alaska Highway.

SNOWBERRY
(Gaultheria hispidula)
(Chiogenes hispidula)

THICK LEAVES 1/16"- 1/4" LONG BRISTLY BENEATH

WHITE BERRY WITH BLACK BRISTLES

REDDISH HAIR ON GREENISH TWIGS

RUNNERS TO 8" LONG

This is a tiny creeping shrub both limited in range and habitat. What it lacks in size is made up in daintiness for its numerous slender runners are only a few inches long. A man's hat might cover it completely. Most times it will be found in a swampy or damp location perched on some hummock or rotting log. Superficially it resembles twin-flower and cranberry but the stem, leaves and fruit are quite different.

The fine greenish stems are covered with short reddish hairs while the thick leathery leaves are alternate, less than 1/4" long and dotted on the underside with small black hairs. The white berry, not to be outdone, bristles with similar short spines. The few berries are usually hidden from view by the mat of leafy runners. Growth in its vicinity might be black spruce, Labrador tea, scrub birch, twin-flower and pyrola.

QUICK CHECK: Thick leaves up to 1/4" long, hairs on stem, leaves and edible fruit.

RANGE: Swampy places in the Rocky Mountains. Mt. Robson, Emerald Lake. Also near edges of Interior Wet Belt Zone. Sicamous.

TRAILING RUBUS
(Rubus pedatus)

This tiny trailing plant hiding under false azalea, white rhododendron and huckleberry bushes on the higher mountain slopes could be regarded as one of the more obscure shrubs in the Province. However its relative abundance under certain conditions, the display of symmetrical leaves against a mossy background, and the tiny red jewel-like berries all contribute in enhancing its appearance.

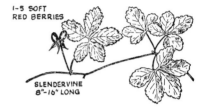

1-5 SOFT RED BERRIES

SLENDER VINE 8"-16" LONG

The wire-thin woody vine may be 8" - 16" long. At intervals an unusual leaf branches off. It has 3 rounded leaflets, 2 of which may be so deeply lobed as to look like 5 complete leaflets. The small, raspberry-like flowers, white in color, grow singly and are replaced by several clear red berries.

QUICK CHECK: Slender vine with rounded "leaflet" leaf about 1" across. One to several clear red berries.

RANGE: Shady mossy places in sub-alpine Coastal forests and Interior Wet Belt Zone. Also North Central B.C. and Rockies. Common along Alaska Highway with berries ripe in September.

RED HONEYSUCKLE
(Lonicera dioica var. glaucescens)

Although having the thin stem and opposite leaves of the honeysuckles, this one is quite different in its habit of stretching along the ground for only a few feet. The variable leaves are from 2" - 3½" long and have a whitish bloom on the undersurface. Leaf edges are finely hairy. The flowers are yellow and red rather than orange and the berries follow through in color. Semi-open, dry forests above 2,000' in elevation provide desirable conditions. Douglas fir, white pine, false box and western teaberry are associates.

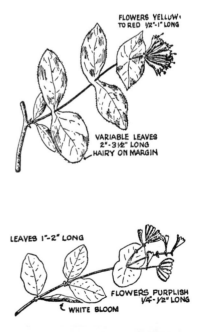

FLOWERS YELLOW TO RED ½"-1" LONG

VARIABLE LEAVES 2"-3½" LONG HAIRY ON MARGIN

LEAVES 1"-2" LONG

FLOWERS PURPLISH ¼"-½" LONG

WHITE BLOOM

QUICK CHECK: Thin straight vine on ground, opposite leaves with bloom below and hairs along edges.

RANGE: Above 2,000' in semi-open forests at Coast and 3,000' in Interior. Mile 26 Hope-Princeton Highway, Field, Peace River, Cariboo.

PURPLE HONEYSUCKLE *(L. hispidula)*: A slender trailing plant up to 12' long. Young stems hairy, oval leaves 1" - 2" long, hairy and with bloom beneath. Pink-purple flowers, red berries. Range— dry open situations on southern Vancouver Island and Gulf Islands.

(63)

SHRUBS

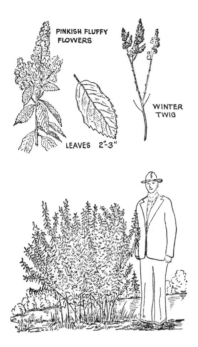

PINKISH FLUFFY FLOWERS

WINTER TWIG

LEAVES 2"-3"

HARDHACK
(Spiraea douglasii)

Steeple Bush — Douglas Spirea

Hardhack usually masses in dense clumps around wet places and is crowned with such a showy display of fluffy pink plumes that it can't help but be noticed. Its slender reddish-brown stems some 3'-4' high show up like a miniature forest during winter months. At this time the pyramidal brownish husks are very noticeable and possibly give rise to the common name. In summer the twigs are covered by narrow oblong leaves with coarse notches on the top half. The coarse teeth on the upper part of the leaf are characteristic of the spireas. Hairy twigs and leaves hairy beneath are features of hardhack which always favors open places where there is plenty of light.

QUICK CHECK: In winter, thin reddish-brown stems with dry pyramidal husk. In summer, upright pink plumes of tiny flowers. Spirea leaf toothed on upper half, woolly beneath.

RANGE: Margins of ponds and meadows at low elevations throughout Coastal Forest and Interior Wet Belt Zones. Damp places in Central B.C.,

SWEET GALE
(Myrica Gale)

There is a good possibility that sweet gale will never be noticed unless a special effort is made to find it. Because it prefers a moist humid climate and a damp habitat, sweet gale is found along swamps and lake margins on Vancouver Island and at low elevations along the Mainland coast. It closely resembles hardhack in form and often loses its identity with the showier shrub.

The slender reddish stems grow up to 4' high. The thin wedge-like leaves, 1/2"-2" long, are coarsely notched along their upper third and have a whitish tinge on the undersurface. Before the leaves appear, clumps of greenish catkins form along the ends of the branches. These later change to brown, cone-like husks prominent in winter.

QUICK CHECK: See habitat limitations. Unmistakable catkins and "cone" seeds.

RANGE: Margins of ponds and lakes. Gulf Island and Coastal Forest Zones. Cowichan Lake, Shawnigan Lake, Bella Coola.

FORM AS ABOVE

GREENISH CATKINS

LEAVES 1/2"-2"LONG

WAX-MYRTLE *(Myrica californica)*: Although growing to a sturdy shrub or small tree waxmyrtle because of its extremely limited range perhaps is the least known of all native shrubs. It is reported from the extreme west coast of Vancouver Island near Tofino and Ucluelet. The leaves are evergreen and shaped like those of sweet gale.

ALDERLEAF BUCKTHORN
(Rhamnus alnifolia)
Buckthorn

Alderleaf buckthorn hasn't thorns and probably takes the buckthorn part of its name from related species to the south. It is a shrub that one might look for in vain unless knowing that it is confined to marshy places like wet meadows. Here where it grows with scrub birch, red-osier dogwood and twin-flower, it may be quite plentiful.

Most shrubs aren't over 5' high and have a loose limb structure something like red-osier dogwood. The symmetrical, 2" - 4" long, dark green leaves with their fine teeth may be noticed before the small greenish flowers or scattered black berries. These plump three-seeded berries usually grow singly and, although juicy, are very bitter.

QUICK CHECK: Marsh habitat. Distinctive symmetrical leaf heavily veined beneath. Small greenish flowers or single black berries in axils of the leaves.

RANGE: Very limited in range but plentiful in Kootenay River Valley. Abundant east of Creston and vicinity of Kimberley. Extends to Rocky Mountains.

LEAVES 2"-4" LONG

SHINY BLACK BERRIES

SCRUB BIRCH
(Betula glandulosa)

"Any resemblance to any birch living or dead is purely co-incidental" might be the descriptive theme for scrub birch... True enough the smooth bark with dull white markings bears some similarity to water birch and there are birch catkins. However, its leaves catch the attention more than anything else for they are almost round and no larger than 10c or 25c coins. Heavy veins give them a ribbed look and add to the thick leathery texture. They turn coppery red in the fall.

Scrub birch brings a picture of wet meadows and swamps sometimes covered almost completely by this shrub. It seldom grows as a lone individual. From the rather compact base a dozen or more crooked branches raise and spread outward to form a loose sprawling top often reaching 15' in height. The height decreases as one goes northward and in Central B.C. it may be only 4' or 5' high.

The slim brown catkins less than 1" long give a colorful touch in late fall to an otherwise drab shrub. Labrador tea, buckthorn and black spruce often keep it company.

QUICK CHECK: A limby shrub of swamps and low grounds. Leaves thick and round, up to 1" across. Twigs rough and sticky.

RANGE: Usually damp ground but occasionally high open slopes. Throughout Province from valley bottom to sub-alpine levels. Sporadic occurrence on Vancouver Island. North to Yukon.

WAXY GREEN LEAVES 1/2"-3/4"

CATKIN

WARTY STEMS

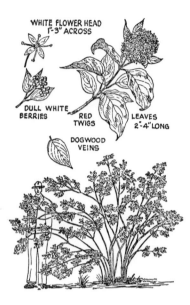

WHITE FLOWER HEAD
1"-3" ACROSS

DULL WHITE
BERRIES

RED
TWIGS

LEAVES
2"-4" LONG

DOGWOOD
VEINS

RED-OSIER DOGWOOD
(*Cornus stolonifera*)

Red-osier dogwood has three eye-catching features. In winter and spring the shiny, bright red bark of the thin stems and symmetrically arranged branches provides welcome color. During June the round heads of dainty flowers are startlingly white against the rich green background of leaves. The graceful vein network of the leaves, characteristic of dogwoods, is the third point.

Usually the red-osier dogwood is massed with other shrubs and trees and so in the summer almost loses its identity in the floral picture. In August it attracts attention by the unusual lead-white color of its berries. Look for this attractive shrub in the Interior along shady creek courses or damp lowlands and mixed with poplar, water birch and willow. Fall weather brings a reddish tint to some of the leaves similar to those of dogwood.

QUICK CHECK: In winter red twig ends and characteristic branching. In summer, "dogwood" leaf.

RANGE: Widespread east of the Coast Mountains. Found from valley bottom to near timberline. Along Alaska Highway.

WESTERN DOGWOOD (*C. occidentalis*) so closely resembles the above that the name red-osier dogwood is generally used for both. However this shrub has leaves with hairs on the underside. It is most abundant west of the Cascades.

WHITE FLOWER
HEADS

RED
SEED HUSKS

LEAVES
1"-3" LONG

SHREDDING
BARK

NINEBARK
(*Physocarpus capitatus*)

Ninebarks receive their name from the supposedly nine thin layers of shreddy bark on the main stems. In Coastal regions ninebark is a rather dense upright shrub 6' - 12' high with long arching branches. Usually it is well scattered and growing with thimbleberry, red-osier dogwood, and other damp-ground shrubs.

The eye-catching, 3-lobed leaves which are quite similar to squashberry, often bring ninebark to notice. During May and into June it is artistically dappled with white rounded balls formed by masses of tiny flowers. By July 15 these have made a startling change to a reddish clump of rough seed husks. The color lasts until August when the seeds are ripe. Mallow ninebark is a small shrub of the Interior. See page 81.

QUICK CHECK: 3-lobed, deeply veined, alternate leaves with fine hairs on undersurface. Shreddy loose bark.

RANGE: Damp places Coastal region and in Interior Wet Belt. Creston.

WESTERN TEABERRY
(Gaultheria ovatifolia)

Bush Wintergreen — Oregon Wintergreen

It requires more than casual observation to find this small sprawling shrub. Even its red berries pass unnoticed for they are hidden beneath the trim little leaves. Western teaberry is a shallow-rooted plant with several thin kinky branches reddish in color. The heart-shaped leaves from 1/2" - 1½" long are artistically arranged in alternate fashion on the hairy twigs. The leaves are minutely toothed and shiny waxy green above but dull beneath. The small white flowers grow singly while the bright red berries are quite unusual being grooved into segments and covered with fine hairs. They are edible.

A preference is shown for dry semi-open forest land above 2,000' elevation in the Coastal Forest Zone with a similar habitat east of the Cascades. Lodgepole pine, white pine and Douglas fir with a sparse undergrowth of false box and twin-flower make a common setting for western teaberry.

QUICK CHECK: Low shrub less than 12" high. Alternate glossy green, heart-shaped leaves on hairy red twigs. Single red berries.

RANGE: Locally abundant in suitable habitat but one of less frequently encountered shrubs. Mt. Benson and Mt. Arrowsmith, V.I.; Mile 23 Hope-Princeton Highway; Mt. Revelstoke; mountains near Nelson. Garibaldi Park at 2,800'.

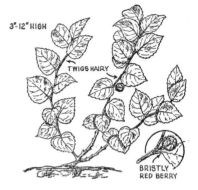

3"-12" HIGH

TWIGS HAIRY

BRISTLY RED BERRY

MOUNTAIN TEABERRY
(Gaultheria humifusa)

Western Wintergreen

This miniature edition of the above usually is found in damp locations at sub-alpine and alpine elevations. It seldom reaches 3" in height. The small leaves from 1/4" - 1/2" long are rounded and very finely toothed. Flowers and fruit are similar to western teaberry.

QUICK CHECK: Note range limitation. Low shrub 1" - 3" high with several short crooked stems. Alternate rounded leaves finely toothed. Red berry.

RANGE: A timberline plant throughout B.C. Manning Park, Garibaldi Park, Mt. Revelstoke, etc.

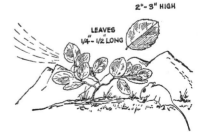

2"-3" HIGH

LEAVES 1/4" - 1/2 LONG

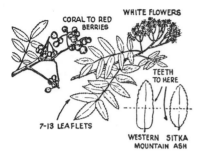

CORAL TO RED BERRIES

WHITE FLOWERS

TEETH TO HERE

7-13 LEAFLETS

WESTERN SITKA MOUNTAIN ASH

SITKA MOUNTAIN ASH
(*Sorbus sitchensis*)

The use of mountain ash as an ornamental tree makes most people familiar with the tree form. The large bunches of red berries which hang on after the leaves have fallen distinguish this tree or shrub from any other. On Vancouver Island and the Lower Mainland, trees up to 20' high will be noticed. These are an introduced tree now widely naturalized on the Coast. The native mountain ash are shrubby growths of the higher mountains.

Sitka mountain ash is the most common and comes into fair abundance on high mountain slopes where the trees begin to thin out—approximately 3,000' at the Coast, 4,000' in the Interior. Sometimes there are only several thin stems up to 8' high with a sparse display of leaves and berries near the top. Under more favorable conditions a brushy thicket is found. In either case an open spot is chosen such as the edge of a meadow or rockslide. The compound leaf has 9 - 13 leaflets which carry coarse teeth almost to the base. Flowers are small, white, and carried in flat-topped clusters 2" - 4" across. These masses of blooms are quite prominent in the high mountains during June. The berries are bright red and suitable for making jelly although having a sour mealy taste when raw.

September sees them at their peak but some hang on until October. Migrating birds sometimes pick off astounding quantities of the berries.

QUICK CHECK: Compound leaf with 9 - 13 leaflets toothed to near base. Flower clusters 2" - 4" across. Berries coral-red.

RANGE: Most abundant above 3,000' at Coast, 4,000' in Interior. General throughout. Very common on high mountains between Grand Forks and Rossland. Northward beyond McLeod Lake.

WESTERN MOUNTAIN ASH (*S. scopulina*) is very similar to the above but has 7 - 11 bluish green leaflets with serrations near the tip only. The flower clusters are usually less than 2" across. The berries have a purplish rather than a coral tinge. The two species occasionally grow together. Western mountain ash is more apt to be found in the Cascade Mountains although it has been recorded on Vancouver Island and in the Interior.

BLUE-BERRY ELDER
(Sambucus cerulea) (S. glauca)

The names of the elders show that they may be distinguished by their berries. Otherwise the individual habitats, ranges and time of blooming can be definite helps. All elders have a large soft pith.

Blue-berry elder partly overlaps red-berry elder in range but grows on dry open situations. Leaflets are generally in nines although fives and sevens often occur. The flower head is white, flat and from 5" - 8" across. This one blooms through the summer and may continue into late August. The berries, in flat-topped clusters, are tinged with a lighter bluish-bloom.

QUICK CHECK: Large flat-topped blooms in June, July and August. Masses of small blue berries August and September.

RANGE: Dry places Gulf Island Zone, Malahat, Duncan, Alberni. Occasional shrubs in upper Fraser Valley. Very abundant from Princeton to Penticton in Dry Interior Zone. Nelson, Trail.

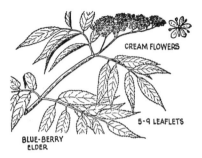

CREAM FLOWERS

5 - 9 LEAFLETS

BLUE-BERRY ELDER

RED-BERRY ELDER
(Sambucus racemosa var. arborescens)

Red-berry elder is a common shrub at the Coast, Vancouver Island and the wetter regions of the Interior, where it raises a spreading mass of stout stems 10' - 20' into the air. The leaves are opposite and formed of 5 - 7 toothed, sharp-pointed leaflets. Vigorous young shoots sometimes have 9 leaflets. The small yellowish-white flowers in their rounded head are in bloom throughout May. The smooth berries tinge with red in early June. They are not edible and even reputed to have poisonous properties.

QUICK CHECK: Compound leaf with 2" - 5" long, toothed, pointed leaflets. Yellowish-white flowers in rounded or pyramidal head. Berries bright red.

RANGE: Coastal Forest and Gulf Island Zone below 2,000'. Interior Wet Belt Zone below 3,500'. North Central B.C. Mt. Robson.

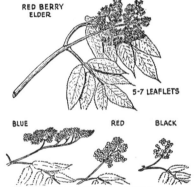

RED BERRY ELDER

5 - 7 LEAFLETS

BLUE   RED   BLACK

COMPARISON OF BERRY CLUSTERS

BLACK-BERRY ELDER
(Sambucus racemosa var. melanocarpa)

Black-berry elder is seldom over 8' high. It has the typical ascending spread and similarity in leaf and bark. Confusion can usually be avoided by noting the high mountain range limitation. The flower cluster differs from the red-berry elder in being more rounded and looser.

QUICK CHECK: Loose flower head. Shiny black berries. Leaflets 5 - 7.

RANGE: Mountain slopes east of the Cascades from 4,000' to timberline. Aberdeen Mountain near Vernon. Mt. Revelstoke Park. Nelson.

RED BERRY ELDER

(69)

OREGON GRAPE
(Berberis spp.)
Mahonia — Holly Grape — Barberry

Mahonia or Oregon grape is immediately distinguished by its evergreen, "holly"-like leaflets for no other shrub in the Province bears any resemblance to it. There may be considerable variation between two of the three species but the main characteristics, "holly" leaf, bright yellow flowers, or waxy blue berries are standard features.

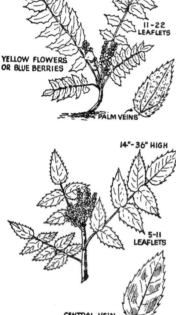

12"-20" HIGH

"HOLLY" LEAFLETS

11-22 LEAFLETS

YELLOW FLOWERS OR BLUE BERRIES

PALM VEINS

14"-36" HIGH

5-11 LEAFLETS

CENTRAL VEIN

3-7 LEAFLETS

6"-12 HIGH

BRISTLE SPINES

DULL BENEATH

OREGON GRAPE (*B. nervosa*): Has leaflets dull both sides, 11 - 21 per leaf. Three central veins. Prefers forest shade. It displays little variation in shape being under 2' high with several fern-like sprays of leaflets. Generally confined to lower elevations in Coastal and Interior Wet Belt forests.

TALL MAHONIA (*B. aquifolium*): Has leaflets shiny both sides, 5 - 11 per leaf. Main central vein. Favors exposed situations like road edges and stony clearings. This species is the one most commonly noticed. Sometimes thick, irregular stems reach 3' - 5' in height but more often a low sprawling shrub is found. Bright yellow flowers are prominent in clusters along the stem during May 15 - June 15. Dark blue berries with whitish bloom are well formed by August 15 and hang on until late fall. They make good jelly when dead ripe or touched with frost. Indians used the bright yellow wood in making a yellow dye. The attactive foliage, flowers, and berries together with the brilliant autumn coloring make it a desirable ornamental. Wide distribution through B.C. on exposed situations with poor rocky soils. Altitude range to 4,000' in the Interior.

CREEPING MAHONIA (*B. repens*): Has leaflets dull beneath, 2 - 7 per leaf. Main central vein. Very similar to *M. aquifolium* but less than 1' high. The spines are thinner and weaker. The underside of the leaflets has a whitish tinge. Widely scattered throughout B.C. on dry places to 6,000' elevation.

SPREADING DOGBANE
(Apocynum androsaemifolium)

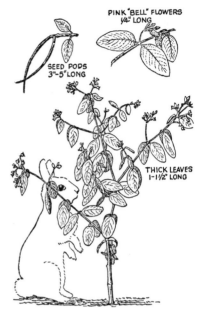

PINK "BELL" FLOWERS ¼" LONG

SEED PODS 3"-5" LONG

THICK LEAVES 1-1½" LONG

The dogbanes send up new stems each year but look so much like shrubs with their fibrous branching stems up to 16" high that they are so treated here. The name results from an unfounded superstition that dogs were repelled by this plant.

If the smooth reddish stem is broken a sticky, milky juice appears as with sumac. The dry exposed habitat along road edges and the prolonged blooming of the end clusters of small, pinkish, bell blossoms help in giving it individuality.

The rather thick, egg-shaped leaves, sharp-pointed and opposite from one another hang down in the summer's heat as if tired and lifeless. The fragrant flowers are in bloom from May to July due to the successive development of new clusters. Bees produce a very fine grade of honey from these. The seed pods are an amazing affair for such a small plant. They are shaped like a smooth, curved green bean 3"-5" long. This brownish husk splits open to allow silky seeds to escape.

QUICK CHECK: A low 2 or 3-branched shrub with opposite, thickish leaves. Milky juice exudes from broken stems. White to rose bell flowers in end clusters. Long curved "string bean" seed pods.

RANGE: Patchy distribution on dry exposed soils throughout B.C. From sea level to 3,000' at Coast and 5,500' in Interior. East of Pine Pass.

INDIAN HEMP (*A. cannabinum*) is a big brother to the above being up to 3' in height. Shadier conditions are preferred and it is not so abundant. The flowers differ in being greenish and slightly smaller than the above. The stems of Indian hemp were once picked in the fall by the Indians, shredded and woven into fishing lines and small ropes. It ranges across B.C.

SHRUBBY CINQUEFOIL
(Potentilla fruticosa)

VELVETY LEAVES 3-7 FINGERS

YELLOW FLOWER ¾" ACROSS

Being abundant only in certain localities or under favorable conditions, shrubby cinquefoil is a common plant to many but a total stranger to others. It is a fine-limbed, sprawling shrub up to 3' high with velvety, "3-7 fingered" leaves and bright yellow, "buttercup" flowers.

QUICK CHECK: Velvety "3-7 finger" leaves and "buttercup" flowers.

RANGE: From Cascade Mountains to Kootenay River Valley. Sporadic occurrence mostly at high exposed places. Common roadside shrub in Windermere Valley. Fairly abundant North Central B.C. and extending to Yukon.

WAXBERRY
(Symphoricarpos albus)

Snowberry

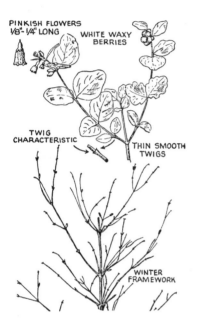

PINKISH FLOWERS 1/8"- 1/4" LONG

WHITE WAXY BERRIES

TWIG CHARACTERISTIC

THIN SMOOTH TWIGS

WINTER FRAMEWORK

Everyone will remember waxberry (often called snowberry) for its clumps of waxy, white berries during early winter months. Even after leaves and berries have fallen the thin twigs branching opposite to one another, provide identification.

Waxberry is one of the most widespread shrubs in B.C. Once started it widens its hold until a low bushy thicket 2'- 3' in height is formed.

The opposite leaves, thin and without teeth are roughly oval in shape and on some plants are irregularly lobed. They show a fine hair on the undersurface. The pinkish, bell flowers are usually clustered near the end of the twigs and in all stages of growth from bud to berry during June and July. The clusters of white, soft berries, irregular in shape and waxy to the touch, don't appear to be sought after by bird or rodent.

QUICK CHECK: A slender-stemmed shrub less than 3' high, locally abundant. Thin, opposite leaves, hairy beneath. Clumps of pinkish, bell flowers or white, waxy berries.

RANGE: Wide range of habitat but not in extreme shade. Throughout B.C. but usually limited to approximately 2,000' at the Coast and 3,000' in the Interior.

WOLFBERRY *(S. occidentalis)* has leaves usually not hairy beneath. Stamen and styles are longer than petals. Sporadic occurrence.

FALSE BOX
(Pachistima myrsinites)

Mountain Lover — Myrtle Box Leaf

Although lacking in conspicuous flowers or leaves, false box makes up for these shortcomings by its abundance in certain forest regions. It is a characteristic evergreen plant of Douglas fir, lodgepole pine or Engelmann spruce forests. In the shade it grows loose and sprawling but rarely reaches a height of 2'. On rocky slopes it forms attractive compact balls of greenery. The opposite, thick, evergreen leaves are comparatively small, 1/4" - 1" long, and grow on thin, angled branches.

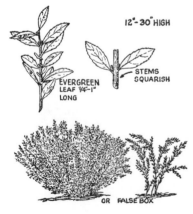

12"- 30" HIGH

EVERGREEN LEAF 1/4"-1" LONG

STEMS SQUARISH

OR FALSE BOX

The small flower clusters are an inconspicuous greenish or reddish color and usually go unnoticed cradled between branch and leaf stem. The fresh, bright-green look and compact form when grown in the open make it a fine shrub for landscaping.

QUICK CHECK: Small, opposite, evergreen leaves on thin, angled twigs. Comparatively abundant in its range.

RANGE: Widespread throughout B.C. in damper coniferous forests from sea level to timberline. Absent in Dry Interior regions.

LABRADOR TEA
(Ledum groenlandicum)

Labrador tea is widely distributed across Canada and the United States. Eastern Indian tribes used it for making a tea and this practice was copied by early explorers and settlers. There is little record of this use in B.C. The leaves are picked and left to dry before being crushed and steeped like tea.

Found generally on mossy, spongy bogs it sometimes occurs on wet, rocky sidehills at high elevations. Its thin, twisting stems, seldom over 3' high, and thick, narrow leaves with their woolly mat of reddish hairs on the undersurface are quite distinctive. This wool and the rolled-over edges of the evergreen, leathery leaves are Nature's way of preventing the loss of water from the underside of the leaves. Although Labrador tea usually grows in a bog the water is so cold that the plant may be unable to absorb any and so adopts a highly specialized leaf to conserve it. The leaves are grouped to give a rough whorl effect.

During June and July, depending on altitude, the twisted little shrub raises a showy head of white, star-like blossoms. These are replaced by clusters of dry husks that often hang on until the following spring. Common associates are swamp laurel, scrub birch and willow.

QUICK CHECK: Thick rusty wool on underside of leaves.

RANGE: Bogs throughout B.C. from sea level to alpine terrain. Common ground cover in northwestern B.C.

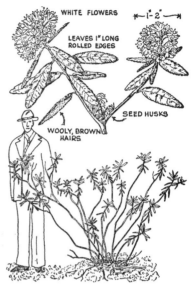

MOUNTAIN LABRADOR TEA
(Ledum glandulosum)

Although slightly larger than the former, this shrub is quite similar in the crooked branching, white flowers, and leaf-whorl characteristics. It lacks the reddish wool beneath the leaves and grows on shady, damp mountain sides where it often forms a brushy tangle. The leaves are deciduous.

QUICK CHECK: Leaf whorls and slightly rolled over edges.

RANGE: Most abundant east of the Cascades on moist mountain slopes. Found up to 5,000' and associated with swamp gooseberry and Engelmann spruce.

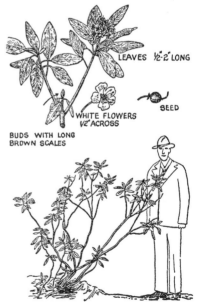

(73)

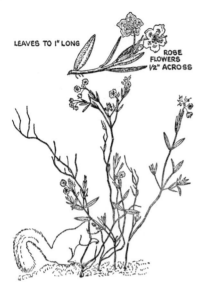

LEAVES TO 1" LONG

ROSE
FLOWERS
1/2" ACROSS

SWAMP-LAUREL
(Kalmia polifolia polifolia)

American Laurel — Alpine Kalmia — Bog Kalmia

Watch for this dainty shrub if you are crossing a bog. The thin, twisting stems up to 2' high and small, narrow leaves easily lose their identity in the thicker tangle of Labrador tea. Of course, if it is displaying its beautiful reddish-purple blossoms you will find it very quickly. The thick, leathery leaves look much like Labrador tea from above but are less than 1" long, have their edges strongly rolled over, and a velvety whiteness beneath rather than the brownish wool.

The star-shaped flowers are worth examining for on some the anthers will be bent back and held by their tips in pits in the petals. Should an insect disturb these the elastic stalk will whip the anther up and spray the disturber with pollen.

QUICK CHECK: A bog shrub; pointed, tough leaves to 1" long, edges rolled under, velvety white beneath. Pink, star flowers.

RANGE: Generally given as "common in bogs throughout B.C." Although widespread to northern B.C. it isn't encountered in every bog.

ALPINE SWAMP-LAUREL *(K. polifolia microphylla)* A miniature edition of the above growing in wet meadows at sub-alpine elevations. Flowers may be only 1/2" above the moss. Leaves are from 1/4" -1/2" long. Most frequent in Cascade Mountains.

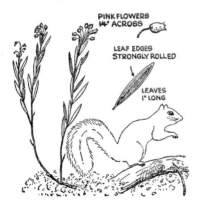

PINK FLOWERS
1/4" ACROSS

LEAF EDGES
STRONGLY ROLLED

LEAVES
1" LONG

MOORWORT
(Andromeda polifolia)

This shrub formerly was called Wild Rosemary, a name now given to *Ledum palustre*. With no other common name in usage, Moorwort was taken from J. K. Henry's "Flora of Southern B.C."

Moorwort closely resembles swamp-laurel in form and habitat. Its crooked, slight stems seldom reach 2' above the peaty bogs it lives in. The dull green leaves with white undersurface are its main distinguishing feature for they are almost like tubes so strongly are they rolled over at the edges. Although approximately 1" long, often they are only 1/8" wide on the top surface. The pink flowers are bell-shaped and form in loose clusters at the end of the twigs. Although relatively widespread it isn't a particularly common plant.

QUICK CHECK: Bog habitat. Slender shrub with narrow leaves strongly rolled over at margin. Pink bell flowers.

RANGE: Peaty bogs north to Alaska. Alice Arm, Prince Rupert, North Central B.C.

MOUNTAIN BILBERRY
(*Vaccinium Vitis-idaea*)

Rock Cranberry

This little known plant with its trailing habit, bright evergreen leaves, and large red berries might easily be mistaken for a puny kinnikinnick plant. However its leaves are usually less than 1/2" long whereas the others are from 1/2" to 1". Most leaves show black dots on the undersurface and the twigs haven't the rough, brownish bark of kinnikinnick. Unlike most mountain blueberries it prefers a fairly damp habitat like muskegs.

Mountain bilberry is a dwarf-like shrub about 6" high. Sometimes it forms a small mat from which protrude a few weak stems. Several small pink flowers cluster near the top of the twigs and later change to large red berries of very poor eating quality.

QUICK CHECK: Note range limits. Alternate, oval, evergreen leaves less than 1/2" long. Black dots beneath. Ripe berries soft and reddish black.

RANGE: Selkirks and Rocky Mountains above 5,000'. Also to Dease and Liard Rivers. Prince Rupert and Peace River. Abundant in muskeg and damp mossy forests along Alaska Highway.

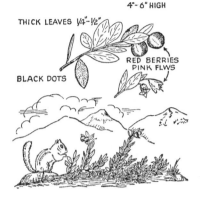

THICK LEAVES 1/4"-1/2"

4"-6" HIGH

RED BERRIES
PINK FLWS

BLACK DOTS

TRAILING AZALEA
(*Loiseleuria procumbens*)

Possibly trailing azalea deserves some special attention for it is the smallest native shrub. Its twiggy matted form may be only an inch high and so is easily overlooked on the rocky slopes of high mountains where it grows. The leaves are in keeping with the dwarf stature of the shrub being from 1/8" - 1/4" long. They cluster abundantly on the twigs and are thickish with rolled-over edges. The small, pink, "bell" flowers in twig-end clusters resemble heather bloom. Dry seed husks form after the flowers.

QUICK CHECK: Tiny sub-alpine or alpine shrub. Leaves less than 1/4" long with rolled edges.

RANGE: Exposed places on high mountains. Mt. Arrowsmith, Mt. Cheam and north to Alaska.

PINK FLOWERS

1"-3" HIGH
LEAF EDGE
ROLLED UNDER

LEAVES 1/8"-1/4" LONG

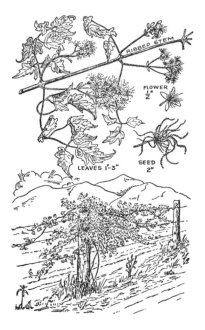

WHITE CLEMATIS
(Clematis ligusticifolia)
Travellers' Joy

Travellers' Joy is an apt descriptive name for this vigorous climber which so artistically decorates the landscape throughout the Dry Interior Zone. It often chooses fences to climb on but when these are not convenient a tree or shrub becomes the support. The slender vines may reach 40' in length and bunch to form mat-like festoons. In spring these owe their beauty to the numerous clusters of small white flowers which are gradually replaced by soft fluffy masses of silver fleece. New shoots with their flower bunches prolong the blooming season from the middle of June to the middle of August, when both flowers and fleece decorate the same vine. The fluffy seed masses last until late October or possibly over winter.

This white clematis chooses the most parched regions of the Okanagan and Similkameen Valleys for its home. Most vines contrive to get their roots into fair soil such as waste places along the edge of farms. Ponderosa pine, black cottonwood and choke cherry, usually grow in the vicinity.

QUICK CHECK: A vigorous climber with leaflets in threes, clusters of small white flowers or white fluffy masses of seeds.

RANGE: Dry Interior Zone. Abundant from Princeton to Keremeos, Osoyoos to Kaleden, Lytton to Kamloops. Lillooet, Cranbrook.

BLUE CLEMATIS
(Clematis columbiana)
Virgins' Bower

Blue clematis is a rather uncommon shrub. Its slender twining form is all but lost on the bushes upon which it climbs. Were it not for the large, showy, blue flowers or white, fluffy seeds it might never be noticed by the casual observer. The shoots branch from the main stems in very symmetrical fashion and carry the tendrils by which it clings to its support. Leaflets are in threes. Unlike the sturdy, white-flowering clematis, this one only raises a few feet into the air. The flowers, set off by a yellow centre, may be 2" - 4" across. Seeds are white and fluffy like miniature dust mops.

QUICK CHECK: A short, slender climber with large blue flowers or fluffy, white "dust mop" seeds.

RANGE: Wide altitudinal range in shady mountain slopes or valley bottoms east of the Cascades. Nickel Plate Mountain, Penticton Creek, Adams Lake, Creston, Quesnel, Fort St. James, Windermere Valley.

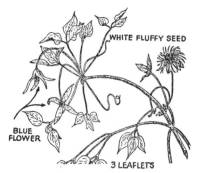

ORANGE HONEYSUCKLE
(Lonicera ciliosa)

Any shrub west of the Cascades or in the Wet Interior Zone that rises from the ground in several thin stems and climbs up shrubs and trees by spiralling tightly around the branches will be orange honeysuckle. Sometimes the stems extend 30' in the air.

The oval, entire leaves are opposite as in all the honeysuckles and have a whitish bloom beneath which rubs off. The twin end-leaves are joined to make an irregular disk with the stem coming through the centre. Orange honeysuckle breaks into leaf early in the season closely following the Indian-plum or oso-berry. During May its clusters of tube-like, orange-red flowers attract attention but then it fades into the background until September when the tidy bundles of orange berries become prominent. Usually 3 or 4 of the berries develop at the expense of the others. They are filled with a reddish pulp and a number of large, yellow seeds.

QUICK CHECK: A supple vine tightly twisted around shrubs or trees. Leaves opposite and with white bloom. Orange-red flowers and orange berries.

RANGE: Below 1,500' elevation west of Cascades and in Wet Interior Zone. Sporadic occurrence eastward to Kootenay River Valley.

BLACK TWINBERRY
(Lonicera involucrata)

Bearberry Honeysuckle

Black twinberry is a shrub 3' - 10' high growing on damp ground. After becoming familiar with its yellow twin-flowers, black twin-berries, and long, light green leaf you will find its presence can almost always be anticipated in the proper habitat.

On Coastal slopes it may be overshadowed in the luxuriant growth of thimbleberry, red-osier dogwood and Pacific crab-apple. In the Interior it grows in more open situations with salmonberry, red-osier dogwood, water birch and cow parsnip.

The 1/2" long, yellow twin-flowers in May and June, and berries with their sticky reddish cape during July and August provide excellent identification features. The long, tapering, opposite leaves are equally good once recognized.

QUICK CHECK: Yellow twin-flowers or shiny, black twin-berries with sticky black or reddish cape.

RANGE: Wet lands throughout B.C. but especially abundant in Coastal and Interior Wet Belt Zones. Ranges from sea level to alpine heights. North Central B.C., Quesnel, Peace River, Bella Coola, Chilcotin.

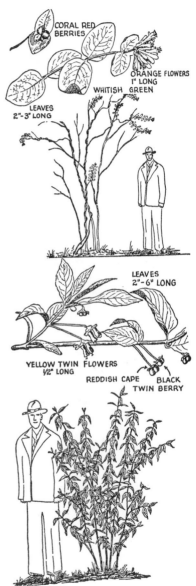

CORAL RED BERRIES

ORANGE FLOWERS 1" LONG

WHITISH GREEN

LEAVES 2"-3" LONG

LEAVES 2"-6" LONG

YELLOW TWIN FLOWERS 1/2" LONG

REDDISH CAPE

BLACK TWIN BERRY

(77)

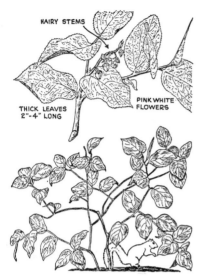

HAIRY STEMS

THICK LEAVES
2"-4" LONG

PINK WHITE
FLOWERS

SALAL
(Gaultheria shallon)

Salal is the Coast Indian word for this plentiful shrub. To them it was of high importance for the dark, mealy berries were made into a syrup or dried in cakes.

Possibly the most abundant shrub of the Coastal Forest Zone, salal may vary from a low sparse growth to an impenetrable tangle 10' or more in height. The pointed, egg-shaped leaves are thick, tough and evergreen and the stems strong and flexible so that the plant can survive the heavy wet snows which may flatten it to the ground.

The pinkish, bell- or urn-shaped flowers hang like beads along the twigs and may be found in bloom from May 15 to July 1. The blackish berries are ripe by August 15 and like the flowers have a very long season.

QUICK CHECK: An abundant shrub with leathery, evergreen leaves, 2" - 4" long. White or pink bell flowers; hairy, blackish berries.

RANGE: Coastal forests to approximately 2,500' elevation. Sporadic occurrence at Kootenay Lake.

INDIAN-PLUM
(Osmaronia cerasiformis)
Oso-berry — Bird Cherry — Skunk Bush

LEAVES
3"-5" LONG

SPRING TWIG

WHITE
FLOWERS

YELLOWISH-RED BERRIES

In March the Indian-plum is the first shrub at the Coast to herald spring. From each separate cluster of leaves there hangs 4-9 small, white flowers in various stages of opening. The flowers have a peculiar odor likened by some to watermelon rind. The crushed leaves also have a pungent smell and the torn bark emits an odor like wood alcohol.

The tapering leaves grow to 3" - 5" in length and show prominent raised veins on their light undersurface. Having such an early start in the spring they are the first to yellow, some as early as July. A scattered string of yellowish-red, plum-like berries replaces the flowers. These ripen to a bluish-black color with a dark blue bloom. A large seed and a flat flavor result in the berries being left for the birds.

Indian-plum develops a bushy, erect form in the open but, if shaded by trees, is sprawling and up to 10' high.

QUICK CHECK: Upright leaf clusters and string of white flowers in early spring. Peculiar flower, leaf and bark smell. Long, tapering leaves and oval berries in summer.

RANGE: Southerly half of Gulf Islands Zone. Common around edges of forests vicinity of Victoria. Lower Mainland eastward to Popkum. Squamish. Vicinity Vancouver.

HAZELNUT
(Corylus spp.)

Within its rather wide Coastal and Interior range it grows abundantly, equally at home on exposed rocky places or in shady glades.

Its numerous slender stems spread in graceful fashion to form a rounded, bushy shrub with heavy foliage. Hazel may reach 20′ in height but generally is from 5′ - 12′ tall.

During February and March conspicuous slender, yellow catkins hang from the slight twigs and so distinguish this shrub from its neighbors. By July the hazel nut is taking shape and is enclosed by a green, stocking-like husk which blends perfectly with the leaves. The edible nut, ripe by fall, is very popular with squirrels.

QUICK CHECK: Yellow catkins in early spring; green "stocking" husk in summer and fall. If "stocking" is twice the length of the nut it is *C. cornuta.* If shorter than this, *C. californica.*

RANGE: *C. californica,* vicinity of Victoria on Vancouver Island. Coastal and Interior Wet Belt Zones ranging from sea level to 2,500′ at the Coast and 4,000′ near Revelstoke. *C. cornuta,* Central B.C., Hazelton, McBride.

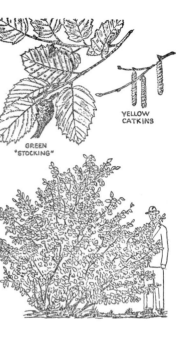

YELLOW CATKINS

GREEN "STOCKING"

GOAT'S BEARD
(Aruncus sylvester)

Goat's beard dies to the ground each year and isn't a true shrub. Its vigorous growth and shrub-like appearance warrant grouping it here.

Goat's beard is found at the Coast in shady, forest borders where the damp soil also supports salmonberry, thimbleberry and red-berry elder. Its common name probably arises from the long, white plumes that make such a showy display during May and June. The 3′ - 7′ high shrub often has a foot or two of its tip in many unmistakable, pencil-like strings of very small flowers. However, the leaves with their short side branches often carrying three leaflets might be mistaken for salmonberry although the golden satiny color of salmonberry bark is quite distinctive.

The thin flower plumes of goat's beard gradually fade from white to a dirty brown as the seeds are formed. These brown strings last until late summer and, although not very conspicuous, do serve as a means of rapid identification from a distance.

QUICK CHECK: Pencils of small white flowers or brown seeds.

RANGE: Low elevations in southern Coastal Forest Zone and Interior Wet Belt. Northward to Central B.C. Very scattered on Vancouver Island.

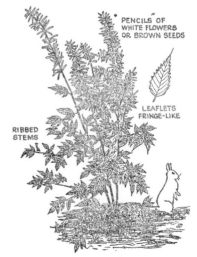

"PENCILS" OF WHITE FLOWERS OR BROWN SEEDS

LEAFLETS FRINGE-LIKE

RIBBED STEMS

SQUASHBERRY
(Viburnum edule)

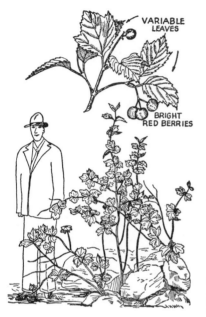

VARIABLE LEAVES

BRIGHT RED BERRIES

Squashberry is usually drawn to the attention through its crinkled, three-lobed leaves or group of bright red berries. In fall the leaves turn crimson and accurately mark its position in the floral picture. Perhaps the rather straggling growth and low height of from 2' - 6' keep it from being noticed by many persons. Once recognized in its damp, shady habitat, it then will be seen over much of B.C. At higher elevations it grows in more open situations and frequently among rocks.

The leaves are long-stemmed and grow opposite from one another. Most are three-lobed but young ones are quite variable in shape. Fine hairs and prominent ribs are characteristics of the underside. The small, white flowers make a cluster an inch or so across. Two to five bright red berries usually mature. They are bitter to the taste and have a large, flat seed in them.

QUICK CHECK: Rounded, 3-lobed leaves, opposite, usually hairy beneath. Flower cluster approximately 1" across. Several smooth, red berries. Ninebarks have somewhat similar leaves but they are alternate.

RANGE: Damp, shady locations at lower levels, more exposed at higher elevations. Throughout B.C. except for Dry Interior and Sub-alpine Zones. Common in northern B.C. and extending into the Yukon.

HIGH-BUSH CRANBERRY
(Viburnum trilobum)

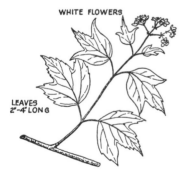

WHITE FLOWERS

LEAVES 2"-4" LONG

This shrub may be fairly abundant in certain limited localities but otherwise is so scarce as to be missed by most people. In general form it closely resembles the above except for leaves and size of flower clusters. The flowers are yellowish white and very showy in their broad clusters.

Central flowers are small while the outer sterile ones are large and showy.

The fruit is bright red and very tart. If cooked it closely resembles cranberry sauce in flavour. Like squashberry the seeds are particularly large.

Shady, brushy thickets along streams is the preferred habitat.

QUICK CHECK: Leaves strongly 3-lobed. White flower clusters 2" - 4" across.

RANGE: Edges of Interior Wet Belt. Salmon Arm, Sicamous, Cranbrook, Quesnel.

RED TWINBERRY
(Lonicera utahensis)

The long, thin stem and opposite leaves of red twinberry are an indication that it belongs to the honeysuckle family. Most shrubs are from 2' - 5' high with a number of irregular "spray" branches. Its straggly limbs, small leaves and dirty, dead-looking bark give it a nondescript appearance only enlivened by the twin, yellowish-white flowers or jelly-like, red berries. Very often one flower grows at the expense of the other and results in one berry being much the larger. Flowers are out as early as May at low elevations but might be delayed a month or more on mountain heights. The 1" - 2" long leaves are very thin and variable in shape. They do not have teeth.

QUICK CHECK: Thin opposite, ovalish leaves with smooth edges. Twin white to yellow flowers or pulpy red berries, one usually undeveloped.

RANGE: Widely distributed from valley bottom to timberline east of the Cascades but also occurring at sub-alpine elevations at the Coast.

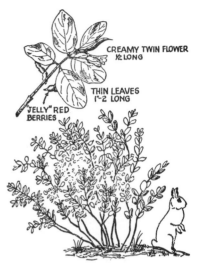

CREAMY TWIN FLOWER ½ LONG

THIN LEAVES 1"-2 LONG

"JELLY" RED BERRIES

MALLOW NINEBARK
(Physocarpus malvaceus)

This shrub, because of its rather limited range in the South Central Interior, will not be very familiar to most people. However, in September when the foliage turns a bright russet red it becomes very attractive and noticeable on semi-open, rocky sidehills. There is considerable similarity to squashberry at this time of the year.

Most shrubs are from 2' - 4' high, stout and bushy, and might easily be taken for a currant from the 3 - 5 lobes and palmate veination of the leaves. The main stems are light grey in color with shreds of loose bark hanging on them. Rounded masses of small, white flowers appear at the twig-ends in June and by August have changed to a cluster of brown seed husks.

Mallow ninebark is often associated with Douglas fir, yellow pine, larch, Douglas maple, Saskatoon berry, mahonia (Oregon grape) and waxberry.

QUICK CHECK: Shreddy bark on stems; leaves alternate, 3 - 5 lobed; white flower head or mass of brown seed husks.

RANGE: Very abundant on mountains east of Christina Lake and scattered on drier regions around Kootenay Lake. Elko, Fruitvale.

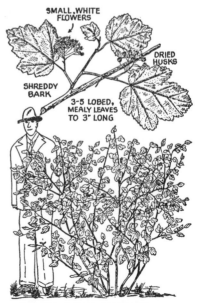

SMALL, WHITE FLOWERS

DRIED HUSKS

SHREDDY BARK

3-5 LOBED, MEALY LEAVES TO 3" LONG

SASKATOON BERRY
(Amelanchier spp.)

June Berry — Shadbush — Service Berry

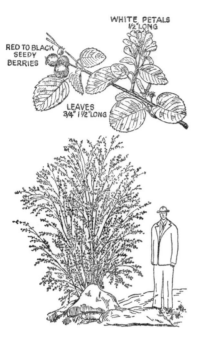

WHITE PETALS
1/2" LONG

RED TO BLACK
SEEDY
BERRIES

LEAVES
3/4" 1 1/2" LONG

Saskatoon berry when either in blossom or fruit can be recognized easily but at other times may be so dwarfed or misshapen from the typical form as to cause confusion. It is under these circumstances that the small, rounded leaf with its big notches on the top half will provide the necessary clue.

Being easily damaged by grazing animals or other means this shrub may often be found less than 2' high All variations in shape are liable to occur but where left undisturbed it forms a loose bush with the upright limbs fanning outward at the crown. It may reach 15' in height but the average is from 6' - 12'. The loose spreading framework, made more noticeable by the small leaves, provides positive identification from the distance.

The fragrant clusters of white blossoms are very abundant and dot the bush from top to bottom during April and May. Berries start to form soon after and by July are a dull red which shades to the ripe black fruit in early August. Unfortunately many of the berries are wormy and their use as an edible fruit has not been popularized. Indians were not so fussy and mixed them with pounded meat to make pemmican. Bears find them a favorite delicacy.

Three species are recognized in B.C.: *A. alnifolia* and *A. cusickii* are east of the Cascades, the latter being the abundant species in the Dry Interior and the former having a more eastern and northern range. They have a smooth, bluish-black fruit; while *A. florida*, the Coastal species has a blackish fruit with bloom. Only an expert can tell them apart from specimens.

QUICK CHECK: Clusters of fragrant blossoms during April and May. Many red or half-black, seedy berries during summer and fall. Typical round leaf notched on top.

RANGE: Widespread through North America. *A. florida*, the only variety west of the Cascades is found on open dry hillsides up to 2,000' elevation. *A. cusickii* is very common in the Dry Interior Zone while *A. alnifolia* ranges from the Rockies north and westward throughout Central B.C. to the Yukon.

SNOWBRUSH
(Ceanothus velutinus)

Mountain Balm — Sticky Laurel — Buckbrush

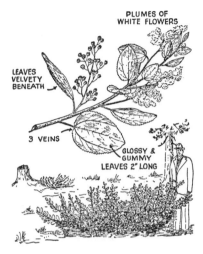

PLUMES OF
WHITE FLOWERS

LEAVES
VELVETY
BENEATH

3 VEINS

GLOSSY &
GUMMY
LEAVES 2" LONG

Snowbrush grows very abundantly on certain sites. Generally it seeks semi-barren gravelly flats or slopes where sunlight is at a maximum. Here the brushy, sprawling shrub may form extensive, irregular mats. The smooth, forked limbs twist upward and carry thick, evergreen leaves about 2" long. These have a glossy but gummy surface which gives rise to the name of sticky laurel. In contrast the undersurface is soft and velvety. The leaf has 3 main veins like central fingers. When the summer's heat becomes intense the leaves curl lengthways along their centre and thus prevent water loss as well as minimizing surface exposure.

During June soft, white heads of tiny flowers rest amongst the glossy green leaves and later turn to small, hard husks. The flowers will make a soapy lather with water and some Indian tribes once used the leaves for a tobacco.

QUICK CHECK: Glossy, evergreen leaves with gummy surface and three main veins.

RANGE: Around the borders of the Dry Interior. Abundant near Princeton, and on roadside flats between Trail and Castlegar. Cranbrook and Lillooet. Ranges to 3,000' in elevation. Very scattered at Coast and on Vancouver Island.

REDSTEM CEANOTHUS
(Ceanothus sanguineus)

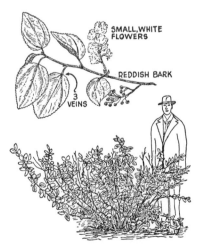

SMALL, WHITE
FLOWERS

REDDISH BARK

3 VEINS

Redstem ceanothus is a nondescript, bushy shrub. With dead limbs and twigs poking out here and there it gives a first impression of being damaged and unhealthy. Preferring semi-shade and well-drained soils it is found along the edge of road clearings, forest openings and rock slides.

This loose ragged shrub may be from 2' - 6' high. Its oval, deciduous leaves have the characteristic 3 main veins evident also in its evergreen relative, snowbrush. The soft, fluffy masses of small, white flowers near the twig ends are out in June. Hard seed pods persist to the following year.

In spring the new twigs have a spicy flavour, and then take on a reddish coloring which leads to the name. It is found growing with Douglas maple, hazel, ocean spray, Saskatoon berry and snowbrush.

QUICK CHECK: Deciduous, toothed leaves with 3 main paralleling veins.

RANGE: Scattered occurrence on Vancouver Island and south Coastal region. Edges of Dry Interior Zone. Alberni, Lillooet, Vernon, Francois Lake.

(83)

SOOPOLALLIE
(*Shepherdia canadensis*)

Soap Berry — Canada Buffalo Berry —
Russet Buffalo Berry

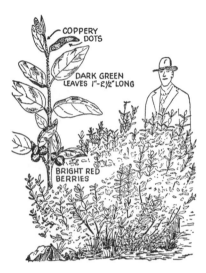

Soopolallie berries when rubbed between the hands make a soapy froth, hence the Indian name: (soop - soap; olallie - berry). When growing in the semi-open it is bushy, upright and 3' - 4' in height. On the westerly slopes of the Rockies a higher, more sprawling form is common. Soopolallie grows abundantly in semi-open forests at medium elevations.

The leaves are opposite, entire, roughly egg-shaped and from 1" - 2½" long. Although dark green above, the undersurface is a combination of silvery hairs and rusty brown spots. Twigs are pebbled with the same brown rust. The small, yellowish-brown male and female flowers are borne on separate bushes. The orange-red, almost transparent fruit grows in small clusters along the stem and twigs.

QUICK CHECK: Dark green, opposite leaves with silvery hairs and rusty brown spots on under-surface. Twigs pebbly with rust. Berries orange-red, transluscent.

RANGE: Throughout B.C. except for Coastal Forest Zone and elevations above 4.500' in the Interior, 5,500' in the Rockies. Alaska Highway.

SILVERBERRY
(*Elaeagnus commutata*)

Silver Buffalo Berry

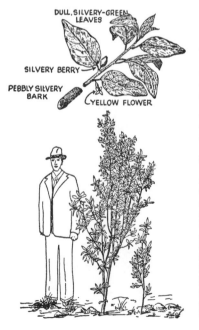

In the Interior one sometimes will see a group of shrubs with leaves so silvery in color that they appear diseased or covered with a fine glistening silt. This will be the foliage of the silverberry, an erect shrub sometimes 12' high but more often from 3' - 5'. It usually forms small groves near stream edges or back channels of the larger creeks and rivers. An occasional appearance on high banks o. mountain slopes usually discloses a seepage area.

Leaves are alternate, from 2" - 4" long and covered with a silvery sheen caused by very small overlapping scales. Smaller limbs are the same color as the leaves but often very young twigs and the main leaf vein are finely pebbled in a beautiful copper color. The small yellow flowers are out in June and the dry, olive-like, silvery berry, in August and September.

QUICK CHECK: Twigs and opposite, entire leaves silvery. Yellow flowers or silvery berries.

RANGE: Main water-courses of Dry Interior Zone. Nicola, Similkameen and Okanagan Rivers. North-ward on Fraser River to Quesnel. Kootenay River Valley, Seton Lake, Cranbrook, Dawson Creek.

SQUAW CURRANT
(Ribes cereum)

Wax Currant

Only the drier slopes of the Dry Interior Zone suit this shrub. Here along the foot of rocky slopes or on almost barren benches the squaw currant can be recognized by its compact. rounded outline, seldom 4' high, and the drab olive-green of its small leaves. By August most shrubs are bright with hundreds of small, red currants.

The crooked, upright stems are brushy toward the top and the bark is greyish with reddish tones and dull white markings. Leaves have a dull, olive sheen to them and vary between the size of a 10c and 25c piece.

QUICK CHECK: Bushy shrub with small, olive-green leaves. Smooth red currants in August and September. With rabbit bush and cactus.

RANGE: Most abundant in Similkameen and Southern Okanagan Valleys. Scattered from Kamloops to Lytton.

GOLDEN CURRANT *(R. aureum)* with yellow berries and strongly lobed leaves is reported near Princeton.

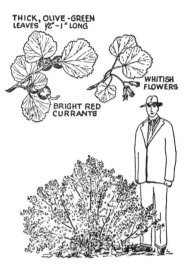

THICK, OLIVE-GREEN LEAVES ½"-1" LONG

WHITISH FLOWERS

BRIGHT RED CURRANTS

SUMAC
(Rhus glabra)

Sumac is a picturesque, low, many-branched shrub found in the drier regions of the Province. Usually a loose thicket develops since new plants shoot up from the long, rambling roots.

It seldom grows over 3' high but along Okanagan Lake bright green masses 6' in height are quite common. The crooked, twisting limb structure looks like some Oriental dwarf shrub. Each stout leaf carries from 13-21, long, toothed leaflets which give the plant its characteristic "plume" foliage. Some plants have a conspicuous conical mass of round seeds near their top. In September and October the seeds are rich red in color from their plush-like covering.

During October the leaflets and stem turn a bright crimson bringing a vivid red rash to lower mountain slopes. Sumac surely leads the way in its flaunting colors of autumn.

Sumac exudes a milky juice when bruised. Some species are used in preparing waxes, dyes and varnishes. "Indian lemonade" is made from the velvety seeds. The husks are steeped in hot water, then the water is strained, sweetened and let cool.

QUICK CHECK: Stout leaf bearing 13-21, toothed leaflets. POISON SUMAC doesn't occur in B.C. It is found in Eastern U.S.A.

RANGE: Dry Interior at lower elevations. Princeton to Keremeos, Nicola Valley, Lillooet, Grand Forks.

13-21 LEAFLETS

REDDISH SEED CONE

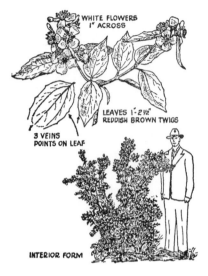

WHITE FLOWERS
1" ACROSS

LEAVES 1'-2½'
REDDISH BROWN TWIGS

3 VEINS
POINTS ON LEAF

INTERIOR FORM

MOCK ORANGE
(Philadelphus lewisii)
(Philadelphus gordonianus)

Syringa — Bridal Wreath

Mock orange with its showy "orange" blossoms is one shrub that invariably arouses the curiosity during June.

P. gordonianus, which is the Coast species, often forms a slender, spreading shrub up to 12' high. It seeks out shady places with fairly good soils. In the Interior, *P. lewisii* seldom grows over 6' high and often is a small, ragged shrub niched into clefts on dry, rocky sidehills.

The profusion of "orange" blossoms are out during June and can hardly be confused with those of any other shrub. The Coast species is very fragrant, the Interior one almost without perfume. The light green leaves are quite distinctive with a few points or teeth on each side of the leaf and the peculiar arrangement of the three main veins. Bark on new twigs is a bright chestnut brown but on older stems is often broken and loose.

QUICK CHECK: White "orange" flowers in June. Points on leaves and vein arrangement.

RANGE: A shrub of low elevations. Sporadic occurrence in southern Vancouver Island. More abundant through Fraser Valley and into Fraser Canyon. Local occurrence in Okanagan and Similkameen Valleys. Also at Shuswap Lake and in the Kootenays.

OCEAN SPRAY
(Holodiscus discolor)

Arrow-wood

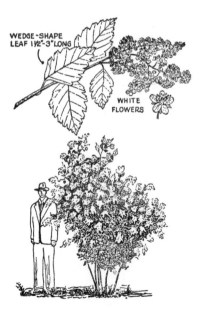

WEDGE-SHAPE
LEAF 1½"-3" LONG

WHITE
FLOWERS

Although dogwood has a showier bloom, ocean spray is more widespread and possibly the most abundant flowering shrub we have. Nearly every dry forest opening or roadside on Vancouver Island and the Lower Mainland is softened during June by masses of loose, creamy plumes. With erect, spreading shrubs to 15' in height almost completely covered with bloom no one can fail to notice ocean spray. In the Interior it is not so abundant and only reaches 6'-8' in height.

In winter months the sparse limb framework still retains a loose cluster of dried husks, a good identifying feature. If before blooming time, the unusual leaves provide the clue. Note how severely the base is wedge-shaped and how coarse are the teeth. Straight young limbs were a source of arrow material for the Indians.

QUICK CHECK: In winter, end twigs with dry husks. Wedge leaves or sprays of small, white flowers.

RANGE: Dry land shrub from Vancouver Island to Columbia Valley.

THIMBLEBERRY
(*Rubus parviflorus*)

Thimbleberry, a widespread shrub, is particularly noticeable because of its large "maple" leaves often 8" across.

In the Coastal or Wet Interior Zones thimbleberry masses in dampish places along the edge of roads or forest openings. East of the Cascade Mountains the same shrub will be found in quite dry places although creek bottoms are preferred.

Ranging from 4' high at the Coast to 2' in the Interior, thimbleberry is an erect, unarmed shrub with short, branching limbs. The stark white flowers, almost 2" across, show up very dramatically from May to July against the background of interlocked leaves, and serve as a means of ready identification. The berries are not "thimble" shaped but round and lumpy. These are bright red and insipid to the taste although sought after by birds and bears during July and August.

QUICK CHECK: Large white flowers or soft, red, rounded berries. "Blotting paper" maple leaf.

RANGE: Widespread in damp shady places. To 2,800' at Coast and to 4,000' in Interior.

WHITE FLWS. 1½" WIDE

LEAVES 4"-8" WIDE ROUNDED RED BERRY

SALMONBERRY
(*Rubus spectabilis*)

Salmonberry, a common shrub of the Coastal forest, is found usually in bottomlands or around the edges of marshes and creeks. In winter its golden, satiny bark with scattered weak spines marks it quite distinctly. Then in early April, it puts forth small bundles of fresh green leaves soon followed by a delicate red flower over 1" wide. As the leaves grow larger the flowers lose their prominence in the landscape, but as new buds develop, continue to bloom an amazingly long time. Flowers might be seen by April 1 and as late as June 1 with berries almost ripe on the same bush. The tender young shoots were eaten raw by Indians and early explorers.

Shrubs usually grow in an erect, branching form 6' - 8' high but where soil conditions are favorable, salmonberry can produce a thicket that would stop Paul Bunyan in his tracks.

The leaflets are mostly in threes and in this respect different from any other native shrub except the thorny blackberries and raspberries. The soft insipid fruit is shaped like a logan or boisonberry and may vary in color from yellow to red. Berries are often ripe by July 1.

QUICK CHECK: Satiny brown stems with very sparse thorns. Leaflets in threes, red "tissue paper" flower 1" across or salmon to red, rounded berry.

RANGE: Wet places below 2,500' in Coastal and Gulf Island Zones.

SALMON TO RED BERRY

LEAFLETS TO 3" LONG

SATINY BROWN STEMS

RED FLOWERS 1" WIDE

BLUEBERRIES, HUCKLEBERRIES
and WHORTLEBERRIES
(Vaccinium spp.)

These three names together with bilberry and cranberry are used in the common naming of the genus *Vaccinium*. A great deal of confusion exists in the names and the following is an attempt to use the more common ones of some descriptive significance.

BLACK MOUNTAIN
HUCKLEBERRY
(Vaccinium membranaceum)

Big Whortleberry — Thin Leaf Huckleberry

As the name suggests this is a shrub of the mountains. At elevations greater than 2,500' on the Coast and 4,000' in the Interior, black mountain huckleberry is often the most common shrub. Tall blue huckleberry may be mixed in with it but is distinguished by the entire leaves.

Black mountain huckleberry ranges from 5' in height at lower elevations to 1' near timberline. It is a crooked plant with smooth limbs and slightly angled twigs. Sometimes a few twisting stems make up its sparse form but often it is a bushy shrub. Leaves are from 1/2" - 1 1/2" long, pointed at both ends and finely toothed. Small, whitish flowers in May and June turn to black berries by September. The leaves turn a beautiful red and purple color in late fall.

QUICK CHECK: Thin leaves with fine teeth. Smooth, black berries. Note approximate elevation ranges.

RANGE: Common throughout on higher mountain slopes.

TALL BLUE HUCKLEBERRY
(Vaccinium ovalifolium)

Tall Huckleberry — Oval Leaf Whortleberry

This huckleberry, the tallest in B.C. is commonly found to 6' where conditions are ideal. Being in the shade for the most part it develops a scraggly form. The pinkish "bell" blossoms grow singly from the axils of the leaves. Berries are ripe by September.

QUICK CHECK: Egg-shaped leaf with smooth edges. Berries with bluish bloom.

RANGE: Widespread throughout cool, shady forests from sea level to sub-alpine heights.

BLUE LEAVED H. *(V. deliciosum)* is a bushy shrub to 12" high. Leaves are 1/4" - 1" long with rounded tips. Berries are single and are a deep blue with a bloom. Near timberline on Coast Mountains and Forbidden Plateau.

THIN LEAVES
1/2" - 1 1/2" LONG

SMOOTH
BLACK BERRY

GREENISH-WHITE
FLOWER

TWIGS
SLIGHTLY
ANGLED

FORM AS

VERY THIN
TWIGS

BLUE-BLACK
BERRIES
WITH BLUE BLOOM

OVAL LEAVES
1/2" - 1 1/2"
LONG

RED HUCKLEBERRY
(Vaccinium parvifolium)

There is no mistaking this lacey, bright green bush even though its bright red berries are not present. It appears limited to cool Coastal forests at elevations below 1,000'. Sometimes 6' in height it grows in a compact upright form, a mass of small oval leaves less than 1" long. On rare occasions they may be toothed. The twigs are as green as the leaves and sharply angled. Sometimes red huckleberry grows in fairly shady places but more often it seeks out the edges of forest openings and roadsides. Old stumps are a favorite perch on the Lower Mainland.

QUICK CHECK: Note range. Angled, green twigs, and tart red berries.

RANGE: Coastal forests below 1,000' in elevation. Common on Vancouver Island.

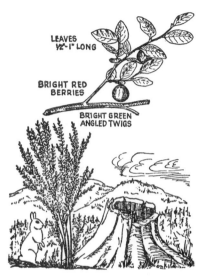

EVERGREEN HUCKLEBERRY
(Vaccinium ovatum)

Scattered specimens of evergreen huckleberry will be found on the Gulf Islands and along the southeast and southwest coast of Vancouver Island. As one proceeds westward near the southern tip of the Island it becomes increasingly abundant and vigorous. Single shrubs are replaced by thickets tightly laced together with salal. Rocky or gravelly soils are preferred.

Indians called the fruit shot oolalie or shotberry on account of its size and shape.

Most shrubs are bushy and thick. Many are 6' high. There is a superficial resemblance to manzanita in that both have thick evergreen leaves, very hairy young twigs and a general similarity in flowers and berries. The crooked, reddish limbs and rounded outline of manzanita quickly distinguish it however.

The fine-toothed leaves are mostly less than 1" long, sharp-pointed, and with very short stems. The many small, pink flowers grow in groups along or near the end of the branches. The abundant berries are small and shiny black. Their sweet flavour makes them very desirable for pies and other domestic uses.

QUICK CHECK: Note limited range. Small sharp-pointed, toothed, evergreen leaves and woolly twigs. Clusters of pink, "bell" flowers during May; shiny, black berries in October and on to mid-November.

RANGE: Scattered through Gulf Island Zone but abundant on southeast portion. Sooke, Jordan River, Little Qualicum Falls Park, Alberni.

BLACK RASPBERRY
(Rubus leucodermis)

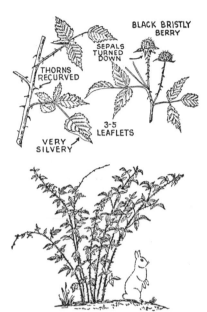

Black Cap

NOTE: Raspberries come off a central core while blackberries are picked with the core.

Not all raspberries are red as this particular shrub will show once the flavorful fruit is fully ripe. Most of the summer its "raspberry" look will serve for rough identification. Many of the shoots are quite straight and may reach 5' in height. Other stems bend over and droop to the ground. Stout thorns with their points turned back bristle on the branches and even creep up on the leaf stems. The white flowers with 5 petals bunch together in small clusters and are out from April to June. The fruit looks like a common raspberry until late summer when it turns almost black. The sharp-pointed, crinkly leaflets are in threes or fives and their contrasting silvery undersurface provides a fairly reliable identity check.

Black raspberry wants lots of sunlight and a coarse dry soil for its roots. Road clearings, forest openings and logged-over areas are favored places.

QUICK CHECK: A mostly upright shrub, thorny, 3 - 5 leaflets with very silvery undersurface. Petals are shorter than hairy, reflexed sepals. Blackish fruit with bloom when ripe.

RANGE: West of the Selkirk mountains to elevations of 2,000' at the Coast and 4,000' in the Interior.

RED RASPBERRY
(Rubus idaeus)

Beyond the fact that this raspberry is red when ripe there is a great similarity in form and leaf to black raspberry. However, the range of red raspberry is east of the Cascade mountains and its preference for very dry places such as rockslides helps distinguish it. Many plants have a very noticeable blue bloom over the brownish stalks. The leaves are hairy beneath but not with the high silvery sheen of black raspberry.

QUICK CHECK: Similar to black raspberry with sepals longer than petals but not folded back. Blue bloom on many stalks. Fruit red. Watch range limitations.

RANGE: Widely distributed east of Cascade summit. North to Peace River. Sporadic west of Cascades.

One variety is a rather uncommon raspberry possibly mistaken for one of the above unless it shows yellow berries. The stems are covered heavily with soft bristles. There are 3 - 5 leaflets less crinkled than the above and almost smooth beneath. The yellow or red berry is about $\frac{1}{2}$" across with rather small velvety druplets. Mt. Revelstoke and North Central B.C.

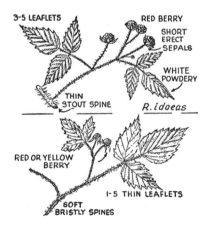

POISON-IVY
(*Rhus radicans*)

12"-20" HIGH

DULL WHITE BERRY

3 GLOSSY-GREEN LEAFLETS

Despite the abundance of poison-ivy in certain regions of B.C. and the publicity given its poisonous properties, there are comparatively few people who can make definite recognition. Being a sun-loving plant poison-ivy is found in a specialized habitat where the careful observer quickly comes to look for it. In the warm climate of the Interior such as the Okanagan and southern Kootenay, rock slides, stony places and road edges are brightened by patches of this low, glossy-leaved shrub.

Its large, wavy-edged leaves in threes and whitish berries in loose clusters part way up the stem are positive identifying features. In the fall the plant turns a colorful scarlet and soon loses its leaves although the berries may remain all winter.

The poison which causes severe irritation to the skin is an oil contained in all parts of the shrub. Poisoning may result from contact with shoes or clothes that have been worn around the shrub or from smoke from the burning plant.

If exposure is suspected, thorough washing in several changes of very soapy water is recommended. A coating of soft soap or a strong solution of Epsom salts over the affected parts are good home antidotes. The standard remedy is calomine lotion obtainable at all drug stores. The poison runs its course and usually clears up in several days' time.

Strangely enough sheep, goats and cattle graze on poison-ivy without harm and may help in its eradication.

QUICK CHECK: Glossy green leaves in threes. Dull white berries close to stem.

RANGE: Dry Interior Zone and southern Kootenay Valley vicinity Trail. Also Kootenay River Valley south of Cranbrook. Quesnel, Seton Lake.

POISON-OAK (*Rhus diversiloba*), fortunately enough is comparatively rare in B.C. Occasional shrubs are found in dry locations in the southern half of Vancouver Island, the Gulf Islands and adjacent to the Fraser River delta. Poison-oak may be a straggly, erect shrub or more commonly a stout climber. The three leaflets are roughly round in outline but sometimes irregularly lobed or toothed often causing a superficial resemblance to an oak leaf.

GREENISH WHITE BERRIES

GLOSSY, LEATHERY LEAFLETS VARIABLE IN SHAPE

LEAVES IN THREE, LET IT BE!

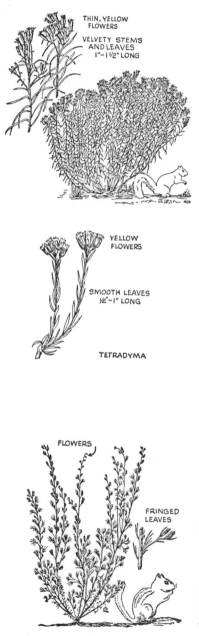

THIN, YELLOW FLOWERS

VELVETY STEMS AND LEAVES 1"-1½" LONG

YELLOW FLOWERS

SMOOTH LEAVES ½"-1" LONG

TETRADYMA

FLOWERS

FRINGED LEAVES

RABBITBUSH
(*Chrysothamnus nauseosus*)

Rabbitbush is often confused with sagebrush because of its similarity in appearance and habitat. From August 15 to September 15 the compact, grey-green plant is topped by a mass of small, yellow flowers whereas sagebrush isn't in drab bloom until the end of September.

Rabbitbush is a compact, olive-green shrub about 2' in height. Numerous finely hairy, erect stems give it a trim look whereas sagebrush has a thick, twisting trunk. Pasture wormwood with which it may be confused also is softer in color and has a much lighter twig framework.

QUICK CHECK: Massed head of yellow flowers from August 15 - September 15. Leaves thin, velvety, and not notched at tip.

RANGE: Common throughout Dry Interior Zone. Drier portions of Cariboo Parklands.

C. viscidiflorus has stems and leaves not hairy. It grows rather sparsely in the Kootenay River Valley. Roadsides, Wasa to Fort Steele. Also vicinity Osoyoos.

TETRADYMA (*T. canescens*) resembles rabbitbush but can be identified by the 4 oblong bracts surrounding the flower head. Leaves are only about half as long. The range is indefinite but does extend from Osoyoos to Penticton.

PASTURE WORMWOOD
(*Artemisia frigida*)

Fringed Sagebrush — Arctic Sagebrush

This beautiful little shrub mingles with sagebrush and rabbitbush but can be picked out by its smaller size (4" - 20" high) and softer shade of color. The "sage" smell of the crushed leaves is very pungent. The leaves differ from rabbitbush in being finely hairy and divided into 2 or 3 thin, fringe-like leaflets. The small, dull flowers cluster along the thin flowering twigs and won't be noticed unless closely examined.

Pasture wormwood extends beyond the range of both sagebrush and rabbitbush. Then dry open slopes with a southerly exposure are favored.

QUICK CHECK: Note limited range. Low shrub less than 20" high with finely divided and hairy leaves, silvery, olive-grey in color and with "sage" smell.

RANGE: Dry Interior Zone and Cariboo Parklands. Into Cariboo to 20 miles south of Quesnel; up North Thompson River to Blue River; Kootenay River Valley, vicinity Fort Steele. Also Peace River, Dawson Creek, Fort St. James. A specimen collected 150 years ago in Siberia led to name "*frigida*".

ANTELOPE BUSH
(*Purshia tridentata*)

SHRUBS

Bitterbrush — Greasewood

The dull green color of this shrub blends very well with the neighboring sagebrush. Actually it is quite different in form having a spreading structure of stiff, awkward branches. The thin, notched leaves are so tiny that the outline of the fibrous limbs is quite distinctive. In the southern Okanagan it may grow 8′ high but in the Kootenay River Valley it seldom reaches 4′ and is more brushy.

In early spring the bush is dotted with small, yellow blossoms that go unnoticed unless a limb is examined.

Greasewood is a common name and arises from the fact that the shrub, even when green, burns with much spitting and crackling. A dark, greasy smoke helps lend authority for this name.

QUICK CHECK: Note limited range. Short leaves up to 1″ long, triple notched like sagebrush. Yellow flowers or "tear-drop" seeds on limbs.

RANGE: Most arid benches of southern Okanagan and Similkameen Valleys. Prominent from Osoyoos north to Kaleden. Altitude limit approximately 1,500′. Kootenay River Valley, vicinity Fort Steele.

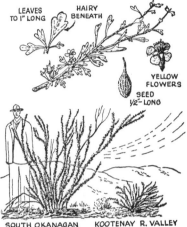

SOUTH OKANAGAN   KOOTENAY R. VALLEY

SAGEBRUSH
(*Artemisia tridentata*)

Sagebrush with its thin, triple or "trident" notched leaves can easily be identified by this one feature. Its gnarled form is so characteristically massed over barren, arid waste land that it just naturally has to be sagebrush. The "sage" smell to its foliage and the twisted, loose bark are other noticeable points. The flowers are extremely small and drab in color and bloom from September 15 to October 15.

Although under favorable conditions it will reach 8′ in height the average shrub is about half that high. Sagebrush is considered an intruding weed plant in overgrazed or otherwise impoverished soils. A rather interesting feature is its occurrence almost always on soils of volcanic origin and seldom on those of granitic formation.

QUICK CHECK: A gnarled, grey-green shrub 2′ - 5′ high with thin, "trident" leaves.

RANGE: Dry Interior Zone. Prominent Ashcroft to Kamloops and in Similkameen and Okanagan Valleys. Usually on lower valley slopes but sometimes to 5,000′

A. trifida differs principally in having the leaves quite deeply notched. The shrub is smaller and generally more bushy. The range possibly is wider than that of sagebrush.

(93)

FALSE AZALEA
(*Menziesia ferruginea*)

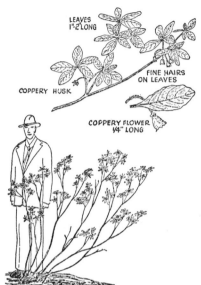

LEAVES 1"-2" LONG

FINE HAIRS ON LEAVES

COPPERY HUSK

COPPERY FLOWER 1/4" LONG

Fool's Huckleberry.

False azalea, although much larger in size than cultivated azalea, bears a resemblance in its loose whorls of small leaves. It is a common shrub on Coast mountains and, where moist conditions prevail, often dominates the undergrowth. Usually 2'-6' high, its slender, ascending limbs support an artistic pattern of blue-green leaves. Young twigs are often coppery in color possibly leading to some confusion with copper bush. The leaves have fine hairs on both surfaces and the base tapers to clasp the stem. In color they are bluish-green on top and light, whitish-green underneath. The bell-shaped flowers, carried on long stems, are an unusual copper color. Shrubs often found with false azalea are copper bush, white rhododendron and black mountain huckleberry.

QUICK CHECK: Leaves 1"-2" long, in rough whorls. Fine hairs on both sides. Copper bush hasn't hairs on the old leaves. White rhododendron has most leaves over 2" long.

RANGE: Moist mountain slopes across the Province. North Shore Mountains, Mt. Revelstoke, Mt. Robson, North Central B.C.

COPPER BUSH
(*Cladothamnus pyrolaeflorus*)

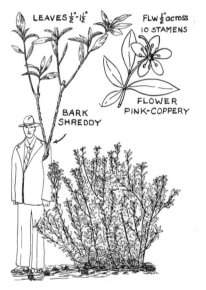

LEAVES 1/2"-1 1/2"

FLW 1/2" across 10 STAMENS

BARK SHREDDY

FLOWER PINK-COPPERY

This is a particularly common shrub of Coastal forests above 2,500' elevation. It mingles with white rhododendron and false azalea to form dense thickets. Being 3'-5' high, bushy, and with its leaves in rough whorls it might be passed up for one of its neighbors. Look closely and you will see it has stout stems with loose coppery bark. The numerous branching twigs have smooth leaves 1/2"-2" long which, when young, are covered with fine, white hairs. Veins show up very prominently on young leaves and older ones have a very noticeable main rib on the underside.

If copper bush is in flower or fruit you will know it immediately by its round coppery flower with the curved, protruding anther. The bumpy, green seed also has this curved protrusion.

QUICK CHECK: Loose coppery bark on shoots. Old leaves not hairy like false azalea or white rhododendron. Copper flower with curved anther. Berry similar in general shape.

RANGE: From sea level to sub-alpine levels. Most abundant with mountain hemlock and yellow cedar forest type. Gulf Island and Coastal Forest Zones. Queen Charlotte Islands, Kootenay Lake, North Central B.C.

WHITE RHODODENDRON
(Rhododendron albiflorum)

Hikers often are so overwhelmed by its tangle of uncompromising branches that the descriptive name, "Mountain Misery," is hardly out of place. This 3'-6' high shrub favors the Coast or Interior Wet Belt but is found also in the Rockies and mountains of the Central and Northern Interior.

The noticeable, rough whorls of 5-7 leaves might be confused with false azalea or copper bush. However, turn the thin leaves so the sunlight glances across the surface. Look closely for fine, coppery hairs glinting in the sun. The main rib on the underside of the leaf is clad in white hairs. Young twigs are hairy also.

In late spring handsome, bell-like, white flowers in clusters of one to three blossoms provide an unmistakable feature. Then the flowers change into dry, brown husks which hang on until next spring.

Many shrubs have yellow mottlings on the leaves, particularly on mature foliage. Associated shrubs are copper bush, false azalea and mountain ash.

QUICK CHECK: Leaves 1"-3" long in rough whorls. Copper-colored hairs on leaf. White flowers in late spring.

RANGE: From 2,500' elevation to timberline on Coastal slopes. From 4,000' to timberline in the Interior Wet Belt. On shady, moist mountains throughout the Rockies and Central Northern B.C.

(R. lapponicum) is a low bush with purple flowers. Northern Rockies, Alaska Highway.

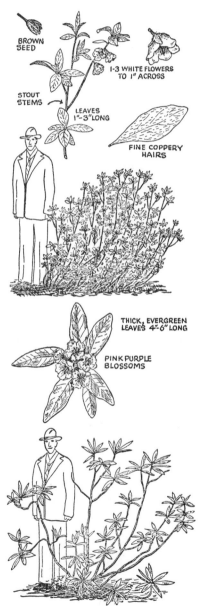

BROWN SEED

1-3 WHITE FLOWERS TO 1" ACROSS

STOUT STEMS

LEAVES 1"-3" LONG

FINE COPPERY HAIRS

THICK, EVERGREEN LEAVES 4"-6" LONG

PINK PURPLE BLOSSOMS

RED RHODODENDRON
(Rhododendron macrophyllum)

Red rhododendron is very similar to the cultivated shrub except for its larger, more sprawling form which may reach 10' into the air. Generally extensive patches grow under the trees rather than widely spaced individuals.

The pink-purple blossoms form in June in round masses strikingly set off by the loose rosettes of long, shiny, evergreen leaves. Sometimes the flower bunches are 6" across and provide a display of color and beauty surpassing all other native shrubs. Like the dogwood, the red rhododendron is protected by law.

QUICK CHECK: Note range. Evergreen leaves 4"-6" long with whitish bloom beneath. Large masses of pink-purple flowers.

RANGE: Most abundant in Skagit Valley bordering Washington. Adjacent to Hope-Princeton Highway, Mile 22 to Mile 24 from Hope. A few shrubs reported on Englishman's River on Vancouver Island. G. M. Dawson, an early geologist found them on mountains above the lower Fraser Canyon.

MANZANITA

VERY HAIRY TWIGS

OLIVE-GREEN LEAVES
1/2"- 1 1/2" LONG

WHITE
FLOWERS

CROOKED
RED LIMBS

HAIRY MANZANITA
(Arctostaphylos columbiana)

Hairy manzanita with its dull green foliage is limited in occurrence to the Gulf Island Zone and then found only on stony slopes or rocky bluffs where the sun's heat is at a maximum. Arbutus and soopolallie are common companions.

It is a rounded, bushy, evergreen shrub seldom reaching 6' in height. The strikingly crooked branches are smooth and have a rich reddish-brown color. Young twigs and leaves are very hairy. The urn-shaped, whitish flowers resemble those of salal and arbutus. In bloom during May they later develop into a blackish-red, mealy berry. Few people know of their edible qualities although they were gathered by the Indians and either eaten raw or cooked.

QUICK CHECK: Note limited range. Thick, evergreen leaves. Twigs and young leaves very hairy. Limbs crooked, reddish-brown.

RANGE: Rocky, southern exposure in Gulf Island Zone. Sooke Hills, Malahat Drive, Hill 60 near Duncan, Great Central Lake.

BROOM
(Cytisus scoparius)

Broom is so widespread on Vancouver Island that it is included here although not a native shrub. It is believed to have been introduced near Victoria, by an early English settler. The brilliant yellow bloom as displayed on massed shrubs on dry slopes, rocky knolls and road edges overshadows the efforts of any native plant. In shape it is a spindly, ragged mass of slender, greenish branches with short, narrow leaves pressed close to them.

The flowers stick out at all angles from the stem and are at their best during May. Some limbs flower as late as July 1. However, by this time most bushes are hung thickly with small pea pods having many hairs along the edges. Some blooms show red and purple shades.

QUICK CHECK: Squarish, green twigs with small leaves, yellow flowers or small, hairy pea pods. Note range limitation.

RANGE: Roadsides and waste places around Victoria and north beyond Campbell River. Sporadic occurrence Lower Fraser River Delta, Kootenay Lake.

GORSE (*Ulex europaeus*) is an introduced shrub somewhat resembling broom by reason of its bushy green form and yellow flowers which often are out in January. It is low and sprawling with sharp-pointed needle leaves. The range and habitat are similar to broom.

GROOVED GREEN
BARK

HAIRY PODS

3/4" LONG YELLOW FLOWERS

BROOM

GORSE

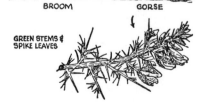

GREEN STEMS &
SPIKE LEAVES

DEVIL'S CLUB
(Oplopanax horridus)

Devil's club stands out because of its large, maple-like leaves and thick, spiny stems. In the mottled shadows of cedar swamps, Devil's club grows abundantly wherever the ground is black, soft and damp. Its light brown stems raise in crooks and twists to support large, exotic leaves which spread like green platters to catch the filtered sun's rays. Long, yellowish spines bristle from the stems and sparse, thin thorns project from the underside of leaf and stem. Terminal clusters of white flowers appear in June. They later change to a pyramid of bright red berries very noticeable during August.

QUICK CHECK: Coarse stems about 1" thick, bristling with light brown, needle-like spines.

RANGE: Vancouver Island and Coastal forests north to Alaska. Interior Wet Belt. Big Bend Highway and generally wherever red cedar grows. Elevation range from sea level to approximately 4,500'.

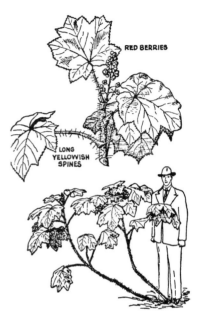

WILD ROSES
(Rosa spp.)

Wild roses are recognized the country over but as individuals only an expert can tell the difference between them. Over 100 different kinds grow in North America and at least 6 in B.C. Each features white to deep rose flowers with a fragrant perfume. The leaves have an odd number of leaflets and a wing-like sheaf clasps the base of the leaf. The fruit or "hips" which hang on all winter are almost as well known as the flowers. Most roses have thorny stems. The following are three of the more common.

COMMON WILD ROSE (*R. nutkana*): Probably the most common bush rose. A bushy shrub to 10' high and armed with stout prickles beneath each leaf. Showy flowers often 2" across, either singly or with one or two others. Fruit, a large showy, scarlet hip. Blooms from May to July. Prefers fairly rich soils. Ranges throughout B.C. at lower elevations. *R. nutkana var. hispida* is the species east of the Cascades.

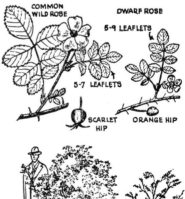

DWARF ROSE (*R. gymnocarpa*): A spindly shrub to 4' high with slender stems prickly with weak straight spines. Leaflets 5 - 9 and pale pink flowers ½" - ¾" across. Fruit smooth and orange in color. Found on rocky exposed situations, it ranges at lower elevations through southern B.C.

SWAMP ROSE (*R. pisocarpa*): Weakly armed with straight spines. Leaflets 5 - 7. Several flowers in twig-end clusters. Fruit smaller than *R. nutkana*. Southern Coastal B.C.

CURRANTS AND GOOSEBERRIES
(Ribes spp.)

Currants and gooseberries have a close resemblance in leaf and fruit to the cultivated variety. The leaves are 3 - 5 lobed, usually toothed and have prominent veins radiating from the base to all the lobes. The pungent, currant smell of the crushed leaves is a help if in doubt. Currants are unarmed while gooseberries carry spines.

STINK CURRANT
(Ribes bracteosum)

Blue Currant

FLOWERS & FRUIT CLUSTERS TO 6" LONG

LEAVES 5-7 LOBED TO 8" WIDE

ROUGH, BLACK CURRANTS

YELLOW SPOTS ON UNDER SIDE

This currant is a more or less erect shrub to 8' high with a few sprawling branches. The large "currant" leaves up to 8" in width are wider than long with from 5 - 7 sharp-tipped lobes. Yellow resin ducts are scattered on the under-surface. The erect, green, saucer-shaped flowers and rough, black fruit in a loose, long cluster of two or three dozen are quite different than the small number of fruit on other species. The smell of the leaves is very pronounced and accounts for the common name.

QUICK CHECK: Large, blue-green leaves, 5 - 7 lobed. Flowers and fruit in 4" - 6" long cluster. Strong currant smell to leaves.

RANGE: Usually confined to low elevations in Coastal Forest Zone and on Vancouver Island.

HUDSON BAY CURRANT
(Ribes hudsonianum)

This shrub resembles the above in leaf shape and in the clusters of flowers and berries. It differs in that leaves are seldom over 3" wide and flowers and fruit are in clusters of from 8 - 16.

This shrub often has sturdy shoots reaching 5' into the air. It may catch the eye in the spring when the numerous, erect clusters of yellowish-white flowers show in advance of the full leaf growth. The flower and berry cluster is only an inch or so long but from this main stalk 8 - 16 short stems branch off. The leaves are seldom over 3" wide and are slightly broader than long. Although smooth textured above they are mealy beneath. Three definite lobes are noticed with usually a minor division into five. The berry is rather small and smooth and black.

LEAVES 1"-3" WIDE

MEALY BENEATH

1"-2" LONG CLUSTER OF WHITISH FLOWERS

SMOOTH BLACK BERRIES

QUICK CHECK: Upright flower and berry stalk. 8 - 16 whitish flowers with long petals and hairy sepals. Smooth black berries.

RANGE: Generally east of the Coast Mountains and along shady water courses.

RED-FLOWER CURRANT
(Ribes sanquineum)

Winter Currant

To persons living at the Coast, this currant will be the one surely to be known. True enough it has only a brief few weeks of glory but it is at a time in early spring when color is much appreciated. The small, red flowers in drooping clusters attract the first migrant humming birds about April 1 but blooms may be seen as late as May 15.

Red-flower currant consists of several crooked stems supporting a loose bush. Cultivated shrubs reach 10' in height but in the woods most are not over 5'. Dry, open woods, logged areas or roadsides are places to look for this shrub. The dull green, mealy leaves are from 1" - 3" across and matted on the undersurface with almost invisible hair. The fruit is a globular, blue-black berry with a whitish, waxy bloom.

QUICK CHECK: Roundish, 3 - 5 lobed currant leaves with fine white hairs beneath. Red flower clusters.

RANGE: Low elevations in southern part of Coastal Forest and Gulf Island Zones. Sporadic occurrence at Arrow Lake and Slocan Lake.

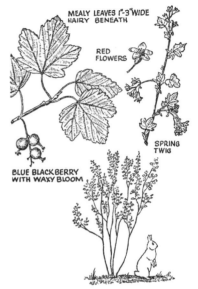

MEALY LEAVES 1"-3" WIDE HAIRY BENEATH

RED FLOWERS

SPRING TWIG

BLUE BLACKBERRY WITH WAXY BLOOM

STICKY CURRANT
(Ribes viscosissimum)

Most bushes are from 2' - 4' high, the few stems twisted and stout at the base. The stems are without thorns but with rather shreddy bark on older branches. Sticky currant grows in semi-open forests on mountains east of the Cascades. Although individual shrubs are well separated the range often covers extensive mountain slopes.

The most noticeable feature is the sticky pores and hairs on the leaves, twigs and fruit. The greenish-white flowers with pinkish tinge are in clusters of from 3 - 8. For some reason very few berries form but those that do are black and covered with short, stiff hairs.

According to an early explorer, David Douglas, 2 or 3 berries will cause vomiting.

QUICK CHECK: "Currant" leaves; twigs, leaves and fruit sticky, hairy.

RANGE: Semi-open mountain slopes from 3,500' to 6,000' from Cascades to Rocky Mountains. Manning Park, Nickel Plate Mine.

Several other currants are found in the Province but different individuals show such variations that a description is not attempted. They are *R. glandulosum, R. triste, R. laxiflorum, R. howellii.*

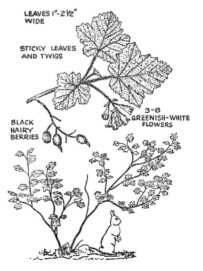

LEAVES 1"-2½" WIDE

STICKY LEAVES AND TWIGS

BLACK HAIRY BERRIES

3-8 GREENISH-WHITE FLOWERS

Wild Gooseberry

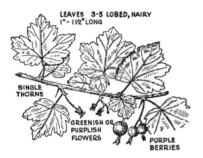

LEAVES 3-5 LOBED, HAIRY 1"-1½"LONG

SINGLE THORNS

GREENISH OR PURPLISH FLOWERS

PURPLE BERRIES

Swamp Gooseberry

LEAVES 1"-2½" WIDE

3-7 SPINES

5-12 WHITISH FLOWERS

BRISTLY, BLACK BERRY

UNRIPE GREEN BERRIES

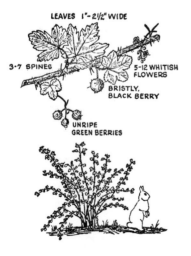

WILD GOOSEBERRY
(Ribes divaricatum)

Common Gooseberry

This shrub sends up several sturdy, "whip" limbs that may reach 6' in the air before bending over. Most of the stem is unarmed but at every joint a single spine (occasionally 2 or 3) is found. Greenish or purplish flowers have five, petal-like lobes that hang down. There may be from 1 - 4 flowers to a cluster. The berry is smooth and wine-colored.

QUICK CHECK: Single thorn at joints. Drooping petal-like lobes on flower.

RANGE: Coastal Forest and Gulf Island Zones below 2,000' elevation.

SWAMP GOOSEBERRY
(Ribes lacustre)

A very plentiful shrub in damp, shady places in the higher mountains. Here it may form an extensive low thicket of weakly upright, spiny stems several feet high. Young stems are bristly with 3 - 7 heavier spines at the nodes. Older branches are almost smooth. The whitish flowers tinged with red are about ¼" across, saucer-shaped, and in clusters of from 5 - 12. The berry is black, bristly and bitter.

QUICK CHECK: Young stems bristly. Flowers and berries as described.

RANGE: Mountain slopes to 6,000' throughout the Province.

R. montigenum is a somewhat similar variety but the fruit is red rather than black.

OTHER GOOSEBERRIES
(Ribes spp.)

GUMMY GOOSEBERRY *(R. lobbii)*: Noticeable in spring because of its handsome flowers with red petals. Spiny stems up to 4' high with 3 large spines at nodes. Leaf deeply 3-lobed and up to 1" across. Leaf and stem sticky. Berry large, hairy and purple. Range—shady forests southern Vancouver Island and Lower Mainland.

MOUNTAIN GOOSEBERRY *(R. irriguum)*: Resembles *R. divaricatum* except for fine thorns all along branches and 1 - 3 large ones at joints. Greenish white flowers, 1 - 3. Berry smooth and purple. Range—along streams in mountains from Hope northward.

SMOOTH GOOSEBERRY *(R. oxyacanthoides)*: A low shrub found along streams east of the Cascade Mountains. Stems are lightly armed but have 3 stout thorns at the nodes. Leaves seldom over 1" across, 3 - 5 lobed with blunt teeth. Flowers, small, greenish and in twos. Berries smooth, blue-black.

TRAILING BLACKBERRY
(Rubus ursinus)

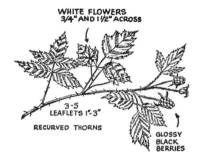

WHITE FLOWERS
3/4" AND 1 1/2" ACROSS

3-5
LEAFLETS 1"-3"

RECURVED THORNS

GLOSSY
BLACK
BERRIES

Here's a long, thorny creeper that has a habit of abruptly bringing itself to one's attention. Its foot-catching and thorn-sticking capabilities might be twined over 15 or 20 feet of ground or draped artistically over logs or rock outcrops. This tough, sinewy shrub is the most abundant and widely distributed blackberry on the Coastal slopes. It shows a very definite preference for recently logged or burned-over forests and comes in with bracken and fireweed as pioneer growth.

During June some confusion as to identity might arise because male and female flowers are carried on separate plants. The male flower is much larger and showier being about 1½" across as compared to ¾" for the female. New runners are often unbranched the first year but thereafter have numerous short side branches.

Most of the dark green, alternate leaves carry 3 leaflets but occasionally 5 are seen. Thorns are stout and curved back at the tip. The glossy black fruit ripens in August and is much sought by humans, bears, birds and even deer.

QUICK CHECK: A slender thorny crawler with alternate, 3-leaflet leaves. Fruit, glossy and black.

RANGE: Most abundant in the burns and logging of the Douglas fir Coastal forests. Altitude range to 3,000' at Coast.

SUB-ALPINE BLACKBERRY
(Rubus nivalis)

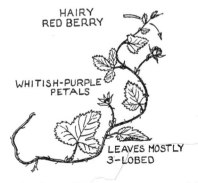

HAIRY
RED BERRY

WHITISH-PURPLE
PETALS

LEAVES MOSTLY
3-LOBED

This slender trailer only grows a few feet long. It is armed with numerous, small, weak prickles. The "blackberry" leaves may be 3-lobed or have three leaflets... Flowers are usually solitary with white or purple petals. The fruit is a finely hairy, red berry.

QUICK CHECK: Note range. Short, prickly trailer with red berry.

RANGE: On dry exposed places near sub-alpine elevations, V.I. and Coastal Mountains.

EVERGREEN BLACKBERRY (*R. laciniatus*) is a common escape from cultivation at the Coast. It has very stout stems with strong, recurved thorns. Dense thickets are a common sight along roadsides on Vancouver Island and through the Lower Mainland.

FLOWERS

SCORCHED PENSTEMON
(Penstemon deustus)

For general features of the penstemons see page 156. Scorched penstemon is the only white-flowered species liable to be encountered. Sometimes there may be a yellow or purplish tinge. The plant has a branching form to 2' high with stout erect stalks. Leaves are dull green, about 1½" long, and variable in shape with distinct jagged teeth. The flowers form clusters along the top 3" - 6" of stem. Each bloom is ½" long and has a hairy throat. It flowers during May and June.

RANGE: Columbia River Valley near International Boundary. Abundant in Washington.

VARIED-LEAVED PHACELIA
(Phacelia heterophylla)

The phacelias range from dry valley bottoms to windswept alpine heights. The long stamens impart a fuzzy appearance and the flowers are usually pastel-colored. Varied-leaved phacelia is a tousled plant to 16" high with a dense cluster of low leaves greatly varying in shape but deeply veined and hairy.

Flowers are usually white but may have a light purplish blush. They too are hairy and grouped in thick fuzzy clusters. The blooming time is middle to late summer depending on elevation.

RANGE: West of the Cascades and to high elevations.

WHITE-LEAVED PHACELIA (*P. hastata leucophylla*) is quite similar but has silvery leaves from dense hairs. The leaves are not lobed or "winged". Dry Interior Valleys.

ELEGANT MARIPOSA LILY
(Calochortus elegans)

Elegant Star Tulip
Cat's Ear, Three Spot

The name "Elegant" is well chosen for the white petals are lushly carpeted with white hairs which become yellow in the throat of the flower. Embellishing this is a purple-violet pouch near the base of each petal, thus the name of Three Spot.

This lily, one of three in B.C. (See page 162) is 6" - 16" in height and carries from 1 - 3 blooms. A ribbed basal leaf provides suitable balance. A few small leaves adorn the upper stem and there is a scattering of purple dots near the base of the sepals. Late June into July is the blooming time.

RANGE: Dryish flats and slopes in south-eastern B. C. Creston, Cranbrook, Fort Steele.

BAKER'S MARIPOSA LILY (*C. apiculatus*) to 16" high, differs in having pale yellow petals densely covered with yellow hairs on the lower half. The gland is round and blackish. Blooms late June into July. Open grassland or forest in south-eastern B.C. Elko, Crow's Nest Pass, Canal Flats.

FLOWERS (WHITE)

8"-24" HIGH

WHITE FLWS. ½" LONG

SCORCHED P.

6"-18"HIGH

CREAMY TO YELLOW FLWS. ¾" LONG 3-4 CLUSTERS

OPPOSITE LEAVES TO 3" LONG

YELLOW P.

8"-16"HIGH

CLUSTERS HAIRY WHITE FLWS. ¼" ACROSS

OLIVE GREEN LEAVES & STEM VERY HAIRY

LEAVES TO 6" LONG, DEEPLY VEINED

WHITE-LEAVED PHACELIA

6"-16" HIGH

PURPLISH DOTS ON SEPALS

WHITE FLOWER 1¼"-1½" ACROSS PETALS HAIRY

PURPLE POUCH ON BASE OF PETALS

2-3 SMALL LEAVES

SINGLE LEAF WITH RIBBED VEINS

FRINGE CUP
(Tellima parviflora)

Fringe cup is one of the early spring wild-flowers that can be confused with several plants with small white flowers such as field chickweed, Siberian miner's lettuce and montia. If you think of the "fringe" part of the name while looking at the five petals, each so deeply fringed as to look like three separate parts, you should be able to remember the name. Fringe cup grows on fairly open ground, such as swales and forest borders. It is one of the first flowers and blooms from April to June. The flowers look like large symmetrical snowflakes with a pinkish tinge. Blooms and buds cluster in profusion at the top of thin stems.

RANGE: Open places on Vancouver Island, Fraser Canyon, Okanagan Valley and eastward to Rockies.

4"-10" HIGH

5 WHITE PETALS "3-FINGERED"

MINER'S LETTUCE
(Montia perfoliata)

Miner's lettuce is a significant name for it means what it says. Indians first used the fresh plant for food. Then the early miners, prospectors, and trappers, often at a loss for green vegetables copied the Indians and found it was a tasty suc-culent green. Several other related species may be called miner's lettuce also. The plant is in bloom and suitable for eating during April and May.

The unusual feature about this species is the saucer-shaped upper leaves through which the stem protrudes. The small white flowers grow along thin stems rising from the centre of the leaf discs. The lower leaves are of more ordinary design and have long stems.

RANGE: Vancouver Island, Coastal Region, Okanagan Valley.

4"-14" HIGH

SMALL WHITE FLOWERS

FLESHY LEAVES AND STEMS

SIBERIAN MINER'S LETTUCE
(Montia sibirica)

You don't have to go to Siberia to find this plant although that is where it was first discov-ered. It differs from miner's lettuce in not having the upper pair of leaves form a disk. However, they are short-stemmed while the lower leaves have long stems.

The flowers, on long thin stems, have 5 petals quite noticeably notched and sometimes pinkish from red lines on them. During April and May you will find this flower in the rich moist soil of meadows or road ditches. Like miner's lettuce it is excellent for salad greens.

RANGE: Vancouver Island and Coastal regions.

5"-12" HIGH

5 WHITE NOTCHED PETALS WITH RED LINES

LEPTARRHENA
(Leptarrhena amplexifolia)
(Leptarrhena pyrolifolia)

This plant is most prominent just as the snow leaves the soggy meadows at and above timber-line. Then its leathery, glossy green leaves make a vivid mat pattern against the dead grasses of the past year... It also finds a suitable habitat along the banks of small creeks. Leaves are 1" - 3" long, with a sheath-like base clasping the short and thick main stem. A marked difference is seen in the dark green surface of the leaf and the whitish green tone displayed beneath.

In early summer the plant is found by its 6" - 12" high stalks carrying dense clusters of small white flowers at their tips. One or two thickish leaves occur on the flower stem.

As frosts grip the meadows, this member of the saxifrage family adds its final decorative touch, a beautiful purplish-red seed stem with a tight packed cluster of seeds of the same brilliant hue. **RANGE:** Sub-alpine and alpine meadows of V.I. and the Cascade Range.

BUCKBEAN
(Menyanthes trifoliata)

The fact that buckbean grows in water enables a person to find it without too much trouble. Marshy places like bogs or around the borders of shallow lakes are a favoured habitat... Its 3-parted leaves are unmistakable. Note how the thick fleshy stems are sheathed at their bases.

The stout flower stem to a foot high carries a dozen or more heavy flowers. These are about ½" long and vary from a drab white to a pale purplish tinge. The five petals have a fuzzy appearance from fine hairs on their surface. Usually the petals curve back disclosing a hairy throat.

Buckbean blooms in May and June.
RANGE: Marshy places across the Province.

BANEBERRY
(Actaea rubra)

Baneberry is a leafy plant to 3' high with an erect stem holding 2 or 3 leaves broken into divisions of three, or ternately compound. Leaves are crinkled and coarsely and sharply toothed.

Small white flowers in a dense cluster make a fuzzy white ball because of the many protruding stamens. Watch for the bloom of this easily recognized plant from April into June. Do not confuse it with a false bugbane. See page 112. By August, handsome scarlet berries, smooth and firm, flaunt their charms. Occasionally white ones are produced. There is a strong possibility that baneberries are poisonous.
RANGE: Moist shady places across B.C and north to Alaska.

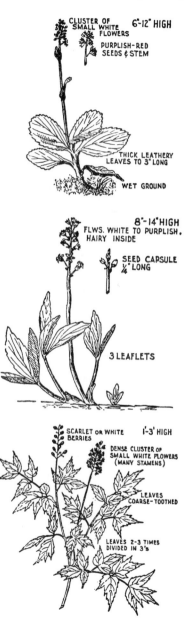

CLUSTER OF SMALL WHITE FLOWERS — 6"-12" HIGH
PURPLISH-RED SEEDS & STEM
THICK LEATHERY LEAVES TO 3" LONG
WET GROUND

8"-14" HIGH
FLWS. WHITE TO PURPLISH. HAIRY INSIDE
SEED CAPSULE ¼" LONG
3 LEAFLETS

SCARLET OR WHITE BERRIES — 1'-3' HIGH
DENSE CLUSTER OF SMALL WHITE FLOWERS (MANY STAMENS)
LEAVES COARSE-TOOTHED
LEAVES 2-3 TIMES DIVIDED IN 3's

FLOWERS (WHITE)

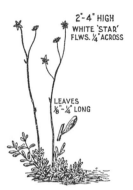

2"-4" HIGH
WHITE 'STAR'
FLWS. ¼" ACROSS

LEAVES
⅛"-¼" LONG

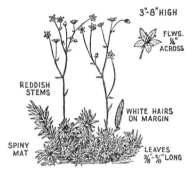

3"-8" HIGH

FLWS. ¼" ACROSS

REDDISH STEMS

WHITE HAIRS ON MARGIN

SPINY MAT

LEAVES ⅜"-⅝" LONG

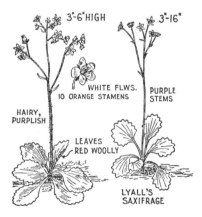

3"-6" HIGH   3"-16"

WHITE FLWS. 10 ORANGE STAMENS

PURPLE STEMS

HAIRY, PURPLISH

LEAVES RED WOOLLY

LYALL'S SAXIFRAGE

TOLMIE SAXIFRAGE
(Saxifraga tolmiei)

Alpine Saxifrage

The saxifrages represent a very widespread group of flowers. Characteristics are basal leaves, sepals in a 5-lobed sheath, 5 entire petals, and generally 10 stamens. A large number of species are less than 6" high and the habitat is mostly on rocky places.

Tolmie saxifrage is quite common on dryish, exposed places above timberline. The leaves form a compact shrubby mat from which slender flower stems rise from 2" - 4". Leaves are evergreen, mealy, ⅛" - ¼" in length, round-tipped, and with a tendency to roll over on the edges. One or several small star-like flowers adorn the stems.

RANGE: High mountains on V.I. Coast and Cascade Mountains and extending north into B.C.

SPOTTED SAXIFRAGE
(Saxifraga bronchialis)

Common Saxifrage

This plant is somewhat similar to the above in mat-like growth but the leaves are spiny and sharp, ¼" - ½" long, and with hairy margins. The small white flowers form a galaxy of sparkling stars atop slim stems. Look closely and you will see that the tiny white petals are artistically speckled with distinct maroon and yellow dots.

There are two varieties, *austromontana* and *vespertina*, distinguished by their range. The former is very abundant in rocky places near and just above timberline. Mountains on V.I., the Coast Range and eastward into the Rockies.

VESPER SAXIFRAGE (*S. bronchialis* var *vespertina*) grows in exposed places along the edge of cliffs and rock slides. Seldom does it ever extend to timberline. The range is not well known. Queen Charlotte Islands, Fraser Canyon.

RUSTY SAXIFRAGE
(Saxifraga occidentalis)

Red Woolly Saxifrage

This plant takes its name from the red woolly appearance of the underside of the leaf. The stem helps the idea along by having a purplish hue. Leaves are thick, leathery, and coarsely but regularly toothed. The branched stem carries a number of white flowers, beautified by 10 orange stamens. Because of its range at comparatively low elevations the blooming time is May and June.

RANGE: Low mountains on V.I.

LYALL'S SAXIFRAGE (*S. lyallii*) is a more abundant plant than the above and bears a close resemblance in flowers. However, the leaves are without hair and the stems are much higher. The range is damp alpine meadows and stream edges from V.I. to the Rockies.

SAXIFRAGE
(Saxifraga integrifolia)

This particular saxifrage is common west of the Cascades. It is found on mossy exposed places during March and April with other early spring flowers such as peacocks, satin flower, and spring gold. The stem is reddish and hairy and the small white flowers form a not too attractive packed cluster. Leaves are thick and shallowly notched. Many are reddish beneath. Other species show a great variety in leaf, some being notched and others lobed.

RANGE: Common on Vancouver Island and Coast. Locally in Dry Interior.

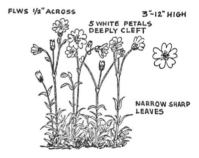

4"-8" HIGH
TIGHT CLUSTER OF SMALL WHITE FLOWERS

FINE RED HAIRS ON STEM

LEAVES PINKISH BENEATH

FIELD CHICKWEED
(Cerastium arvense)
Star of Bethlehem

This fresh white little flower rising on thin stems from a mat of leaves has a world-wide distribution but nevertheless makes a convincing display at being a native wildflower.

Each flower is about 1/2" across and has 5 petals which are so deeply cleft in two that they are easily mistaken for a total of 10. The hairy stems carry narrow sharp-pointed leaves but a leafy mat-like growth is not uncommon. Field chickweed often is found with other spring wildflowers which grow on the drier rockier places. It has a prolonged blooming season from April into June.

RANGE: Sporadic throughout B.C.

FLWS 1/2" ACROSS
3"-12" HIGH
5 WHITE PETALS DEEPLY CLEFT

NARROW SHARP LEAVES

WILD LILY-OF-THE-VALLEY
(Maianthemum unifolium dilatatum)

The twisting veiny leaves are sufficient aid in recognizing this small plant which generally masses together in shady places. Each short stem holds one or two waxy leaves. During May a 2"-4" long spike of small white flowers rises above the leaves. This display is short-lived but even so is embellished by each flower having knobby protruding anthers and a delicate scent. The berries that follow are first mottled with brown but later change to ruby beads.

RANGE: Vancouver Island and Coast.

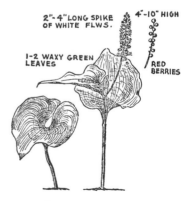

2"-4" LONG SPIKE OF WHITE FLWS.
4"-10" HIGH
1-2 WAXY GREEN LEAVES
RED BERRIES

(107)

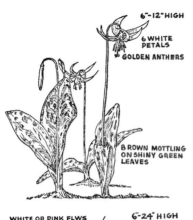

6"-12" HIGH
6 WHITE PETALS
GOLDEN ANTHERS
BROWN MOTTLING ON SHINY GREEN LEAVES

EASTER LILY
(*Erythronium oregonum*)

Dog-tooth Violet

In spring many forest glades are carpeted by this regal white lily. Almost as showy as the flower are the mottled glossy leaves. Well out of sight deep in the ground is a bulb which requires 5 - 7 years to develop before raising its first flower stem. Seed dropped from the flowers accounts for the great masses of lilies often seen in secluded surroundings.

The Easter lily blooms in April and is particularly abundant within 30 miles of Victoria. This condition can hardly be expected to continue for many unthinking people go to great trouble to pick every flower they can find.

RANGE: North to Comox on Vancouver Island and on the Gulf Islands. Vicinity Langley Prairie. PINK EASTER LILY (*E. smithii*) has pink petals and grows from Cowichan Lake northward. Sooke.

A Plea . . . Leave them be, for others to see!

WHITE OR PINK FLWS 1 1/2"- 2" ACROSS
6"-24" HIGH

WESTERN TRILLIUM
(*Trillium ovatum*)

Wake Robin

There is no chance of confusing the trillium with any other flower. Its stout stem carries three large, net-veined leaves which form a whorl to cradle the short-stemmed white flower. There are three petals from 1" - 2" long and 6 dark, fuzzy stamens in the centre. The pure white flower undergoes a change to purple or pink as it ages. The blooming season is from mid-April to the end of May.

RANGE: Vancouver Island, the Gulf Islands, and Coastal Forest Zone. Sporadic in Kootenays. Creston to Moyie Lake and vicinity of Fernie.

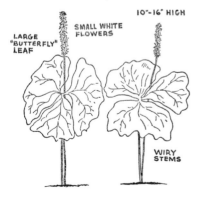

10"-16" HIGH
SMALL WHITE FLOWERS
LARGE "BUTTERFLY" LEAF
WIRY STEMS

VANILLA LEAF
(*Achlys triphylla*)

May Leaves — Sweet-after-death

The masses of large 3-winged "butterfly" leaves will be seen here and there at lower elevations throughout shady coniferous forests. A thin wiry stem about a foot high holds a single leaf artistically divided into 3 wavy-edged segments. The leaves start to take shape by mid-April and in May a thin flower stem unerringly pokes its way between a narrow leaf cleft to hold aloft a spike of small white flowers.

The name comes from the faint vanilla odor of the dried leaves as does sweet-after-death, another name sometimes used. A bundle of dried leaves hung in a room is supposed to repel flies.

RANGE: Low and middle elevations on Vancouver Island and Coastal Region.

(108)

BUNCHBERRY
(Cornus canadensis)
Pigeon Berry

Bunchberry is a relative of the flowering dog-wood tree. In its few inches of height are con-tained all the dogwood tree features except size. See how similar are the leaves with their parallel curved veins. The "flower" too has a greenish centre of tiny flowers surrounded by a number of showy white bracts. This produces the effect of a white blossom about 1" across.

Bunchberry is one of the more abundant forest flowers and carpets many forest dells and glades. Sometimes it will grow on old stumps and logs where soil has collected. Flowers may be well out in May and, like the tree dogwood, the tiny plant sometimes blooms again in late summer. By August most plants have developed a cluster of brilliant red berries, a showpiece more impressive than the flowers. These, although insipid and mealy, are in no way poisonous.

RANGE: From sea level to sub-alpine forests throughout the Province.

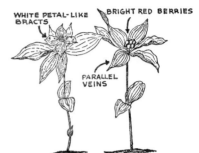

3"-8" HIGH

WHITE PETAL-LIKE BRACTS

BRIGHT RED BERRIES

PARALLEL VEINS

QUEEN'S CUP
(Clintonia uniflora)
Alpine Beauty

Queen's Cup is a widespread forest flower that is bound to come to the attention of every mountain hiker. Its two or three shiny green leaves from 4" - 8" in length mark it immediately. From May to July a slender stem about 6" high carries one pure white flower about 1" across. This is followed by a most unusual oval berry. Its deep, china-blue color is one not often seen in nature.

RANGE: Most abundant at middle mountain elevations where it may carpet the mossy forest floor. It ranges across the Province and far north-ward.

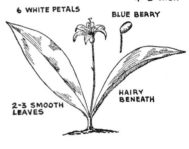

4"-8" HIGH

6 WHITE PETALS

BLUE BERRY

2-3 SMOOTH LEAVES

HAIRY BENEATH

RATTLESNAKE PLANTAIN
(Goodyera oblongifolia)

Mossy but fairly dry places in coniferous forests are home to this plant with the peculiar name and leaves. The long ovalish leaves which grow close to the ground are a dark green color laced with a criss-cross network of white. This mark-ing is supposed to resemble that on a rattlesnake.

Often the leaves are the only feature to be seen for the plant does not bloom every year. When it does it produces a thickish stalk with small greenish-white flowers loosely scattered along the spike. There is a tendency for the flowers to favor one side of the stem. The bloom-ing time is midsummer.

RANGE: Dry coniferous forests across B.C.

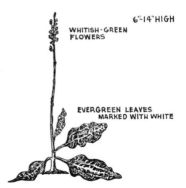

6"-14" HIGH

WHITISH-GREEN FLOWERS

EVERGREEN LEAVES MARKED WITH WHITE

FLOWERS (WHITE)

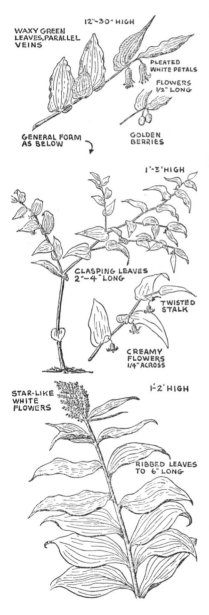

WAXY GREEN LEAVES, PARALLEL VEINS

12"-30" HIGH

PLEATED WHITE PETALS

FLOWERS ½" LONG

GENERAL FORM AS BELOW

GOLDEN BERRIES

1'-3' HIGH

CLASPING LEAVES 2"-4" LONG

TWISTED STALK

CREAMY FLOWERS ¼" ACROSS

STAR-LIKE WHITE FLOWERS

1-2' HIGH

RIBBED LEAVES TO 6" LONG

OREGON FAIRY BELLS
(Disporum oregonum)

Smooth Fairy Bells

Glossy veined leaves cover its several branches and effectively hide the creamy 2 - 3 flowers. During May and June look for the pairs of drooping, bell-shaped flowers near the tips of each branch. After the flowers are over an oblong smooth berry will form. It varies from yellow to orange and its pulpy centre surrounds several large seeds. The berry looks edible but its taste doesn't bear out the appearance.

RANGE: Moist woods on Vancouver Island and Coastal Forest Zone.

ROUGH FAIRY BELLS (*D. trachycarpum*) has larger and more greenish flowers than the above. The berry is more rounded and has a velvety fuzz to it. When ripe it turns a rich red color. The range is east of the Cascades and across B.C. Cariboo Parklands and Central B.C.

TWISTED STALK
(Streptopus amplexifolius)

Twisted stalk gets its name from the curious sharp twist in the hair-like stems carrying the flowers and berries. This oddity of structure serves for immediate identification whereas the leaves are confused easily with other plants. The alternate leaves clasp the stem and grow so close together they often hide the flowers or berries. The white or cream-colored flowers which hang one to the stem, are about ¼" long and will be found in bloom during May and June. Even when the oblong bright red berries are formed the kink in the stems still remains.

RANGE: Shady damp woods across B.C. and into North Central B.C.

FALSE SOLOMON'S SEAL
(Smilacina amplexicaulis)

False Solomon's seal may attract the attention by reason of its size, the large glossy leaves, or plume of creamy flowers. Each stout unbranched stem carries two rows of alternate broad leaves from 2½" - 5" long. These clasp the stem at their base. Parallel veins impart a touch of the exotic. The small whitish flowers are packed into a pyramidal cluster which emits a sweet scent. They will be found from May into June. Later in the season mottled greenish-red berries are carried which slowly turn an unusual red color. They are edible but rather tasteless with one or two seeds.

RANGE: Damp shady habitat throughout B.C.

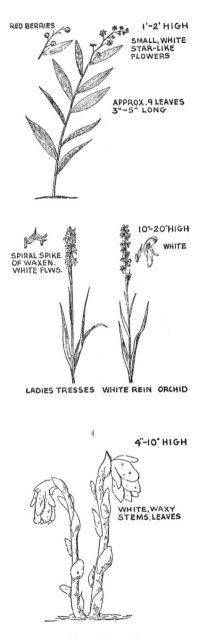

STAR - FLOWERED SOLOMON'S SEAL
(Smilacina stellata)

This plant, because of similarity of name or leaf, is liable to be confused with twisted stalk, fairy bells and false Solomon's seal. The plant is fairly uniform in size being a single stem 1' - 2' high. The thin leaves 2" - 5" long clasp the main stem and point upward. It gets its name from the several white, star-like flowers at its tip. From April until June these tiny sprites make their appearance. Later, the berry becomes green with darkish stripes and slowly changes to bright red.

RANGE: Moist woods throughout B.C.

LADIES' TRESSES
(Spiranthes romanzoffiana)

The distinguishing feature about ladies' tresses is the 3 vertical rows of flowers which spiral around the central stem. The suggestion of the twisting of a hair braid has led to the common name. The white or pale cream flowers are almost ½" long and have a sweet fragrance. It bears a slight resemblance to white rein orchis. The blooming season is July to August.

RANGE: Across B.C. and into northern regions.

WHITE REIN ORCHID
(Habenaria dilatata)

Almost a dozen rein orchids are found in B.C. The Latin, *habena* means a bridle or rein alluding to the narrow lip of some species. The beautiful little orchids vary from white to greenish-yellow in color. The white rein orchid has flowers of the purest white and a perfume to match. Most species are lovers of moist soils thus leading to the common name of bog orchid.

RANGE: Wet places throughout B.C.

INDIAN PIPE
(Monotropa uniflora)

A person finding Indian pipe for the first time is sure his senses are deceiving him. The waxy white clump of "pipes" can hardly be likened to any other growing plant. The stout brittle stems twist over at the tip and droop in a massed cluster of thick waxy scales. The leaves are white also and press closely to the stem. Indian pipe may be found in late spring or midsummer. It gets its nourishment from growing on decaying matter from other plants.

RANGE: Sparsely distributed in shady places on Vancouver Island, Coastal and Cariboo region.

FLOWERS (WHITE)

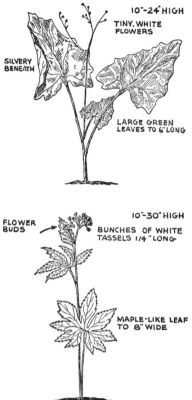

10"-24"HIGH

TINY, WHITE FLOWERS

SILVERY BENEATH

LARGE GREEN LEAVES TO 6"LONG

SILVER - GREEN
(*Adenocaulon bicolor*)

Pathfinder

The most noticeable feature about silver-green is the contrast in color between the two sides of the leaf. Its alternate name of pathfinder comes from the marked path that is left when a person disturbs these plants. The dark green weedy leaves when turned over attract immediate attention by their silvery sheen and can be seen from afar. The flashing color comes from a mat of fine white hairs.

The small white flowers on their thin stems aren't noticed very often but later may prove an annoyance through the sticky seeds catching in the clothing.

RANGE: Vancouver Island and Coastal forests, also wetter portions of Interior.

FLOWER BUDS

10"-30"HIGH

BUNCHES OF WHITE TASSELS 1/4"LONG

MAPLE-LIKE LEAF TO 8"WIDE

FALSE BUGBANE
(*Trautvetteria caroliniensis*)

False bugbane prefers shady moist places giving rise to luxuriant vegetation. For this reason the plant is usually hidden except for its head of small white bristly flowers. The bristles are formed by tufts of long stamens which are a good distinguishing feature. After blooming during late spring, bright red berries are formed.

The single leaves are maple-like and from 2" - 6" across. Generally they are wider than long and have from 5-9 lobes. Stem leaves are few and short stemmed.

RANGE: Vancouver Island and Coastal Forest Zones from low to middle elevations.

The true bugbane or baneberry is described on pege 105.

10"-24"HIGH

WHITE COTTONY HEADS

GRASS-LIKE LEAVES

COTTON GRASS
(*Eriophorum chamissonis*)

Although there are several species of cotton grass in B.C. the peculiar white cottony head and swamp habitat dispel any doubts as to general recognition. Often wet meadows are covered so thickly with this sedge that they appear like a field of cotton.

The springy green stems from 1' - 2' high carry a puffy ball of cotton which obscures the small flowers hidden in its depths. Leaves are short and grass-like. Cotton grass has a wide altitudinal range being found from sea level to sub-alpine meadows.

RANGE: Sedgy, wet meadows throughout Coastal Region and in North Central B. C.

FOAM FLOWER
(*Tiarella unifoliata*)

Laceflower

The fine erect stems carry only a single leaf on them but the plant is provided with a group of long-stemmed leaves growing from its base. Often masses of this delicate flower are found in favorable locations. The tiny white flowers dance on the ends of short wire-like branchlets grouped airily near the top of the stem. They have a prolonged blooming season during May to July.

RANGE: Mostly middle and high elevations in damp coniferous forests across B.C.

T. trifoliata has 3 leaflets instead of a single leaf. Coastal Forests and Central B.C.

SMALL - FLOWER ALUMROOT
(*Heuchera micrantha*)

Alumroots with creamy or yellow flowers are given on page 149.

Alumroots are quite easily recognized from their basal group of long-stemmed, oval to heart-shaped leaves with irregular lobes and rounded notches. Long tap roots with an astringent, alum taste make a firm anchor. Often alumroot is the first plant of any size to establish itself on inhospitable cliffs. The leaves have rounded lobes and a heart-shaped base. The slender stems are reddish from fine hairs. Tiny white globes on short, delicate side branches bloom from May to July.

RANGE: Common alumroot west of Cascades.

ALUMROOT (*H. glabra*) has sharp-pointed leaf lobes and smooth stems. Abundant in Coastal Forest Zone, Interior Wet belt and north to Smithers.

SUNDEW
(*Drosera spp.*)

The low tuft of small leaves are bristly with reddish hairs each with a tiny sticky globe at its tip. This secretion attracts insects which are caught fast when they alight and absorbed into the leaf. The inconspicuous white flowers droop near the tip of one or more thin stems. They only open in strong sunlight. The blooming period is from late spring to midsummer.

RANGE: Coastal regions and North Central B.C.

ROUND LEAF SUNDEW (*D. rotundifolia*) has small round leaves. Sphagnum bogs.

SUNDEW (*D. anglica*) has long narrow leaves shaped like a canoe paddle. It too is found mostly in bogs or wet soils around the shores of lakes.

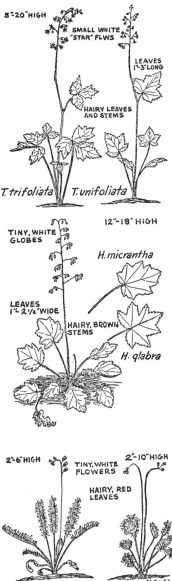

5"-20"HIGH
SMALL WHITE "STAR" FLWS
LEAVES 1"-3"LONG
HAIRY LEAVES AND STEMS
T.trifoliata *T.unifoliata*

12"-18" HIGH
TINY, WHITE GLOBES
H.micrantha
LEAVES 1"-2½"WIDE
HAIRY, BROWN STEMS
H. glabra

2"-6"HIGH
TINY, WHITE FLOWERS
HAIRY, RED LEAVES
2"-10"HIGH
D.anglica *D.rotundifolia*

(113)

FLOWERS (WHITE)

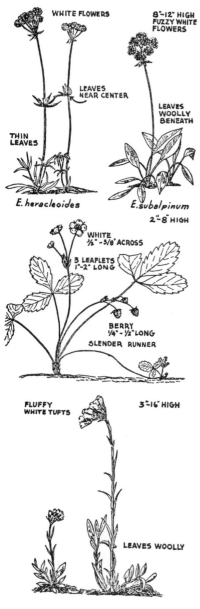

WHITE FLOWERS

8"-12" HIGH FUZZY WHITE FLOWERS

LEAVES NEAR CENTER

LEAVES WOOLLY BENEATH

THIN LEAVES

E. heracleoides

E.subalpinum
2"-8" HIGH

WHITE ½"-⅝" ACROSS

3 LEAFLETS 1"-2" LONG

BERRY ¼"-½" LONG
SLENDER RUNNER

FLUFFY WHITE TUFTS

3"-16" HIGH

LEAVES WOOLLY

TALL WHITE ERIOGONUM
(*Eriogonum subalpinum*)

Eriogonums have a shrubby, mat-like base and white hairs on one or both sides of the leaves. The flowers are in shades of white, cream or yellow but often a reddish tinge is seen toward the end of the season.

Tall white eriogonum raises a stout stem from a dense mat of ovalish leaves which are noticeably woolly beneath. The small, white to cream flowers bunch in a compact rounded cluster supported by a series of short umbrella stems. Flowers are on display from June to August.

RANGE: On rocky or poor soils at middle elevations throughout B.C.

E. heracleoides has a wisp of leaves near the centre of the stem. It grows at lower elevations and is quite common on poor soils in open places throughout the Dry Interior Zone.

See page 143 for two eriogonums with yellow flowers.

BLUELEAF STRAWBERRY
(*Fragaria glauca*)

The wild strawberries are much like the cultivated varieties except for their sparseness and smaller size, particularly that of the berry. Of possibly 6 different species in B.C., *F. chiloensis* and *F. bracteata* are the two most common ones west of the Cascades while blueleaf strawberry ranges widely east of these mountains.

There is no plant stem for everything seen above ground is either a flower, leaf stem or runner since these branch almost directly from a scale cluster attached to the roots. The flowers have 5 white petals and later produce a very small but sweet berry.

RANGE: East of Cascades through the Dry Interior, Cariboo and into North Central B.C.

WHITE PUSSYTOES
(*Antennaria spp.*)

White pussytoes attracts attention in the spring because of its odd woolly head. The tight ball of flowers is dry and furry and very soft to the touch. There are over a dozen species in B.C. but all of these flannelly plants seek out rocky, dry places on which to grow. The leaves are alternate and entire with wider leaves at the base of the stem. Some species are so woolly as to appear quite white. One has very attractive pink flowers (page 132) and all possess "everlasting" qualities after being picked.

RANGE: Dry exposed places throughout B.C. from sea level to mountain tops.

(114)

PEARLY EVERLASTING
(Anaphalis margaritacea)

This is a vigorous roadside plant with a flat-topped mass of white flowers. It waits until the more colorful spring flowers have faded and then in July bursts into bloom. The stems and the underside of the long thin leaves are covered with a white wool which is usually hidden from sight by the bushy mass of dark green leaves.

The tightly packed flower head, perhaps 6" across, is worth more than a passing glance. Each pearly white ball has a yellowish or brownish centre flanked by a large number of beautifully arranged parchment-like scales of delicate pastel shading. The flowers, if picked in full bloom, remain without wilting thus leading to "Everlasting" as an alternate name.

RANGE: Throughout B. C., particularly along roads and wherever there is settlement.

YARROW
(Achillea millefolium)

This plant may be thought of as a flower or weed depending on the ideas of the individual. Perhaps the weed concept arises from the wide range of yarrow over waste areas and on the poorer soils.

Arching from its stout unbranched stem are a number of leaves so finely divided into fringes that they look like large fuzzy pipe cleaners. These have a very pungent odor if crushed. The flower head of numerous small flowers is from 2" - 4" across and slightly rounded. A casual glance shows small, scaly, white flowers with yellow centres. Actually each tiny part of the flower is itself a complete flower. Both the white "ray" flowers and the yellow "disk" flowers produce seed. Yarrow blooms about June at the Coast and August elsewhere.

RANGE: Throughout B.C. on dry and poor soils.

MEADOW SPIREA
(Luetkea pectinata)

This small plant, so abundant in damp open places in sub-alpine and alpine regions, differs greatly in outward appearance from the several other common spireas in the Province. The fresh green clumps only several inches high are composed of a large number of individuals. Leaves are so divided as to appear fringed like those of a fern. The slender stems carry small white flowers in bloom during midsummer.

RANGE: High mountains at the Coast, North Central B.C. and extending to Alaska.

HEADS 1"-6" ACROSS

12"-24" HIGH:

WHITE FLWS. 1/4" ACROSS

WHITE WOOLLY STEMS

LEAVES 2"-6" LONG WOOLLY BENEATH

8"-20" HIGH

FLAT, WHITE FLOWER HEAD 2"-4" ACROSS

2"-4" HIGH

SMALL, WHITE FLOWERS

FRINGED LEAVES

(115)

1'-2' HIGH

FLWS 1½-2" ACROSS

WHITE "DAISIES" WITH YELLOW CENTERS

OXEYE DAISY
(Chrysanthemum leucanthemum)

The feeling that this flower would look quite at home in a garden is perfectly right for it is a naturalized plant now widely distributed on Vancouver Island and the Lower Mainland. Its erect graceful stems, branching near the top, carry symmetrical white daisies. The combination of yellow centre and white ray petals make up a gay bloom almost 2" across. The leaves are dark green and lobed.

Sometimes entire fields are taken over by the oxeye daisy. Then the massed blooms, all at an even height, present an unforgettable sight as they shimmer in the sunshine or ripple to the touch of a breeze. The blooming season is from May to July, after the bulk of spring flowers has passed.

RANGE: Roadsides and fields on Vancouver Island, Lower Mainland and Kootenays. Extends into Central B.C.

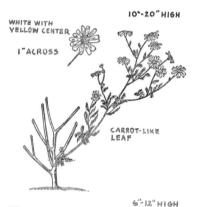

10"-20" HIGH

WHITE WITH YELLOW CENTER

1" ACROSS

CARROT-LIKE LEAF

FIELD CHAMOMILE
(Anthemis arvensis)

This flower also is daisy-like in appearance and an introduced plant but differs from the oxeye daisy in not having such large crisp flowers. It is more tousled in form being much branched and lacking the long erect stems. The white flower, about 1" across, has a yellow centre. New buds are continually developing and so lead to a prolonged blooming season during June and July. The leaves are shredded like those of carrots.

RANGE: Waste places such as roadsides throughout Vancouver Island and the Coastal region.

6"-12" HIGH

WHITE TO PINKISH FLOWERS 3/4"-1" ACROSS

FINE HAIRS ON LEAVES AND STEMS

WHITE FLEABANE
(Erigeron caespitosus)

This bushy little plant, about one foot high, will be found along roadsides and in waste places in the more arid parts of the Province. The clusters of round white flowers are daisy-like and sometimes with a pink tinge. Close inspection shows numerous thin ray petals, a feature of the fleabanes. The flowers are almost an inch across and have yellowish-green centres. They are in bloom from May to July.

As with many flowers found in dry regions, the long narrow leaves and branching stems are dull green and covered with fine hairs.

RANGE: East of Cascades and north to Yukon.

BLACK NIGHTSHADE
(Solanum nigrum)

Many people believe this plant has poisonous properties, but the glossy black berries are quite edible and even cultivated in some places.

A close relative to the tomato, grows to 2' high in a bushy erect shrub. The older leaves, to 4½" long and 2" wide, generally have several irregular shallow teeth. Three to eight small white flowers protruding anthers are carried in a loose drooping cluster.

RANGE: A summer bloomer on the south half of V.I. Dry places east of Cascades. Merritt.

THREE-FLOWERED NIGHTSHADE (*S. triflorum*) is a sprawling plant with deeply lobed leaves to 2½" long. Two or three white flowers develop into green berries. Dry Interior.

DRUMMOND'S ROCKCRESS
(Arabis drummondii)

Rock cresses, of which there are about 12 species in B.C., have small flowers in pastel shades of white, pink, or purple. Rock cresses belong to the *Cruciferae,* referring to the cross-like arrangement of the petals. Other family characteristics are a single erect stem, 4 sepals, 4 petals, and 6 stamens of which 2 are short ones. Leaves have a distinctive bitter taste. The ting seeds are usually formed in two rows in long narrow flattened pods.

RANGE: Sub-alpine zone of Cascades and Rockies.

TOWER MUSTARD (*A. glabra*) is much coarser than the above. Leaves are to 2½" long and ½" wide and seed pods average between 3" - 4" long. The tiny white flowers form a dense cluster. Sporadic appearance on dry ground.

GLOBE ANEMONE
(Anemone multifida) *(A. globosa)*

The widespread anemones or wind flowers generally have a basal group of toothed or lobed hairy leaves and one or two leaf whorls on the slender stem. The single flowers haven't petals but carry 5 or more petal-like sepals often with a bluish tinge. Stamens are numerous and protrude from a small central cushion. The seed head is a soft feathery mass.

The chameleon-like flowers in June and July vary from shades of red and purple to white or greenish yellow. The young seed head is a symmetrical globe shape.

RANGE: Mt. Arrowsmith, Cariboo, Peace River.

DRUMMOND'S ANEMONE (*A. drummondii*) grows from 2" - 8" high. Flowers are white on the inside but with a distinct blue tinge on the outside. Rocky places near and above timberline, on V.I., Cascades and Invermere Mountains.

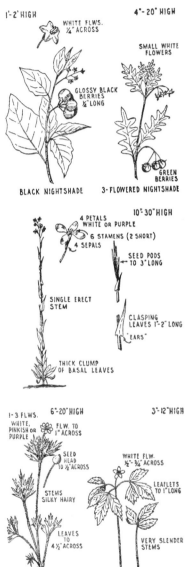

1'-2' HIGH — WHITE FLWS. ¼" ACROSS — GLOSSY BLACK BERRIES ¼" LONG — BLACK NIGHTSHADE

4"-20" HIGH — SMALL WHITE FLOWERS — GREEN BERRIES — 3-FLOWERED NIGHTSHADE

10"-30" HIGH — 4 PETALS WHITE OR PURPLE — 6 STAMENS (2 SHORT) — 4 SEPALS — SEED PODS TO 3" LONG — SINGLE ERECT STEM — CLASPING LEAVES 1"-2" LONG — "EARS" — THICK CLUMP OF BASAL LEAVES

1-3 FLWS. 6"-20" HIGH — WHITE, PINKISH OR PURPLE — FLW. TO 1" ACROSS — SEED HEAD TO ½" ACROSS — STEMS SILKY HAIRY — LEAVES TO 4½" ACROSS

3"-12" HIGH — WHITE FLW. ½"-¾" ACROSS — LEAFLETS TO 1" LONG — VERY SLENDER STEMS

(117)

FLOWERS (WHITE)

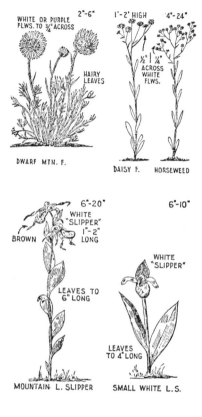

WHITE OR PURPLE FLWS. TO ¾" ACROSS — 2"-6"

HAIRY LEAVES

DWARF MTN. F.

1'-2' HIGH

½" ¼" ACROSS WHITE FLWS.

DAISY F.   HORSEWEED   4"-24"

6"-20"
WHITE "SLIPPER"
1"-2" LONG
BROWN

LEAVES TO 6" LONG

MOUNTAIN L. SLIPPER

6"-10"
WHITE "SLIPPER"

LEAVES TO 4" LONG

SMALL WHITE L.S.

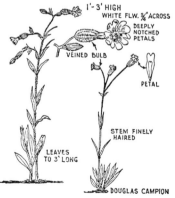

1'-3' HIGH
WHITE FLW. ¾" ACROSS
DEEPLY NOTCHED PETALS
VEINED BULB

PETAL

STEM FINELY HAIRED

LEAVES TO 3' LONG

DOUGLAS CAMPION

DWARF MOUNTAIN FLEABANE
(Erigeron compositus)

This dainty flower with either white or purple ray petals is less than ¾" across and has a yellow center. Generally low and many branched, the leaves are velvety and branch into thin fingers. Blooming time is from mid-summer on. There are several varieties with minor changes in leaves and hairyness.

RANGE: Across the Province on dry mountain slopes from medium to high elevations.

DAISY FLEABANE (*E. strigosus*) grows to 2' high and has white or creamy flowers about ½" across. Leaves are scant and from 1"-1½" long. It blooms in July and occurs spasmodically across the south half of the Province.

HORSEWEED (*E. canadensis*) is a common weed growing stiffly erect with a many branched stem carrying a large number of white "fleabane" flowers about ¼" across. Leaves are slender and up to 2½" long. South half of the Province.

MOUNTAIN LADY'S SLIPPER
(Cypripedium montanum)

This exotic plant supports large waxy green leaves with parallel veins. Surmounting this are 1-3 pure white slippers veined with purple and sometimes reaching 2" in length. Several long brown petals and sepals are twisted like coppery ribbons.

There is an exquisite perfume to this unusual flower.

RANGE: V.I., Okanagan, Falkland, Bella Coola.

SMALL WHITE LADY'S SLIPPER (*C. passerinum*) carries a pure white slipper tinged with purple on the inside. Blooms in July. Windermere Valley, Peace River, Central and Northern B.C.

NIGHT-FLOWERING CATCHFLY
(Silene noctiflora)

The catchfly's or campions are a widespread group of about a dozen rather weedy plants all with prominently veined bulbs formed by the 5-lobed calyx beneath the flowers. The five petals are either lobed, divided or fringed and have a scale at their base which gives the appearance of an inner row of shorter petals. Flowers may be white, pink or red. There are 10 stamens and the leaves are opposite. This catchfly is hairy throughout with white petals deeply cut into the two lobes.

RANGE: V.I., Coastal regions and Interior.

Silene dichotoma is similar but the flowers have no stems. A weed pest in the Kootenays.

DOUGLAS CAMPION (*S. douglasii*) is a high mountain species from 2"-2' high. Flowers are white, notched, and usually 3 to a stem. Most common east of the Cascades.

WHITE MARSH MARIGOLD
(*Caltha leptosepala*)

Frigid ice water trickling about its roots does not discourage this succulent plant with its stout fleshy leaves and reddish flower stems, nor its companions, the snow lily, western anemone, buttercup and globe flower. The abundant leaves, 2″ - 4″ long are characteristically folded and twisted. They are a light waxy green color. The showy flowers are from ¾″ - 1¼″ across and average about 8 white petals tinged blue on the underside. The flower center is greenish-yellow from a large number of yellowish stamens.

RANGE: Wet places above timberline from V.I. to Rockies.

2″-6″HIGH

WHITE FLOWER
¾″-1¼″ ACROSS

THICK REDDISH
STEMS

WAXY LEAVES
TO 4″ LONG

GLOBE FLOWER
(*Trollius laxus*)

Globe flower sometimes even pokes its precocious way through the melting snow of alpine meadows. It superficially resembles the above and should not be confused with the anemones which have a bluish tinge to the outside of the petals.

The white flower 1″ - 1½″ across has a beautiful golden center. This collar of gold is a circlet of from 15 - 25 tiny petals while the showy white bloom is composed of 5 to 6 sepals. These soon discolor and wilt. Leaves are deeply lobed. Note the group of leaves just below the flower.

The common plant of the Rockies often has a pinkish tinge to the petal-like sepals. It doesn't grow over a foot in height and prefers moist borders of alpine streams.

RANGE: Mountains of V.I., Coast Range and East to Rockies.

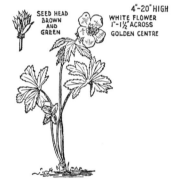

4″-20″HIGH

SEED HEAD
BROWN
AND
GREEN

WHITE FLOWER
1″-1½″ACROSS
GOLDEN CENTRE

AMERICAN BISTORT
(*Polygonum bistortoides*)

Mountain Dock

Mountain Meadow Knotweed

The white "bottle brush" about 1″ long and ½″ thick is formed of tightly packed small white flowers with protruding stamens.' The flower stem is wiry and jointed below each of the several small tapering leaves, a characteristic of the *Polygonum* or knotweed family. Blooming time is during July and August. There are several dozen knotweeds in B.C. See also page 129.

RANGE: Extending from Washington into Cascade Mountains vicinity Chilliwack.

ALPINE BISTORT (*P. viviparum*) seldom exceeds 12″ in height. Its flowers vary from white to rose and are loose-clustered. Protruding stamens impart a fuzzy look. Small reddish bulblets form close to the stem below the flowers. Coast Mountains and east to Rockies.

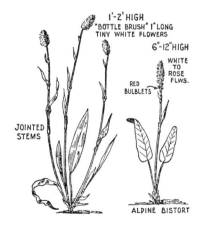

1′-2′ HIGH
"BOTTLE BRUSH" 1″ LONG
TINY WHITE FLOWERS

6″-12″HIGH

WHITE
TO
ROSE
FLWS.

RED
BULBLETS

JOINTED
STEMS

ALPINE BISTORT

FLOWERS (WHITE)

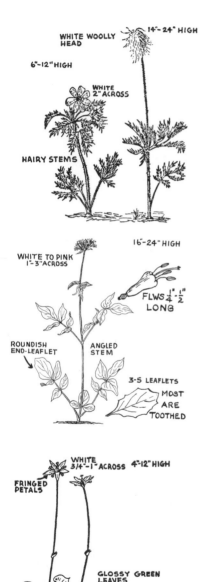

WHITE WOOLLY HEAD

14"–24" HIGH

6"–12" HIGH

WHITE 2" ACROSS

HAIRY STEMS

WHITE TO PINK 1"–3" ACROSS

16"–24" HIGH

FLWS ¼"–½" LONG

ROUNDISH END-LEAFLET

ANGLED STEM

3–5 LEAFLETS
MOST ARE TOOTHED

WHITE ¾"–1" ACROSS   4"–12" HIGH

FRINGED PETALS

GLOSSY GREEN LEAVES

WESTERN ANEMONE
(Anemone occidentalis)
Tow-head Baby

Most people never see the flower because the plant pops up immediately the snow has left the ground. The thick stems are hairy and the leaves finely divided. A typical anemone flower with white sepals tinged with blue on the outside adorns the top of the stem. Seed is a fluffy "dust mop."

RANGE: Eastward from the Cascade Mountains at sub-alpine and alpine elevations.

ALPINE ANEMONE (A. drummondii) is usually less than 6" high. Flowers are white on the inside, blue on outside. Lower leaves long-stemmed and finely divided. Vancouver Island, Coast Mountains, Selkirks and Rockies.

MOUNTAIN VALERIAN
(Valeriana sitchensis)

Among the gay alpine blooms the sweet-scented valerian raises its head of tiny white or pinkish flowers. One of the more common plants at sub-alpine and alpine heights, the blooming period may be any time during the summer. The flowers have a very fragrant perfume which is in strong contrast to the disagreeable smell of the roots.

RANGE: Approximately from 4,000' to 7,000' in Cascades and eastward to Rockies.

FRINGED GRASS OF PARNASSUS
(Parnassia fimbriata)

Grass of Parnassus in no way resembles a grass. Instead a single white flower tops a stem rising from an artistic cluster of glossy green, kidney-shaped leaves. One distinguishing feature is a clasping leaf half way up or more on each stem. The white flower, about 1" across, has 5 white petals veined with yellow or light green. The bottom portion of each petal is fringed artistically on each edge which, together with the odd arrangement of the stamens, makes a most unusual flower. Look for this plant in damp mountain meadows and along alpine streams.

RANGE: Sub-alpine and alpine elevations in B.C.

ALPINE P. (P. kotzebuei): No leaf on stem. Petals not fringed and shorter than sepals. Selkirk and Rockies.

MARSH G. of P. (P. palustris): Petals nearly twice as long as sepals. Clasping leaf is usually below middle. Wide range through the mountains.

MOUNTAIN G. of P. (P. palustris var. montanensis): Petals slightly longer than sepals. Rockies.

SMALL-FLOWERED G. of P. (P. parviflora): Bottom leaves oval, not kidney-shaped, clasping leaf below centre. Columbia Valley.

(120)

WATER-PARSNIP,
WATER-HEMLOCK,
POISON-HEMLOCK

The first two of these poisonous plants grow in marshes or brackish ponds; the latter prefers drier ground. The water-hemlocks in particular are regarded as the quickest acting poisonous plants in North America. A piece of root the size of a walnut might kill a cow in less than 15 minutes. Stems, leaves and root are all poisonous with the greatest concentration being in the thick, fleshy roots. Poison-hemlock was used by the ancient Greeks in putting to death their condemned prisoners. Indians sometimes used it in a mixture to poison their arrows.

WATER-PARSNIP
(Sium cicutaefolium)

A common plant of marshes and ponds noticeable in July and August because of its large size and masses of flattish, white flower heads. The "umbrella" flower stems carry very small flowers less than 1/8" across. Leaflets are long and finely toothed and the main leaf stems branch from heavy sheaths. Sometimes a few lower leaves are submerged. These differ from the other leaves in being finely fringed. Seeds are round with raised ribs.

RANGE: Vancouver Island and southern Interior, northward to Central B.C.

WATER-HEMLOCK
(Cicuta douglasii)

Although similar in general form to water-parsnip, the leaves branch into side branchlets which may branch again to short stems holding three leaflets. The tapering leaflets may be to 4" long and have coarse teeth. An important point to notice in the water-hemlocks is that the veins on the leaflets run toward the bottom of the teeth notches rather than forward to the points. The flower head is a rounded ball of small white flower clusters. Most of the thick shallow roots when cut open will show horizontal chambers.

RANGE: Widespread throughout B.C.

OREGON WATER-HEMLOCK (*C. vagans*) puts up a cluster of stout leaf stems. The foliage is generally tinged purple. Range as above.

POISON HEMLOCK (*Conium maculatum*) found in waste places around Victoria. An introduced plant which is slowly spreading. Its chief difference from the above is the habitat and very fringed leaflets which give a fern-like appearance.

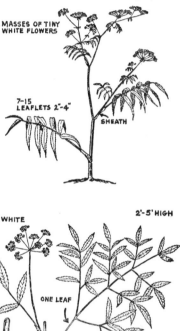

2'-4' HIGH

MASSES OF TINY WHITE FLOWERS

7-15 LEAFLETS 2"-4"

SHEATH

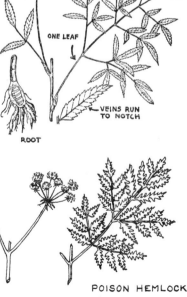

2'-5' HIGH

WHITE

ONE LEAF

VEINS RUN TO NOTCH

ROOT

POISON HEMLOCK

FLOWERS (WHITE)

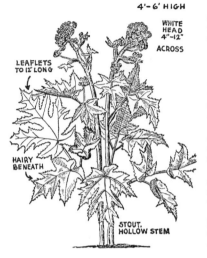

4'-6' HIGH

WHITE HEAD 4"-12" ACROSS

LEAFLETS TO 12" LONG

HAIRY BENEATH

STOUT, HOLLOW STEM

COW PARSNIP
(Heracleum lanatum)

This Hercules of a plant often may reach 6' in height. Its thick coarse stems, large leaflets and wide head of flowers are all in such grand scale that possibly it qualifies for the largest perennial plant in the Province.

It will be seen on moist rich soils from sea level to almost sub-alpine elevations. A common error is that cow parsnip is poisonous. However, cattle will seek it out and the thick flower stems can be used by humans either cooked like carrots or eaten as greens.

The leaves arch from the main stem through a large sheath and hold 3 tremendous leaflets, each of which may be a foot long. At the top of the plant the main stalks divide into an umbrella of short stems each of which branches again into another umbrella framework supporting small, white flowers. The massive slightly rounded flower head may be from 4" - 10" across. After blooming in May at the Coast or several months later in the high mountains, a large number of flattened oval seeds appear, a good identifying feature when only the stalks are standing.

RANGE: Throughout B.C. at low and middle elevations.

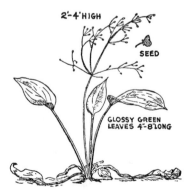

2'-4' HIGH

SEED

GLOSSY GREEN LEAVES 4"-8" LONG

WATER PLANTAIN
(Alisma plantago-aquatica)

Plants growing in marshes are always interesting because they are not observed as often as those on firm ground where most people choose to walk. The water plantain can't claim fame by its branching head of tiny white flowers but its glossy green leaves appear as if belonging in a tropical jungle. They spring from the base of the flower stem and carry a large ovalish leaf at the end of a long thick stem.

Most times the plant is in shallow water or the muckiest of soils such as roadside ditches or low-lying swales.

RANGE: Common in suitable habitat at lower and middle elevations throughout the Province.

MOUNTAIN SANDWORT
(Arenaria capillaris)

Rock Sandwort

The wide ranging sandworts are represented by more than a half dozen species. Nearly all tend to have a tufted or matted base. The leaves are needle-like and those on the stem opposite. Flowers are white with 5 petals, 10 stamens, and 3 styles.

Mountain sandwort is quite common on dry places and rocky ridges near and above timberline. The thin erect stems to 6" high carry dainty starlike blooms about ½" across.

RANGE: Exposed dry places. Cascades to Rockies.

VERNAL WHITLOW GRASS
(Draba verna)

Flat Pod

The dozen or more whitlow grasses occur from sea level to mountain heights. They have either white or yellow flowers, 4 short petals, 6 stamens, wide sepals, and produce dainty round to narrow flat pods which stick out alternately from each side of the stem. When the two rows of seeds have blown away, flat gauze-like pods are left. Some species have yellow flowers.

Probably the first to greet the spring around March 21st is vernal whitlow grass a dainty wildflower 2" - 4" high. The small leaves ½" - 1" long are finely hairy, lobed or toothed.

This is the only one of the many whitlow grasses that has notched petals.

RANGE: Abundant southern V.I. in oak tree glades and edges of forest.

TWISTED WHITLOW GRASS
(Draba lonchocarpa)

There are several whitlow grasses quite similar to this but having yellow flowers. The alternate seed pods make a good identifying feature for the flat pods.

A plant of dry rocky places above timberline, it has a compact bunch of tiny narrow leaves about ¼" long with prominent midribs. Flower stems a few inches high carry a loose head of small white flowers.

RANGE: Rocky places above timberline from Cascade Mountains to Rockies.

FEW-SEEDED WHITLOW GRASS (*D. oligosperma*) has small leaves with prominent midribs and covered with star-like hairs. Flowers are light yellow. Cascades to Rockies and north to Alaska.

GOLDEN WHITLOW GRASS (*D. aurea*), 3"-12" high, has hairy leaves about 1" long and yellow blooms. Seed pods are narrow and often twisted. Rockies and extending far northward.

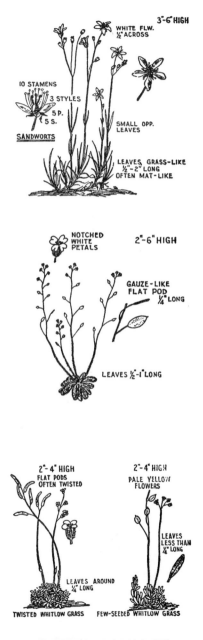

FLOWERS (WHITE)

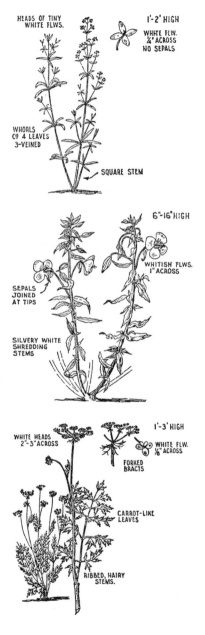

HEADS OF TINY WHITE FLWS.

1'-2' HIGH

WHITE FLW.
¼" ACROSS
NO SEPALS

WHORLS
OF 4 LEAVES
3-VEINED

SQUARE STEM

6"-16" HIGH

WHITISH FLWS.
1" ACROSS

SEPALS
JOINED
AT TIPS

SILVERY WHITE
SHREDDING
STEMS

1'-3' HIGH

WHITE HEADS
2"-3" ACROSS

WHITE FLW.
⅛" ACROSS

FORKED
BRACTS

CARROT-LIKE
LEAVES

RIBBED, HAIRY
STEMS.

NORTHERN BEDSTRAW
(Galium boreale)

There are more than a half dozen bedstraws in B.C., but all can be quite easily recognized by their square stems and whorls of 4-8 leaves at the joints. Actually the two opposite leaf-like bracts give the appearance of a whorl of four.

Flowers carried in branching end clusters range from ⅛" - ¼" across and have 4 spreading petals. They may be white, pinkish, or greenish. There are no sepals. Often the stems and fruit have short hooked spines which stick to one's clothes.

Northern bedstraw may reach 2' in height and is usually branched at its base into several stems. It may be in bloom from June to September.

RANGE: Wide altitudinal range and widespread throughout B.C. Northward to Alaska.

PALLID EVENING PRIMROSE
(Oenothera pallida)

This evening primrose is a gnarled and woody, much branched plant to 16" in height. Sandy or gravelly banks with a direct southern exposure to the parching sun are the customary habitat. The 1" wide flowers are a dirty white color but the buds have a pinkish tinge. The long sepals are generally twisted and joined at their tips. Blooming time is early summer.

RANGE: The dry Interior country from Penticton southward is its most common range.

WILD CARROT
(Daucus carota)

Queen Anne's Lace

The abundance of this coarse yet dainty plant along roadsides and in waste places coupled with its late blooming time demands the attention.

Growing to 3' high it has a number of stout ribbed stems. The fern-like leaves are finely divided like the domestic carrot. The massed heads of white flowers are 2" - 3" across but the individual 4-petaled bloom is very tiny. The flowers may be seen from July into September and often are the only conspicuous blooms of that particular season.

There may be considerable variation in leaves and size of the plant in these escapes because of hybridization.

RANGE: Dry places around Victoria and scattered here and there in the Interior.

LITTLE WILD CARROT (D. pusillus) is a smaller edition of the above with finer dissected leaves and flower heads hollowed in the center to form a shallow bowl. It blooms in late summer and ranges on souther V.I. and the lower mainland.

PEACOCK
(*Dodecatheon spp.*)

Shooting Star

Although there are about 6 species in the Province the unusual shape of the flower is sufficient to accurately mark a peacock or shooting star. All have thick succulent stems with a group of thin smooth leaves at the base.

Some species may have one or two small flowers branching out near the top, others display a half-dozen or more gaudy blooms. One has white petals but it is found only in the southern Cascades near the International Boundary. All the others have pink or purplish petals which stream-line out behind like an Indian head-dress. The dark stamens and style cling together to form a spear-like point. Peacocks will be found in bloom from March to May.

RANGE: Valley to alpine heights throughout B.C.

SATIN FLOWER
(*Sisyrinchium grandiflorum*)

Grass Widows

The southern part of Vancouver Island and adjacent islands enjoy a climate that produces an abundance of spring wild flowers. Camas, stonecrop, saxifrage, Easter lily, violets, trillium, and peacocks are some of the more common and no doubt satin flower should be included. Almost every rocky knoll with its springy carpet of fresh moss is further enlivened in April by clumps of beautiful satin flower. From a spray of long thin leaves that look like stout grass blades there arises a stem or two bearing several reddish-purple flowers with unusual satin-like petals. A single flower may be from 1" - 1½" across and when massed they are particularly attractive. Unlike most flowers they have a very short life and start to wither after a day or two of full bloom.

RANGE: Dry places near Victoria.

MONTIA
(*Montia parviflora*)

Miner's Lettuce

This plant differs from the other Miner's lettuce (page 104) in having a basal clump of fleshy bright green leaves. The flower is characteristic however, having five thin pale-pink petals. The thin stem imparts a dainty look which, with the blooms, is reminiscent of other spring flowers such as fringe cup and field chickweed also blooming during May and June.

RANGE: Rocky places on Vancouver Island and Coastal Region. Manning Park, Mt. Revelstoke.

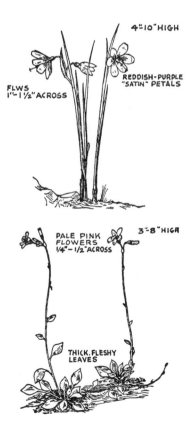

FLOWERS (PINK)

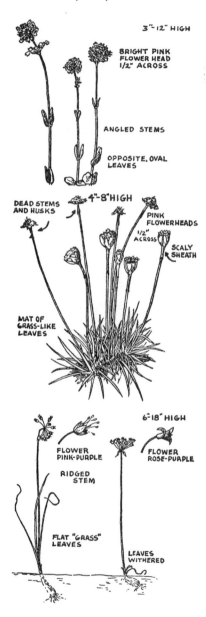

3"-12" HIGH

BRIGHT PINK
FLOWER HEAD
1/2" ACROSS

ANGLED STEMS

OPPOSITE, OVAL
LEAVES

DEAD STEMS
AND HUSKS

4"-8"HIGH

PINK
FLOWERHEADS

1/2"
ACROSS

SCALY
SHEATH

MAT OF
GRASS-LIKE
LEAVES

6"-18" HIGH

FLOWER
PINK-PURPLE

FLOWER
ROSE-PURPLE

RIDGED
STEM

FLAT "GRASS"
LEAVES

LEAVES
WITHERED

SEA BLUSH
(Plectritis congesta)
(Valerianella congesta)

Sea blush is an early spring flower blooming during April and May with blue-eyed Mary, satin flower, stonecrop, camas, peacock and Easter lily. It favors rocky knolls capped by moss.

The stems are squarish and rise between opposite oval leaves which are without stems. Tiny pink flowers are clustered together forming a compact rounded head.

RANGE: Abundant on Vancouver Island, the Gulf Islands, and Lower Mainland. Other species have slender branching stems and paler flowers. Some range into the Interior.

THRIFT
(Armeria maritima)   *(Statice armeria)*

Sea Lavender

Anyone who grows the garden variety of thrift will be struck by the similarity to the wild species. There is the same compact clump of needle-like leaves about 2" long and stiff flower stems each with its pinkish dome of tiny flowers. After the flower has faded its parchment texture keeps it intact for months leading to some use for thrift in "everlasting" decorations. New shoots keep thrift in bloom for several months in the late spring.

RANGE: Open, grassy bluffs along the sea coast from Victoria to Alaska.

NODDING ONION
(Allium cernuum)

Nodding onion, which usually stands about a foot high, is easily recognized by its nodding or bent flower head of a dozen or so pink blooms. Six stamens with hair-thin stems protrude far out of the pink cup. Each petal and sepal has one thin vein down its centre line. The blooms will be found from May 15 - July 15. The few "grass" leaves rise from a thin bulb something similar to a green onion. Of the half-dozen wild onions in B.C. this is the most common and widespread.

RANGE: Central B.C., the Cariboo, Dry Interior Zone and into the Kootenays.

HOOKER'S ONION *(A. acuminatum)* differs from the above in several ways. If not in bloom the bulb can be examined. It is rounded and has a hexagonal tracing or marking on its outer coat. The few leaves wither by the time the rose-purple flowers are out. The flower head is an erect mass of beautiful, bell-like blooms. It is in bloom in late spring. The range is on dry slopes on the Gulf Islands and Coastal Forest Zones.

(126)

GEYER'S ONION
(Allium geyeri)

There are about a half dozen species of onions in B.C. and despite their characteristic odor, telling them apart is very difficult. An important means of identify is the pattern of the bulb covering.

Geyer's onion is the only one with a bulb covered with a weave of loose fibres. Other points more easily seen are the 2 - 4 narrow leaves and cluster of rose flowers often mixed with pink-tinged bulblets. The two broad bracts under the flower head are usually joined on one edge. Notice that the stamens protrude about three-quarters the length of the petals.

RANGE: Variable from moist ground to rocky exposed places. Sporadic in south part of V.I.

FILAREE
(Erodium cicutarium)

Storksbill, Heronsbill

This introduction from Europe appears widely scattered on dry open ground. There it grows as a mat of finely cut leaves with flower stems an inch or two high, bearing from 2 - 10 small bright pink to purplish flowers. This relation to the geraniums may reach a foot in height or put out branches a foot or more in length. Most commonly seen in bloom from March to May but flowers might be found all summer.

The most distinctive feature are the long sharp seed pods from 1" - 1½" long. These stick up in groups reminding one of a bird's nest full of hungry, long-billed young. Flowers and seed pods may be found at the same time on a plant.

RANGE: Common in waste places on V.I. Spreading on Mainland, Penticton, Chilcotin.

MOUNTAIN SORREL
(Oxyria digyna)

Like the closely related sorrels (*Rumex spp.*) the leaves of mountain sorrel have a bitter acid taste. Some plants on very poor situations may only reach 2" in height and have leaves hardly larger than ½" across. Generally it is from 4" - 14" high with about six thin rounded basel leaves from ½" - 1" wide.

The small, green flowers are inconspicuous and unattractive but give rise to distinctive seed masses. Each seed is flat, circular, and about ⅛" across. The margin or wing is a pale red imparting a blush to the entire seed mass.

RANGE: Blooming July to September near or above timberline. Mt. Arrowsmith, Cascades, Smithers.

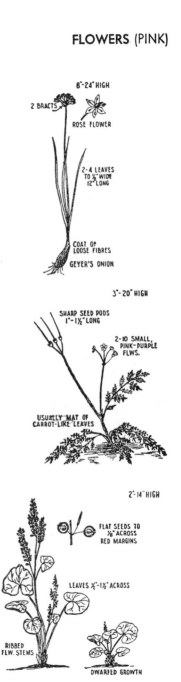

8"-24" HIGH
2 BRACTS
ROSE FLOWER
2-4 LEAVES TO ½" WIDE 12" LONG
COAT OF LOOSE FIBRES
GEYER'S ONION

3"-20" HIGH
SHARP SEED PODS 1"-1½" LONG
2-10 SMALL, PINK-PURPLE FLWS.
USUALLY MAT OF CARROT-LIKE LEAVES

2"-14" HIGH
FLAT SEEDS TO ⅛" ACROSS RED MARGINS
LEAVES ½"-1½" ACROSS
RIBBED FLW. STEMS
DWARFED GROWTH

PIPSISSEWA
(Chimaphila umbellata)

Princes' Pine

Pipsissewa, often associated with pyrola, grows in cool evergreen forests. It is 5" - 10" high with attractive leathery, evergreen, sharply-toothed leaves which cluster around the stem in loose whorls. The 3 - 9 flowers, which bloom in May or June, are bunched near the top of the stem. They have an artificial look from their waxy petals which vary from white to pink in color.

RANGE: Throughout B.C. in cool, damp, evergreen forests.

MENZIES' PIPSISSEWA (*C. menziesii*) is a smaller species with fewer leaves, 1 - 3 flowers, and growing to 6" high.   Coastal Forest Zone.

5"-10" HIGH

WHITE TO PINK WAXY FLOWERS

THICK, EVERGREEN LEAVES 1-2" LONG

PYROLA
(Pyrola spp.)

Wintergreen

There are at least 9 species in B.C. Two of these may be without leaves but in general, pyrola has distinctive thick evergreen leaves which cluster at the bottom of the slender stem.

Plants may be from a few inches in height to over a foot high. The flowers, arranged singly along the stem, droop down and have thick waxy petals varying from greenish white to red. Every flower has a long curved beak protruding from it. Even the seed carries this distinctive beak.

RANGE: General across the Province but most abundant at mountain elevations.

SINGLE DELIGHT OR ONE-FLOWERED PYROLA (*Moneses uniflora*) has leaves like the pyrolas but is only 2" - 4" high. The single saucer-shaped, whitish or pinkish flower has a forked beak. Blooms June to August. East of Cascades and north to North Central B.C.

2"-14" HIGH

CREAM FLOWER

PINKISH WAXY FLOWERS

RIBBED SEEDS

GREENISH WHITE FLOWERS

ONE-SIDED WINTERGREEN

WAXY, EVERGREEN LEAVES

SINGLE DELIGHT

BLEEDING HEART
(Dicentra formosa)

Its delicately fringed leaves sweep upward and almost hide the drooping row of pinkish "hearts." Each flower is a symmetrical jewel formed by the petals being held together near their tip. Matching their timid look at the world is the faint fragrant perfume. Depending on altitude, the bleeding heart may bloom from May to June.

RANGE: Rich shady woods from sea level to middle mountain elevations west of the Cascade Mountains. Spotty in wet Interior. Armstrong. *D. uniflora* growing sparsely in the Kootenays has only one or two flowers. Phoenix.

8"-16" HIGH

PINK "HEARTS"

THIN, LIGHT GREEN LEAVES

STOUT, TRIANGULAR STEMS

ARCTIC RASPBERRY
(Rubus arcticus)

The crinkled three-parted leaves and pink-to rose-colored blossom with its narrow petals are typical "raspberry" in form. However, this is an unarmed dwarf model seldom reaching 6" in height. The flower is replaced by a bright red berry of indifferent flavour. The dainty pink blooms bring welcome dabs of warm color in May and June to the fresh green of spring growth. Most commonly it is found in or on the borders of mossy boggy places. Also known as Arctic Dock.

RANGE: Wetter portions of Province east of Cascades to Rockies and north to Alaska. Wells Gray Park, Lake Louise. From low to high elevations.

CLARKIA
(Clarkia pulchella)

This flower might qualify for the oddest looking bloom in the Province. At first glance it appears as if the flowers have been torn to ribbons but actually there are 4 deeply lobed petals of a bright pink-purplish hue. Notice how the flower stems are swollen and the sepals joined together at their tips. The plant is fairly uniform in height ranging from 6" - 12". Dull green leaves 1" - 2" long almost pass unnoticed compared to the attraction of this unmistakable plant. It gets its name from William Clarke of the famed Lewis and Clarke Expedition into the far Northwest.

RANGE: Very scattered along rocky exposed places. Grand Forks — Rossland Road above Christiana Lake, Castlegar.

KNAPWEED
(Centaurea spp.)

The knapweeds, particularly those with rose or purplish flowers, will often be mistaken for thistles. However, the leaves which range from thin narrow ones to wide and serrated are not spiny. The bulb or involucre beneath the tousled flower is formed of triangular scales, in some species satiny smooth, and in others with fine bristles. The showy flowers may be yellow, blue, violet, or white and range in size from small blooms ½" across to others close to 2". Notice how they are usually at the tips of the many branched plant. Seed heads are a white fluffy mass like thistles at seed. These plants bloom from mid summer to early fall.

RANGE: Scattered throughout B.C.

BATCHELOR'S BUTTON *(C. cyanus)* is plentiful in some areas as an escaped garden flower. Although most often blue in color it does vary to white, purple or red. Don't confuse this with Blue Sailors. See page 148. Batchelor's Button has narrow leaves most of which are not toothed and is not as coarse and large a plant.

3"-8" HIGH
PINK TO ROSE FLW. ½"-1" ACROSS
LEAFLETS ½"-1½" LONG
STEM UNARMED

6"-16" HIGH
BRIGHT PINK FLW. 1½"-2" ACROSS
SEPALS JOINED
DULL GREEN LEAVES 1"-2" LONG

1'-2' HIGH
BRISTLY PINK FLOWERS

FLOWERS (PINK)

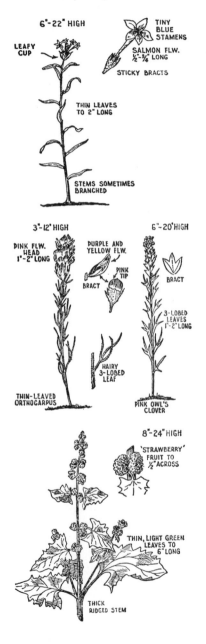

6"-22" HIGH

LEAFY CUP

TINY BLUE STAMENS

SALMON FLW. ½"-¾" LONG

STICKY BRACTS

THIN LEAVES TO 2" LONG

STEMS SOMETIMES BRANCHED

3"-12" HIGH

PINK FLW. HEAD 1"-2" LONG

THIN-LEAVED ORTHOCARPUS

PURPLE AND YELLOW FLW.

PINK TIP

BRACT

HAIRY 3-LOBED LEAF

6"-20" HIGH

BRACT

3-LOBED LEAVES 1"-2" LONG

PINK OWL'S CLOVER

8"-24" HIGH

'STRAWBERRY' FRUIT TO ½" ACROSS

THIN, LIGHT GREEN LEAVES TO 6" LONG

THICK RIDGED STEM

COLLOMIA
(Collomia grandiflora)

There are several species of collomias. All are annuals with rather small trumpet-like flowers in dense terminal clusters. The gilias are very close relatives.

This collomia is the showiest of the group with very unusual salmon- or orange-colored flowers often fading to white. Flowers form a cluster of up-pointing trumpets in an overlapping leafy base somewhat resembling half of a miniature cabbage. The calyx is rough and sticky. Blooming time is June and July.

Plants are usually unbranced and grow singly and well scattered in dry exposed places.

RANGE: Very scattered at low elevations on V.I. More plentiful east of the Cascades and to the Rockies. Princeton, Penticton.

THIN-LEAVED ORTHOCARPUS
(Orthocarpus tenuifolius)

The genus *Orthocarpus* with its head of colored bracts bears a close resemblance to the paint-brushes, with shades of yellow, pink, red, and purple. Behind the bracts tiny trumpet-shaped flowers are almost hidden from sight. Typically they have an erect or curving upper lip and a lower one with three divisions.

In this species the hairy leaves are divided into three narrow fingers replaced near the top by delicately tinged pink bracts. Behind these may be seen flowers ½" - ¾" long, yellow and purplish in color, and with a hooked nose or beak. Blooming time is June and July.

RANGE: Eastern B.C. from vicinity of Cranbrook south into Washington and Montana.

PINK OWL'S CLOVER (*O. bracteosus*) has a head of triangular bracts shaded a dull purple. The few flowers are a reddish purple color. Victoria region, and in bloom throughout the summer. YELLOW ORTHOCARPUS (*O. luteus*) is a thin-stemmed plant to 16" high. Flowers are yellow and about ¼" long. Bracts are greenish and divided into 3 - 5 pointed lobes. Blooms July and August. Dry places. Cariboo, Chilcotin.

STRAWBERRY BLITE
(Chenopodium capitatum)

This plant with the bright red "strawberries" stuck to its stem belongs to the Goosefoot Family —a fanciful resemblance relating to the shape of the large triangular leaves. It may grow upright to 2' high or be sprawling.

The fruit forms in August and September after inconspicuous small greenish flowers. A red dye was made by the Indians from the "strawberries" which are edible raw or cooked.

RANGE: Grows best on upturned ground. Across B.C. Abundant north of Prince George to Yukon.

RED MONKEY FLOWER
(Mimulus lewisii)

Lewis Monkey Flower

This red mimulus often displays a spectacular mass of color many feet across. It is quite common in alpine terrain along wet banks or stream edges. The stems cluster together thickly and hold opposite, purplish-red flowers from 1" - 2" long. These "snapdragon" flowers have five petals of which two turn up and the other three down. The throat has a touch of yellow in it and may be quite hairy. A succession of new buds keeps it a profusion of bloom during July and August. The leaves are opposite and have parallel ribs which add to their beauty.

RANGE: Wet places in high mountains throughout B.C.

STAR FLOWER
(Trientalis latifolia)

Here is a forest sprite that is fashioned in manner both neat and delicate. The simple slender stem bears a symmetrical whorl of thin oval leaves each from 1" - 3" long. These are glossy green in color and number from 4 - 7. From the centre of the leaf whorl there arises 1 - 4 thin graceful stems each carrying a single star-like flower of charming simplicity. Sometimes it is pure white, again with a pinkish tinge. Look for star flower in shady moist forests from May into June.

RANGE: Common on Vancouver Island and the Coastal region. North Central B.C.

UPLAND STAR FLOWER *(T. arctica)* is much smaller than the above being only a few inches high. It grows on sphagnum moss or boggy soils and has a white waxy flower about ½" across which is out in June to July. The range is as above.

WATER KNOTWEED
(Polygonum amphibium)

Water Buckwheat

On occasion water knotweed grows so thickly that the surface of the water is given a pinkish blush from the short rosy spikes of flowers. Shallow lake edges or ponds are home to this aquatic plant which roots in the mud and raises to the surface stems up to 20' long. Often the leathery oblong leaves aren't noticed for they usually lie flat on the water. Look for the rose-pink spikes during July and August. They can be seen from afar and water knotweed is a plant everyone should know because of its unusual aquatic nature and attractive bloom.

RANGE: Across B.C. and northward to Peace River.

FLOWERS (PINK)

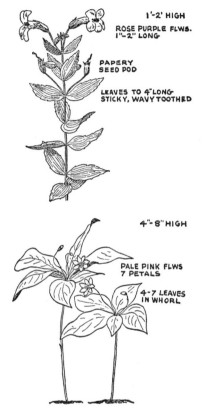

1'-2' HIGH
ROSE PURPLE FLWS. 1"-2" LONG
PAPERY SEED POD
LEAVES TO 4" LONG STICKY, WAVY TOOTHED

4"-8" HIGH
PALE PINK FLWS 7 PETALS
4-7 LEAVES IN WHORL

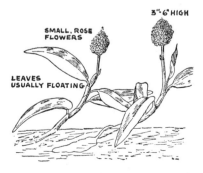

3"-6" HIGH
SMALL, ROSE FLOWERS
LEAVES USUALLY FLOATING

FLOWERS (RED)

2'-3' HIGH

ORANGE SPURS

YELLOW PETALS

10"-30" HIGH

ORANGE PETALS WITH PURPLISH BROWN DOTS

SOME LEAVES IN WHORLS

10"-18" HIGH

FLWS. ORANGE WITH BLACK SPOTS

3" ACROSS

UPPER LEAVES WHORLED

COLUMBINE
(Aquilegia formosa)
Sitka Columbine — Western Columbine

Among the amazing floral works of Nature, columbine surely leads the way. The word columbine, which refers to a dove, is most apt for the five scarlet petals that arch backward do have a fancied resemblance to five perched doves. The "head" is a honey gland which can only be reached by humming birds or long-tongued butterflies. Moist, partly shaded roadsides and glades are sought. In alpine meadows vast areas often are covered almost completely with this prolific bloomer. Flowers show from May to August.

RANGE: Throughout B.C. in moist places.

BLUE COLUMBINE *(A. brevistylis)* with blue and cream flowers is found near timberline through the Cariboo and Central B.C. Peace River.

YELLOW COLUMBINE *(A. flavescens)* is more rare than the above. The flowers are almost completely yellow. At middle to high elevations east of the Okanagan Valley.

WILD TIGER LILY
(Lilium parviflorum)

The wild tiger lily is very suggestive of the cultivated plant. Sometimes there are from 6 - 9 drooping blooms. The long anthers stand out from the flower. Since wild tiger lily grows from low to high altitudes the blooming season may range from June to August. Most of the narrow leaves form whorls up and down the stem. The plant grows from a large scaly white bulb that is edible when cooked.

RANGE: From sea level to 4,000' in damp soils. Vancouver Island to Rockies. North to Quesnel.

MOUNTAIN LILY
(Lilium montanum)
Wood Lily — Red Lily

The mountain lily has the largest and most colorful bloom among native wildflowers. Its orange-red flaming trumpets with their dark markings are often 3" across and several may be carried on one branching stem. Leaves are narrow and pointed. Wood lilies prefer a moist soil and bloom from June to July.

RANGE: Interior Wet Belt, Big Bend Highway and Kootenay River Valley.

INDIAN PAINTBRUSH
(Castilleja spp.)
Painted Cup

Many different species grow in B.C. with colors ranging through shades of yellow, orange, pink and crimson. The tiny flowers are hidden by crimson, leaf-like bracts which give the plant the look as if having been dipped in a pot of bright paint. Two of the most common are given below:

C. angustifolia is from 6" - 12" high with lower leaves very noticeably lobed. Throughout B.C. at lower elevations.

C. miniata may be 2' high and has narrow, sharp-pointed leaves. It favors moist places and is most abundant at high elevations.

YELLOW PAINTBRUSH may be one of several species growing in open places above timberline. Other species are creamy in color.

SCARLET GILIA
(Gilia aggregata)

The vividness of the scarlet trumpets is beyond belief and many persons think they have found something of great rarity when first seeing it. Actually it is quite common in certain ranges. The thin stems are usually quite straight with a number of slender branches near the top. The leaves are narrow, drab and hardly noticed. Thin trumpets about 1" long flare into 5 petals with small white marks dabbed on the red. The blooming season is from May 15 - July 15.

RANGE: Open slopes in Dry Interior. To elevations of 6,000' where there is a southern exposure. Manning Park, Merritt, Oliver, Penticton, Kamloops, Grand Forks.

SPREADING PHLOX
(Phlox diffusa)
Carpet Pink

The green cushions of short thin leaves designed with small pink blossoms show from June to August. The flowers are less than 1/2" across and sit close to the leaves.

RANGE: Open rocky places in high mountain forests to alpine heights. Throughout B.C.

TUFTED PHLOX (*P. caespitosa*) forms a low mat like the above. The many flowers may be white, pink or mauve and bloom in May. Dry exposed places, Kootenay River Valley. This species or a variety also occurs at alpine heights.

MOSS CAMPION (*Silene acaulis*) closely resembles the above species. It usually forms a compact dome up to 12" across. Masses of bright rose flowers are eye catching at alpine heights to Alaska.

(133)

FLOWERS (RED)

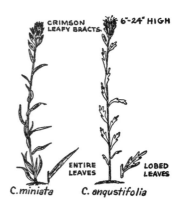

CRIMSON LEAFY BRACTS. 6"-24" HIGH
ENTIRE LEAVES LOBED LEAVES
C. miniata   C. angustifolia

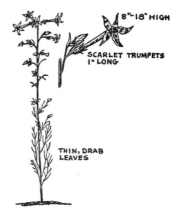

8"-18" HIGH
SCARLET TRUMPETS 1" LONG
THIN, DRAB LEAVES

NEEDLE-LIKE LEAVES 1"-3" HIGH
PINK-PURPLE FLOWERS 1/2" ACROSS

FLOWERS (RED)

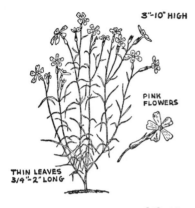

3"–10" HIGH

PINK FLOWERS

THIN LEAVES
3/4"–2" LONG

PHLOX
(*Phlox longifolia*)

Phlox is one of the welcome spring wildflowers of the Dry Interior. It grows on the lower mountain slopes where yellow bells and spring sunflowers also are found earlier in the season. Usually the plant forms a low rounded tuft covered with a mass of small pink or lavender flowers.

Leaves are long and thin. When crushed they emit a pungent odor. After blooming from May into June the plant becomes quite inconspicuous amongst the range plants.

RANGE: Dry Interior Zone. Abundant from Penticton to Peachland.

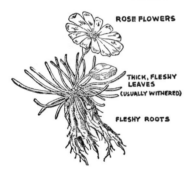

1"–3" HIGH

ROSE FLOWERS

THICK, FLESHY LEAVES
(USUALLY WITHERED)

FLESHY ROOTS

BITTERROOT
(*Lewisia rediviva*)

Rock Rose

Bitterroot is an abundant spring bloom on the most exposed places throughout the Dry Interior. It suddenly appears in May as if by magic and disappears in the same fashion. The rose-pink flowers hug close to the ground, their 10 - 15 petals spread wide in the sunshine. By the time the flowers appear the tufts of fleshy leaves have dried up. The root is thick and fleshy and was used in large quantities by the Indians. When the roots are boiled they swell up and become jelly-like. An early explorer says that a sack of roots would buy a good horse. The bitterroot is the state flower of Montana.

RANGE: On rocky places through the Dry Interior Zone. Ashcroft, Penticton, Cranbrook.

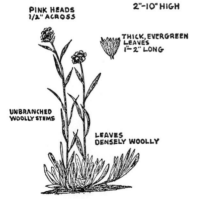

PINK HEADS
1/2" ACROSS

2"–10" HIGH

THICK, EVERGREEN LEAVES
1"–2" LONG

UNBRANCHED WOOLLY STEMS

LEAVES DENSELY WOOLLY

ROSY PUSSYTOES
(*Antennaria rosea*)

Most of the pussytoes are white. See page 114. All have the whitish matted stems and leaves characteristic of plants that live in bright sunshine and withstand drought. The fanciful name comes from the resemblance of the soft roundish heads to the hairy toes of a cat. Pink pussytoes sometimes is dwarfed to a few inches in height but otherwise may reach to 8". The alternative leaves are very narrow and almost white with a soft wool. They form a thick mat at the base. The flowers bunch in a rounded head of rosy balls which get their color from the outer papery bracts. If the plant is picked it will retain its natural color for years.

RANGE: Lower elevations, Dry Interior.

HAIRY CAT'S EAR
(Hypochaeris radicata)

There is a close resemblance to a dandelion in the form and color of this flower. However, thin wiry green stems, often branched, hold it aloft rather than thick milky ones.

The scalloped and hairy leaves spread in a fanciful rosette pattern. Hairy cat's ear has an extended blooming season lasting from mid-summer to mid-September. Its dandelion-like characteristics are followed through by a white ball of downy seeds.

RANGE: Common on V.I. and Lower Mainland.

SMOOTH CAT'S EAR (H. glabra) is a smaller plant to 12″ high. The flowers are less than ¾″ across and the leaves aren't hairy. It is found on V.I. and along the Coastal area into California.

AGOSERIS
(Agoseris spp.)

Mountain Dandelion

The half-dozen agoseris all display great variety in the leaves. Characteristics of the group include dandelion-like flowers, a milky juice and a white fluffy seed head. In dandelions the bracts are in one main row with an outer shorter row being bent back. Agoseris have several rows of bracts in a "shingle" effect.

ORANGE-FLOWERED AGOSERIS (A. aurantiaca): Usually less than 1′ high with a deep orange-colored flower. Cascade Mountains, Okanagan, Cariboo, and far northward. Often alpine.

SLENDER AGOSERIS (A. a. var. aurantiaca) grows to 2′ high and has bright yellow flowers with a dull reddish tinge on the under parts. Sea level to middle mountain elevations across B.C.

SMOOTH AGOSERIS (A. glauca): Flowers may reach 2″ across and are pale yellow with a purplish tinge beneath. Blooms July to August. Fairly dry ground east of the Cascades. Edges of Dry Interior Zone, Cariboo, Cranbrook, Peace River.

COMMON ST. JOHNSWORT
(Hypericum perforatum)

An European introduction, St. Johnswort is becoming a serious weed. There is a supposition that this plant always bloomed on June 24, St. John the Baptist's Day. It is moderately poisonous but only to white-colored animals.

The several different species all have yellow flowers with an abundance of protruding yellow stamens. In this case the stamens form clusters. The petals are faintly black-dotted on the margins as are the leaves. June into August.

RANGE: At low elevations across B.C. from V.I. to the Kootenays. Victoria, Yale, Kamloops.

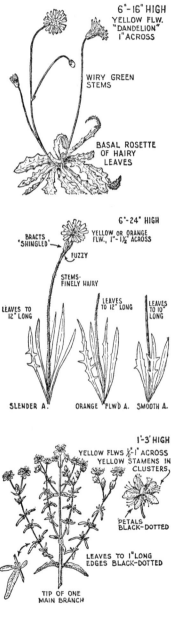

6″-16″ HIGH
YELLOW FLW. "DANDELION"
1″ ACROSS

WIRY GREEN STEMS

BASAL ROSETTE OF HAIRY LEAVES

6″-24″ HIGH
YELLOW OR ORANGE FLW., 1″-1½″ ACROSS

BRACTS 'SHINGLED'
FUZZY
STEMS· FINELY HAIRY

LEAVES TO 12″ LONG
LEAVES TO 12″ LONG
LEAVES TO 10″ LONG

SLENDER A.   ORANGE FLW'D A.   SMOOTH A.

1′-3′ HIGH
YELLOW FLWS ½-1″ ACROSS
YELLOW STAMENS IN CLUSTERS

PETALS BLACK-DOTTED

LEAVES TO 1″ LONG
EDGES BLACK-DOTTED

TIP OF ONE MAIN BRANCH

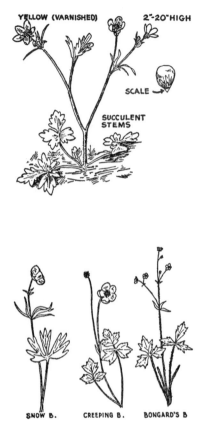

YELLOW (VARNISHED)   2"-20"HIGH

SCALE →

SUCCULENT STEMS

SNOW B.   CREEPING B.   BONGARD'S B

WESTERN BUTTERCUP
(*Ranunculus occidentalis*)

Of course everyone recognizes a buttercup or do they? There are over 30 species in B.C. excluding those known as water crowfoots which have white petals and no basal scale. A feature of the buttercups is the varnished golden petals with a little scale at the base of each petal. The leaves vary in shape very noticeably. In some species they are lobed while others display leaves finely dissected. Potentilla's have compound leaves and avens have 5 green sepals with 5 bractlets between. Buttercups are found in a wide variety of habitat and blooming from March to July. Some choose very wet places, others prefer open dry fields. They may be only an inch or two high or on stems that lift them 20" into the air.

RANGE: Widespread at low and middle elevations. Some species confined to certain regions.

SNOW BUTTERCUP (*R. eschscholtzii*) : This flower of brightest gold bejewels the fresh greenery around the edges of snowbanks. The several lower leaves are fancifully lobed but another group of narrow leaves make a circlet halfway up the stem. This buttercup is perhaps the most common one above timberline and will be found in bloom from early to late summer as the snow recedes. Common on mountains throughout.

CREEPING BUTTERCUP (*R. repens*): The creeping stems which root here and there account for masses of this buttercup in wettish situations. The stem and leaves are slightly hairy. Leaves are divided into 3 separate leaflets or merely 3-parted. The flower is a bright golden yellow. Common on V.I. and lower elevations west of Cascades.

BONGARD'S BUTTERCUP (*R. bongardi*): The small pale yellow flowers not more than ¾" across and the deeply 3-lobed leaves, again 3-lobed, distinguish this buttercup. Usually the 1' - 2' high stems and leaves are hairy. It ranges across the Province in shady, moist forests of lower elevations.

SPRING GOLD
(*Lomatium spp.*)

Hog-fennel

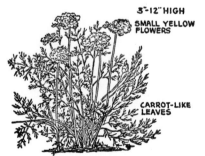

3"-12" HIGH

SMALL YELLOW FLOWERS

CARROT-LIKE LEAVES

The heads of tightly packed small flowers are a brilliant yellow nicely set off by the dark green carrot-like leaves. In early spring the plant usually forms a low, rounded tuft but later in the season the flower gains height and the flower stems raise into the air showing the umbrella framework holding the blooms. Mossy rocky places are where to look for spring gold during April and May.

RANGE: South half of Vancouver Island and adjacent islands. Also several similar species found in the Dry Interior.

NARROW-LEAVED PARSLEY
(Lomatium triternatum)

Nineleaf Biscuitroot

There are a half-dozen or more lomatiums. Most species like dry exposed places and are early bloomers. Leaves and flower stems spring from the ground for there is little or no true stem. Leaf stems are broadened at the base and divided into segments. Some resemble parsley leaves, others fern leaves, and two species still differ as shown. Flowers may be white, yellow, or purple, and have no or hardly visible sepals. Note the absence of bracts at the main flower hub, but see how they are present below each of the flower heads. Seeds are smooth and flat with thin side wings.

Narrow-leaved parsley may reach 2′ in height and blooms from April to July. The root is edible raw or cooked or ground into flour.

RANGE: East of Cascades to Rockies.

INDIAN CONSUMPTION PLANT *(L. nudicaule).* Note the shape of its leaves and the stem swelling at the main flower hub. It blooms from April to July. Indians used the ground-up seeds as a medicine for consumptive diseases. Dry places on V.I. and east of the Cascades.

WOOLLY SUNFLOWER
(Eriophyllum lanatum)

This bright little sunflower is supported on slender hairy stems which rise from a twisted mat of olive-green leaves. The leaves are very woolly beneath and give the flower its common name. Those on the stem are 3-7 lobed while the lower ones are entire.

The flower, which is 1″ - 1½″ across, has 9 - 11 broad golden-yellow petals and a beady yellow centre. Like most sunflowers it loves bright sunshine and is found on dry exposed places.

RANGE: Grassy knolls on Vancouver Island and the southern part of the Coastal Forest Zone.

GOLDEN FLEABANE
(Erigeron aureus)

This cheery little midget sunflower greets the hiker in the high mountains. Only a few inches tall, it adorns rocky ridges and gravelly pockets. The dull green leaves are basal except for a small one on the stem. This plant blooms during the late summer.

RANGE: From the Cascades to the Rockies in alpine terrain of southern B.C.

LYALL'S GOLDENWEED *(Haplopappus lyallii)* is liable to be confused with golden fleabane. However it has leaves well up on the stem and both leaves and stem are sticky and hairy. It ranges from the Cascades to the Rockies on rocky soils at high elevations.

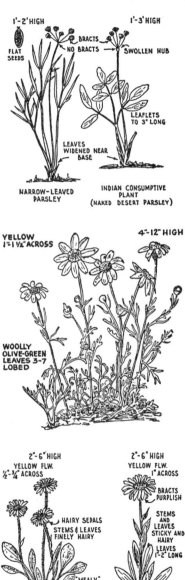

1′-2′HIGH 1′-3′HIGH
FLAT SEEDS BRACTS NO BRACTS SWOLLEN HUB
LEAFLETS TO 3″ LONG
LEAVES WIDENED NEAR BASE
NARROW-LEAVED PARSLEY
INDIAN CONSUMPTIVE PLANT
(NAKED DESERT PARSLEY)

YELLOW 1″-1½″ACROSS 4″-12″HIGH
WOOLLY OLIVE-GREEN LEAVES 3-7 LOBED

2″-6″HIGH YELLOW FLW. ½-¾″ ACROSS 2″-6″HIGH YELLOW FLW. 1″ ACROSS
HAIRY SEPALS BRACTS PURPLISH
STEMS & LEAVES FINELY HAIRY STEMS AND LEAVES STICKY AND HAIRY
LEAVES 1-2″ LONG
"MEALY" LEAVES ½″-2½″ LONG 3-NERVED
GOLDEN FLEABANE LYALL'S APLOPAPPUS

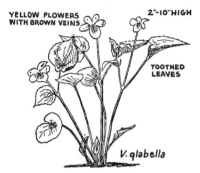

YELLOW FLOWERS WITH BROWN VEINS

2"-10"HIGH

TOOTHED LEAVES

V. glabella

2"-5" HIGH

YELLOW STAR-LIKE FLOWERS

½"ACROSS

COAST FORM

FLESHY, OLIVE GREEN LEAVES

INTERIOR FORM

6-24" HIGH

YELLOW FLOWERS ½"-1" LONG

2-LOBED STIGMA

SESSILE LEAVES

STALKED

ANGLED, REDDISH STEMS

YELLOW VIOLETS
(Viola spp.)

Besides the three yellow violets in B.C. there are other species having white, pale mauve or deep blue flowers.

TRAILING YELLOW VIOLETS (*V. sempervirens*): This slender creeper produces a mat-like growth, attractive because of the evergreen, heart-shaped leaves. The lower petals are delicately veined with brown. Vancouver Island, Gulf Islands and in Wet Interior.

JOHNNY-JUMP-UP (*V. nuttallii*) forms a tuft of beautiful upright leaves. They are short-stemmed and usually hairy. The flower is faintly marked with purple veins. Dry grassy places on Vancouver Island and Rockies.

YELLOW VIOLET (*V. glabella*) is distinguished by toothed leaves of which 2 or 3 branch out near the top of the stems. It grows to 10" in height. The single large flowers have brownish veins. Common across the Province.

STONECROP
(Sedum spp.)

During May and June rocky bluffs are enlivened by dabs and fringes of brightest yellow. Stonecrop with its irregular head of star-like flowers and bursting buds is strictly a rock plant at the Coast. Probably the most noticeable feature is the rough rosettes of thick fleshy leaves which cling tightly to the thin moss layer on the rocks. The thick leaves, acting like the cactus, store enough water to tide the hardy flower over dry periods.

RANGE: Various species are found throughout B.C. with the plant ranging in altitude to subalpine slopes.

YELLOW MONKEY FLOWER
(Mimulus guttatus)

Yellow mimulus grows from sea level to alpine heights. The clear yellow "snapdragon" flower is about ¾" long with brown or crimson dots in a bearded throat. The petals drop almost immediately after it is picked. The stem is angled and very succulent as are the opposite leaves, thus leading to its use in salads. The blooming period is from May to August.

RANGE: Vancouver Island, Coastal Mountains and through Central B.C. to the Yukon.

BABY MONKEY FLOWER (*M. alsinoides*) only grows a few inches high. The curious little yellow face is spotted with one or two purplish dots on the lower lip. Most flowers bloom in April. The range is Vancouver Island and the Coastal Zone.

MUSK FLOWER
(Mimulus moschatus)

This plant is the least attractive of the numerous mimulus or monkey-flowers. Its weak drooping stems are sticky and hairy and often slimy. The reputed musky odor varies considerably in strength.

The yellow flowers are two-lipped; the upper two-lobed, the lower three-lobed. The hairy throat is very narrow and marked with dark lines or spots. It blooms from May to late July.

RANGE: Widespread on V.I. and generally west of the Cascades in ditches and marshes.

CLUSTERED OR ALPINE MONKEY FLOWER (*M. tilingii var. caespitosus*) one of the loveliest flowers of sub-alpine and alpine meadows. Flourishes along cold streams often forming mats of bright gold. V.I. and Cascade Mountains.

LEMONWEED
(Lithospermum ruderale)
(Lithospermum pilosum)

Western Gromwell

In open country from May to July watch for an outstanding bushy plant 1'-2' high having a rough hairy appearance. The small pale yellow funnel-like flowers will be seen almost hidden among the small flowers at the tips of the stems.

The general bushy appearance is brought about by the very leafy stems. Leaves are alternate but bunch together toward the top until becoming tightly packed. Those at the tip of the flower head protrude beyond the small flowers.

RANGE: Open slopes in the Dry Interior Zone. Also Cariboo and Chilcotin.

CARROT LEAF
(Leptotaenia dissecta multifida)
(Lomatium dissecta multifida)

This spring plant looks like a very vigorous lomatium. It is separated on the basis of narrow thickened corky wings on the seed rather than the thin wings of lomatiums. It blooms in April and May and the big tousled ball of fern-like leaves usually slightly less than 2' high is very decorative on rocky ridges and slopes. Some plants have yellow flower heads—others purple. The heavy aromatic roots were once roasted by Indians.

RANGE: East of Cascades in dry places. Manning Park, Kamloops, Cranbrook.

LACE-LEAVED LEPTOTAENIA (*L. dissecta*) ranges on both sides of the Cascades. It differs in having thicker leaf segments and shorter seeds. Flowers generally purple, occasionally yellow. South end of V.I. Spences Bridge, Cariboo, Kaslo.

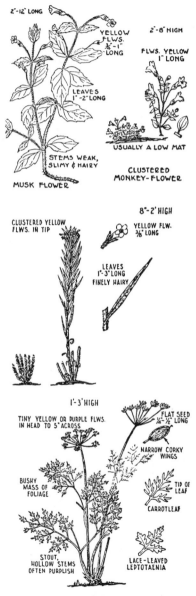

2"-12" LONG

YELLOW FLWS. ¼"-1" LONG

2"-8" HIGH

FLWS. YELLOW 1" LONG

LEAVES 1"-2" LONG

USUALLY A LOW MAT

STEMS WEAK, SLIMY & HAIRY

MUSK FLOWER

CLUSTERED MONKEY-FLOWER

CLUSTERED YELLOW FLWS. IN TIP

8"-2' HIGH

YELLOW FLW. ⅜" LONG

LEAVES 1"-3" LONG FINELY HAIRY

1'-3' HIGH

TINY YELLOW OR PURPLE FLWS. IN HEAD TO 5" ACROSS

FLAT SEED ¼"-½" LONG

NARROW CORKY WINGS

BUSHY MASS OF FOLIAGE

TIP OF LEAF

CARROTLEAF

STOUT, HOLLOW STEMS OFTEN PURPLISH

LACE-LEAVED LEPTOTAENIA

FLOWERS (YELLOW)

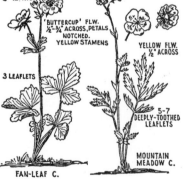

16"-24" HIGH

FLWS. 1/2" ACROSS

YELLOW 3/4" ACROSS

5 SEPALS WITH 5 SHORTER BRACTS

5-7 TOOTHED LEAFLETS

6-7 LEAFLETS

P. nuttallii

P. milleqrama

6"-16" HIGH

LEAFLETS SILVERY BENEATH 1/2"-11/2" LONG

YELLOW 1"ACROSS

SEED

THIN RUNNERS

3"-12" HIGH

4"-12" HIGH

'BUTTERCUP' FLW. 1/2"-3/4" ACROSS, PETALS NOTCHED. YELLOW STAMENS

3 LEAFLETS

YELLOW FLW. 1/2" ACROSS

5-7 DEEPLY-TOOTHED LEAFLETS

MOUNTAIN MEADOW C.

FAN-LEAF C.

CINQUEFOILS
(*Potentilla spp.*)

Fivefinger — Potentilla

A common name, fivefinger, is descriptive of leaves of species which have five leaflets. There are over 20 in B.C., but all have the same shiny buttercup flower. Only one is purple colored. Five green sepals show their tips around the flower. Five shorter bracts alternate with these and by this arrangement it is possible to make sure of the cinquefoils. The leaves differ widely, some being finger-like, the others with leaflets opposite one another.

P. milligrana is a fairly common rangeland plant in the Dry Interior and Kootenays. The height is from 12" - 24". Blooming period July.

NUTTALL CINQUEFOIL (*P. nuttallii*) has 5 - 7 finger-like leaflets each 2" - 3" long. The leaves are hairy on both sides. East of Cascades, and north to Central B.C.

P. gracilis similar to the above is distinguished by densely hairy stems and leaflets. Vancouver Island, Coast, Cariboo and Central B.C.

MARSH CINQUEFOIL (*P. palustris*) has purple flowers. The stout stems are almost flat on the ground but the tips turn up. Margin of bogs and lakes through Southern and Central Interior.

SILVERWEED (*P. anserina*) has single flowers on a long stem. The leaflets are fringe-like, green above but strikingly silvery beneath. Saline meadows and marshes throughout B.C.

FAN-LEAF CINQUEFOIL
(*Potentilla flabellifolia*)

This very common flower of alpine meadows might be mistaken for a buttercup unless the notched petals and green sepals are noticed. The flower is more than 1/2" across and adorned by a cluster of a dozen yellow stamens. Usually several flowers branch from the main stem.

The leaves are reminiscent of a strawberry plant, being formed by 3 leaflets, wedge-shaped at the base and coarsely toothed above. Fan-leaf cinquefoil blooms during the summer while most alpine flowers are at their height of color.

RANGE: Sparse on V.I. but very common in Cascade Mountains.

MOUNTAIN MEADOW CINQUEFOIL (*P. diversifolia*) grows to 12" high and is sparsely hairy. Long-stemmed leaves carry 5 - 7 deeply toothed leaflets. Common in moist situations near and below timberline from Cascades to Rockies and far northward.

GROUNDSELS AND RAGWORTS
(*Senecio spp.*)

These include a large number of plants with smallish yellow to orange flowers, alternate leaves and bracts in one row.

WESTERN GOLDEN RAGWORT (*S. pseudaureus*) has flat-topped heads of numerous yellow flowers and brownish centres. Note the two types of leaves. Kootenays and Rockies.

GIANT RAGWORT (*S. triangularis*) is 2′ - 3′ high, leafy to the top and crowned with flat-topped heads of small yellow flowers. It is a plant of high mountains and blooms in late summer. Across B.C. and into the North Central Region.

COMMON GROUNDSEL (*S. vulgaris*) is a common weed less than 2′ high and with branching stems. The bracts have a shorter row around the base and these are black tipped.

1′-3′ HIGH

ORANGE-YELLOW FLOWERS 1/2″ - 3/4″ ACROSS

MAIN BRACTS IN ONE ROW THICKENED ON BACK

SOFT, BRISTLY SEED

LEAVES 2″-6″ LONG

LEAVES VARIABLE

S.pseudaureus S.triangularis S.vulgaris

SLENDER HAWKWEED
(*Hieracium gracile*)

Other flowers such as the groundsels (*Senecio spp.*) and hawksbeard (*Crepis spp.*) also have yellow flowers turning to untidy seed heads. In hawkweeds the cup that holds the flower has one main row of flat, sharp-pointed bracts. In this species the cups are black and hairy. Flowers are pale yellow, about 1″ across. The light green leaves form a rough rosette. The blooming period is July and August.

RANGE: High mountains throughout B.C.

HAIRY HAWKWEED (*H. scouleri*) has 2-3 rows of bracts covered with long hairs. This hairyness is continued on leaves and stem. Range country, Kootenays and Similkameen Valley.

WHITE HAWKWEED (*H. albiflorum*) has a dozen or more white flowers. The height is from 2′ - 3′. Leaves and lower stem are hairy. Across B.C.

8″-14″ HIGH

PALE YELLOW FLOWERS WITH BLACK COLLAR ABOUT 1/2″ ACROSS

BLACK HAIRS

ONE MAIN ROW OF BLACK HAIRY BRACTS TO 1/2″ LONG

SLENDER STEMS

LEAVES LONG-STEMMED

GUMWEED
(*Grindelia spp.*)

Several gumweeds are found in B.C. Most plants are bushy with a bright yellow flower on a rough, sticky bur. This bur has 5 or 6 rows of gummy bracts which curl outward at their tips.
G. squarrosa is most likely to be found in the Dry Interior and *G. nana* at the Coast. *G. integrifolia* has basal leaves 2″ - 8″ long and is found on high beaches along the sea coast.

10″-18″ HIGH

YELLOW 1/2″-1 1/2″ ACROSS

GUMMY GREEN BURR

1″-2″ LONG

THICK, GUMMY LEAVES TO 2″ LONG

2″-8″ LONG

G.squarrosa   G.nana G.oregana

FLOWERS (YELLOW)

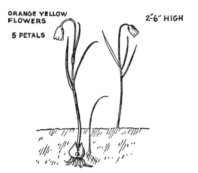

ORANGE YELLOW FLOWERS

5 PETALS

2"-6" HIGH

YELLOW BELL
(Fritillaria pudica)

Mission Bell — Yellow Fritillary

The slopes and benches of the Similkameen and Okanagan Valleys are liberally sprinkled with this shy little yellow bell from April into May. It seldom grows over 4" high and has one nodding fragrant orange to yellow flower about $\frac{1}{2}$" long. The 2 or 3 long narrow leaves are olive-green in color and start well up on the flower stem. The tiny white bulb giving rise to the flower is about 1" beneath the ground. Like the Easter lily at the Coast it suffers from thoughtless over-picking.

RANGE: Throughout the Dry Interior Zone. Osoyoos to Kamloops, Lytton, Lillooet. Scattered occurrence in the Kootenays.

SPRING SUNFLOWERS
(Balsamorhiza sagittata)

Balsam-Root

1-2' HIGH

YELLOW FLOWERS 3"-4" ACROSS

THICK LEAVES TO 10" LONG

During May, acre upon acre of open mountain slopes in the Dry Interior are covered with bunches of these bright yellow flowers. A dozen or so large flowers may rise from each bunch of big olive-green leaves and the individual clumps may almost touch. These dry up during the hot summer and the twists of parched leaves remain as poor evidence of their former glory.

Indians ate the rich oily seeds either raw or mixed with deer fat and boiled by means of hot stones. The roots were eaten raw or roasted with much care and ceremony in large pits.

RANGE: At low and middle elevations throughout the Dry Interior Zone. Osoyoos to Kamloops, Grand Forks, Cranbrook to Columbia Lake.

CACTUS
(Opuntia fragilus)

The spiny clumps of wrinkled fleshy cactus are a characteristic plant of the arid sagebrush rangelands. The beautiful yellow tissuey blossoms give the otherwise drab cactus a brief period of glory from June into July. The whole spiny mass is often covered with these bright blooms. The thick, spongy stem carries on the function of leaves and is designed for storing precious water. Spines protect the succulent stems from animals.

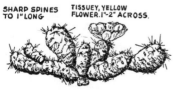

1"-3" HIGH

SHARP SPINES TO 1" LONG

TISSUEY, YELLOW FLOWER. 1"-2" ACROSS.

RANGE: Similkameen, Okanagan and Nicola Valley extending northward to Kamloops, Clinton, and Peace River region. Southward to Lytton. Abundant on some southern Gulf Islands. Saturna Island and north to Denman Island.

DEATH CAMAS
(*Zigadenus venenosus*)

Death camas bears a resemblance to camas through its long grass-like leaves and main stem with a spike of flowers at the tip. When not in flower the two plants have a close resemblance. The several long thin leaves have a deep groove which forms a keel on the opposite side. The creamy colored flowers are less than ½″ across and have 3 sepals and 3 petals which simply appear as 6 petals. The dark-coated bulb, shaped like an onion, is very poisonous. Young leaves can be fatal to grazing stock.

Death camas may be found wherever camas grows. It blooms from April 15 to June but later in the Interior.

RANGE: Gulf Islands and Dry Interior Zone up to 4,000′. Cariboo Parklands and Chilcotin.

SULPHUR ERIOGONUM
(*Eriogonum umbellatum*)

This species flourishes at high elevations where the winds beat at the compact mass of leaves and stout flower stems. The sulphur-yellow color of the flowers is one not seen often in flowers. Sometimes a rosy tinge suffuses the yellow providing a rather bizarre effect.

RANGE: Sub-alpine and alpine elevations from Cascades eastward.

CUSHION ERIOGONUM (*E. ovalifolium*) is a very low plant with a compact mass of small oval leaves less than ½″ long. Both leaves and stem are white with dense woolly hairs. The flowers are a soft yellow color sometimes touched with red. High mountains east of Cascades.

OYSTER PLANT
(*Tragopogon dubius*)

Salsify — Goat's Beard

This weedy plant, widely cultivated throughout Europe and North America, is generally called salsify. The thick root is edible in early spring or late fall or the young stem and leaves may be eaten as a cooked vegetable.

A stout flower stem carries a bright yellow dandelion-like flower about 2″ across. The seed head that follows is similar in shape and form to that of a dandelion but may be 3″ wide. Several long alternate grass-like leaves clasp the stem near the base. This species has a thickened flower stem near its top and thus may be distinguished from *T. pratensis*. *T. porrifolius* has purple flowers.

RANGE: *T. dubius* and *T. pratensis*, throughout Dry Interior and near Victoria.

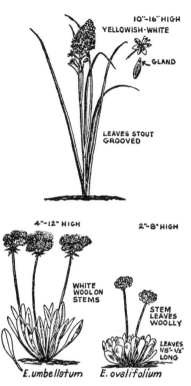

10″-16″ HIGH
YELLOWISH-WHITE

GLAND

LEAVES STOUT GROOVED

4″-12″ HIGH

2″-8″HIGH

WHITE WOOL ON STEMS

STEM LEAVES WOOLLY

LEAVES 1/8″-1/2″ LONG

E. umbellatum *E. ovalifolium*

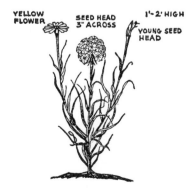

YELLOW FLOWER

SEED HEAD 3″ ACROSS

1′-2′ HIGH

YOUNG SEED HEAD

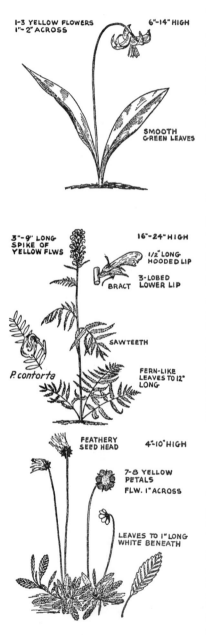

3"-9" LONG
SPIKE OF
YELLOW FLWS

1-3 YELLOW FLOWERS
1"-2" ACROSS

6"-14" HIGH

SMOOTH
GREEN LEAVES

16"-24" HIGH

1/2" LONG
HOODED LIP

3-LOBED
BRACT   LOWER LIP

SAWTEETH

P. contorta

FERN-LIKE
LEAVES TO 12"
LONG

FEATHERY
SEED HEAD

4"-10" HIGH

7-8 YELLOW
PETALS
FLW. 1" ACROSS

LEAVES TO 1" LONG
WHITE BENEATH

SNOW LILY
(*Erythronium grandiflorum*)
Glacier Lily—Fawn Lily

This bright flower of the purest yellow has two glossy green leaves contrasting with the one to three flowers with their six long recurved petals. Like the avalanche lily and western anemone it blooms soon after the snow has left the ground. **RANGE:** In western B.C., seldom seen below 3,500'. At Shuswap Lake and in the Kootenays it descends to valley elevations.

AVALANCHE LILY (*E. montanum*) is larger with white flowers. Although common in Washington and Oregon, B.C. is at the edge of its range.

WOOD BETONY
(*Pedicularis bracteosa*)
Northern Fernleaf

Wood betony, a plant of the high mountains, has an unusual spike of flowers. These hook-beaked oddities are pale yellow in color but occasionally with a pinkish tinge. They present a series of quaint little faces one peeping over top of the other. This arrangement and a twisting beak is characteristic of the louseworts or *Pedicularis spp.* The leaves are finely divided.

RANGE: High moist mountains throughout B.C.

CONTORTED LOUSEWORT (*P. contorta*) has soft yellow flowers about 1/2" long and with a remarkably twisted beak. The plant is from 8" - 15" high. Kootenays and Rockies.

SICKLETOP LOUSEWORT (*P. racemosa*) has white or pink flowers with a beak that curves inward. Foliage purplish. Westerly half of B.C.

ELEPHANT HEAD (*P. groenlandica*) has purplish or reddish flowers with a long, upcurved beak. See page 162.

YELLOW DRYAS
(*Dryas drummondii*)

Yellow dryas is usually found on high rock slides or hard-packed gravel bars. The leaves, less than 1" long, are distinctly crinkled and so densely hairy beneath that they appear silvery. The round yellow flowers about 1" across have 7 or 8 petals. The seed head is a fluffy white tuft.

RANGE: Cariboo and edges of Dry Interior. Windermere Valley. Northern Coast. Muncho L.

WHITE DRYAS (*D. octopetala*) is a few inches high and the leaves less than 1/2" long. The single white flower has 8 petals and a fluffy seed head. Common alpine plant on rockslides. East of Cascades and northward to the Yukon.

BROAD-LEAF ARNICA
(Arnica latifolia)

The straight stem to 2′ high is unbranched and carries flowers about 2″ across. The large oval coarsely toothed leaves branch opposite from one another, the lower ones having short stems. The showy flowers have a light brown center. Medicinal arnica for cuts and bruises is from an European species.

RANGE: Most abundant at sub-alpine heights. Widespread through B.C.

HEART-LEAF ARNICA (*A. cordifolia*) grows at lower elevations but still in moist forested mountains. It is only 10″ - 18″ in height but has a slightly larger flower than broad-leaf arnica and often 3 to a stem. The large, heart-shaped leaves grow near the ground and have long stems. Abundant along Hope-Princton Highway and widely distributed throughout the Province.

A. fulgens differs in having long thin leaves. Rocky Mountains near sub-alpine elevations.

A.cordifolia A.fulgens A.latifolia

GOLDEN ASTER
(Chrysopsis hispida)

Here is a plant with flowers much like an aster except it has yellow rather than purple or violet rays and an overall greyish color of stems and leaves. This peculiar tinge results from fine matted hairs, a protection from the intense exposure and drought. The fibrous roots penetrate many feet into the soil. The blooming period is midsummer.

RANGE: Exposed places at low and middle elevations throughout the Dry Interior and bordering areas. Fraser Canyon, Manning Park.

C. villosa is more hairy and shaggy than the above and occurs in the same range.

BROWN-EYED SUSAN
(Gaillardia aristata)

Gaillardia

When most of the early flowers have disappeared and the sidehills and fields are taking on the dehydrated look of summer in the Interior then brown-eyed Susan appears to charm the eye. To most people it is a bright little yellow sunflower with a reddish brown center. The drab rough leaves are not very noticeable so the flower reposes without detraction at the top of a long erect stem. The bloom is from 1½″ - 2″ across and the yellow ray flowers are deeply notched at their tips. Dry open fields during June and July.

RANGE: Throughout the Dry Interior and in vicinity of Cranbrook, Seton Lake.

FLOWERS (YELLOW)

BUTTERCUP FLOWERS

1'-2' HIGH

3-5 PARTED LEAVES

COARSE AND HAIRY STEMS AND LEAVES

2'-3' HIGH
FLAT YELLOW FLWS 1/4" ACROSS

SMALL YELLOW FLOWERS

DWARF THIN GOLDENROD

3 VEINS

LARGE-LEAVED AVENS
(Geum macrophyllum)

Large-leaved avens produces a bright yellow buttercup-like flower. Otherwise the plant is coarse and hairy with large ragged leaves. The leaves growing from the base are about 6"-9" long with small toothed leaflets on either side and a large terminal one. Leaves off the stem are rounded with 3-5 lobes.

Avens generally have 5 green sepals with 5 small bractlets between.

The flowers, either singly or in a few-flowered cluster, grow at the tip of the branches and will be seen in bloom during May at the Coast or to July in the north. The flower develops into a round burr with hooked prickles.

RANGE: Vancouver Island eastward to Rockies and into North Central B.C. McLeod Lake.

TANSY
(Tanacetum vulgare)

Usually between 2' and 3' high, it becomes very prominent when the compact clusters of flattish yellow flowers burst into full bloom. Each bloom is only 1/4" across but the bunched grouping is very effective above the thick mass of dark green carrotty leaves. The flowers are out during the latter part of August and the first half of September.

RANGE: Vancouver Island eastward to Creston, northward through Cariboo. Abundant in Lower Fraser Canyon.

GOLDENROD
(Solidago canadensis)

A widespread belief that pollen from goldenrod caused hay fever has been proven wrong. The 100 or so species in North America contain some exceptionally beautiful flowers.

The common goldenrod often forms masses of golden bloom during midsummer where there is rich moist soil for its roots. The pyramid of small yellow flowers was used once as a source of yellow dye and a bright dye it must have made.

RANGE: Vancouver Island and Coastal Zone.
THIN GOLDENROD (*S. canadensis* var. *elongata*) has the typical goldenrod flower but is usually less than a foot high. It grows on well drained soil and ranges from Vancouver Island to Nelson and northward through Central B.C.

DWARF GOLDENROD (*S. spathulata*) has a tousled head of rather large yellow flowers. One point to notice is the bend in the lower part of the stem. Common on high mountain slopes east of the Cascades and into the far north, also Kootenay River Valley.

(146)

MOCCASIN FLOWER
(Cypripedium parviflorum)
Small Lady's Slipper

The pouch-like yellow flower of satiny texture can be very well likened to a dainty moccasin. Enhancing its beauty are the claret-purple streaks and markings which are found on the lining. A bizarre touch is added by the long twisted sepals. The leaves are rich green and artistically arranged. The moccasin flower is comparatively scarce in B.C.. Usually moist shady sites or high mountain stream banks provide a suitable setting. It blooms from June to July.

RANGE: Edges of Dry Interior and into Big Bend, also Windermere Valley and Rockies.

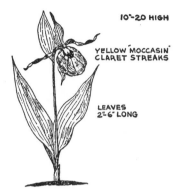

10"-20" HIGH

YELLOW 'MOCCASIN' CLARET STREAKS

LEAVES 2"-6" LONG

SKUNK CABBAGE
(Lysichiton kamtschatcense)

Skunk cabbage is most noticeable in March and April before the shrubs have come into leaf. Then almost every swampy or mucky place is dotted with soft yellow sheaths which give off a sickish sweet smell. The thick fleshy club inside the sheath carries a large number of small green flowers. Later the club will show a cluster of bright red berries. The leaves probably are the largest of any native plant. Some may grow to 3' in length and be a foot wide. If crushed the plant gives off a pungent odor thus leading to its common name.

RANGE: Wetter regions of B.C. Generally under or near cedar trees.

6"-24" HIGH

YELLOW CAPE

LEAVES TO 3' LONG

GREENISH FLOWERS

YELLOW POND LILY
(Nymphaea polysepalum)

The large scaly roots of this native plant are anchored firmly in the mud. From them long stems reach upward to the lake surface. The yellowish-green flowers are cup-like and have a knob in their center. This is formed of petals and the other plant organs. The blooms will be seen from May through the summer. The seeds were gathered once by the Indians and ground into flour. The large flat leaves, either ovalish or heart-shaped, float on the water and provide convenient docking facilities for dragon flies and frogs.

RANGE: Throughout B.C. and far north in the smaller lakes and marshes. Upper Liard River.

2"-6" HIGH

GREEN, FLESHY PADS TO 12"LONG

YELLOW CUPS

(147)

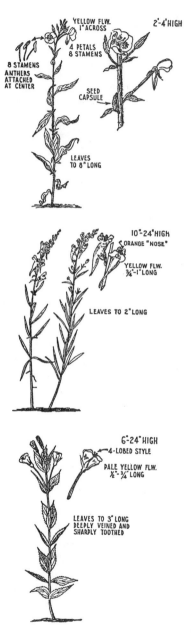

EVENING PRIMROSE
(*Oenothera biennis*)

Watch for possible confusion between the evening primroses and godetias. The stamens of the evening primrose hold the anthers at the center while in the godetias they are attached at one end. Most godetias are pink in contrast to the yellows and whites of the evening primroses.

Plants are generally so widely scattered that they are missed unless a person looks closely for them although the stout and occasionally branched stem may reach 4' in height.

The satin-like flowers are an exquisite soft yellow color and about 1" across. They are at their best on a cloudy day or in the early morning or evening. See how the flower stem swells at its base and eventually withers away to leave an upright 4-sided seed capsule. Leaves are numerous and to 8" long. The lower ones usually have "wings" near their base.

RANGE: Mostly west of the Cascades but also occurring in Dry Interior Zone.

BUTTER AND EGGS
(*Linaria vulgaris*)

There's no chance of mistaking butter and eggs for anything else. The intricate yellow flower with its orange "nose" is a close match to the yellow of butter and orange of an egg yolk. The blooms are in rich profusion on the top of an erect stalk to 2' high. The inch-long flowers have a graceful yellow spur and two lips, the upper being two-lobed and the lower three-lobed and pouch shaped. The "egg" color comes from an orange swelling almost closing the throat. Leaves are narrow and up to 2" long. Although they are regarded as being alternate there are times when they appear opposite.

RANGE: A naturalized European weed now widely spread on exposed places at lower elevations across the Province.

YELLOW WILLOW HERB
(*Epilobium luteum*)

The luxuriant growth along mountain streams is similar in habitat and form to red mimulus. Stems are erect and to 2' high. Leaves are to 3" long, heavily veined, sharply toothed, and generally in opposite pairs.

The modest flowers are held erect on long stems near the top of the plant. They are pale yellow and 1/2" - 3/4" long. The 4 folded petals suggest a closed flower. Four long narrow sepals support the reticent bloom. Depending on elevation the blooming period varies from early to late summer.

RANGE: Moist meadows and stream edges from middle mountain to high elevations. Cascade and Selkirk Mountains ranging northward to Alaska.

GREAT MULLEIN
(*Verbascum thapsus*)

The tall thick stem of the great mullein and its large flannelly leaves quickly attract the attention. The stem often reaches 5' in height and is sometimes branched near the top into several upright arms. Dead stalks often stand all winter. Leaves are up to a foot long and have a coarse blotting paper texture with a covering of fine woolly hairs. They are rather repelling to the touch. Leaf bases form long ribs running down the stalk.

Tiny yellow flowers bursting out here and there on the flowering spike have a pleasant smell and the formation of new buds at the top keeps the great mullein in ragged bloom for several months from mid-summer onward.

RANGE: Scattered in pastures in Lower Mainland. Widespread on poor land east of Cascades.

FALSE ASPHODEL
(*Tofieldia intermedia*)
Western Tofieldia

A close watch during July and August along the lush growth bordering streams, swamps, or meadows often reveals the small yellowish flower head of the false asphodel, although the finely ribbed grass-like leaves are usually lost from sight. The unbranched flower stem has a slightly dirty look and sticky touch. The small pale-yellowish flowers about 1/4" across form a loose cluster. The stamens are darkish and provide a dainty touch.

RANGE: Widespread from low to high elevations in wet places throughout B.C.

NORTHERN ASPHODEL (*T. palustris*) has a tuft of short spiny leaves from 1" - 2" long. The flowers are greenish-white and so small the whole cluster is often not more than 1/4" across. Throughout B.C. in northern two-thirds of the Province.

OVAL - LEAF ALUMROOT
(*Heuchera cylindrica*)

Alumroots with white flowers are on page 113.

This hardy plant grows on rock slides and the poorest of soils producing its leaves and flowers before the extreme heat of midsummer. The oval leaves with their irregular lobes grow at the bottom of the stem and are thick, sticky and hairy. Small yellowish flowers form a cluster along the upper part of the slender hairy stems. They bloom in early June in the Dry Interior.

RANGE: Drier parts from Cascades to Rockies.

H. glabella has smooth, rounded leaves 1" - 2" long which, in the fall, often turn striking crimson shades. The flowers are a light yellow. Vancouver Island to the Rockies.

H. parvifolia is similar except the flowers may cover the greater part of the stem. Kootenay River to Rockies.

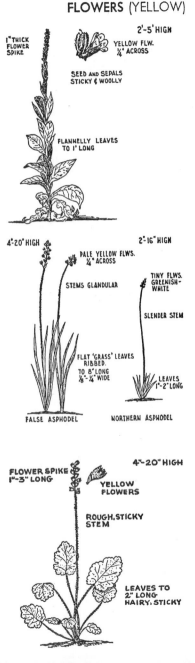

2'-5' HIGH — 1" THICK FLOWER SPIKE — YELLOW FLW. 1/4" ACROSS — SEED AND SEPALS STICKY & WOOLLY — FLANNELLY LEAVES TO 1' LONG

4"-20" HIGH — PALE YELLOW FLWS. 1/4" ACROSS — STEMS GLANDULAR — FLAT 'GRASS' LEAVES RIBBED. TO 8" LONG 1/8"-1/4" WIDE — FALSE ASPHODEL

2"-16" HIGH — TINY FLWS. GREENISH-WHITE — SLENDER STEM — LEAVES 1"-2" LONG — NORTHERN ASPHODEL

4"-20" HIGH — FLOWER SPIKE 1"-3" LONG — YELLOW FLOWERS — ROUGH, STICKY STEM — LEAVES TO 2" LONG HAIRY, STICKY

FLOWERS (BLUE)

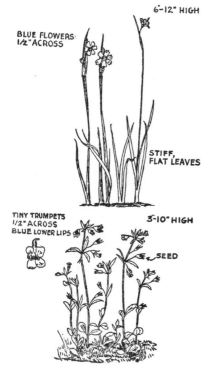

6"-12" HIGH

BLUE FLOWERS: 1/2" ACROSS

STIFF, FLAT LEAVES

TINY TRUMPETS 1/2" ACROSS BLUE LOWER LIPS

3"-10" HIGH

SEED

1'-2' HIGH

PURPLISH-BLUE 1"-1 1/2" ACROSS

GRASS-LIKE LEAVES

BLUE-EYED GRASS
(*Sisyrinchium spp.*)

The flowers are about 1/2" across and appear to protrude from a seam in the stem. Depending on their exposure to the elements they are in bloom from April into May at the Coast but a month or two later elsewhere.

RANGE: One species on open grassy bluffs and along sea coast of Vancouver Island. Other species in valleys of eastern B.C.

BLUE-EYED MARY
(*Collinsia grandiflora*)
Innocence - Blue Lips

Blue-eyed Mary brings a picture of rocky openings and knolls green with fresh moss and bright with spring sunshine. Usually the dainty plant has a number of branched and spreading stems which produce a mat effect. The lower leaves are oblong to nearly round while the upper are almost stemless. Sometimes under ideal growing conditions an erect stem 8" or 10" high is found.

The fragile little flower, less than 1/2" long, is trumpet-like with two lower blue petals. Very often a single flower adorns the thin stem but in other plants a whorl of flowers rises from the leaf axils. The blooming period at the Coast is during April and May.

RANGE: Abundant on dry exposed locations in the Coastal Forest Zone. Related species range widely through the Province, being possibly the most common spring wild flower.

CAMAS
(*Camassia quamash*)

The range of camas coincides quite closely with that of arbutus and garry oak which are typical trees of the Gulf Island Zone. The plant grows from a large, deep-seated bulb which once formed an important food item of the native Indians. The leaves are long and narrow and resemble coarse grass.

The flowers have three sepals and three petals, so similar in appearance that they are not ordinarily differentiated. The blue-purple flower is about 1" across and from 10 - 30 flowers and buds will be found on one stem. Occasionally a plant with white blooms will be seen but most often it will belong to the following species.

RANGE: Most abundant in the vicinity of Victoria but extending to Alberni and Comox. Gulf Islands. *C. leichtlinnii* is a larger species that blooms a little later than the above. The range is the same.

(150)

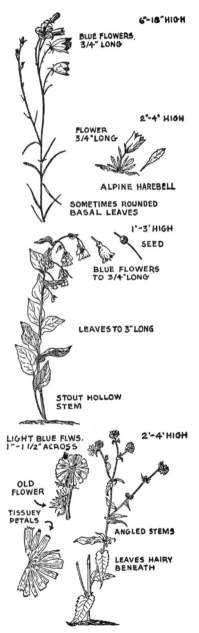

BLUEBELL
(*Campanula rotundifolia*)

Harebell

This flower, the real "Bluebell of Scotland", is widely distributed throughout North America. The slender stems carry several beautiful blue bells near their tops. The stem leaves are thin and narrow but younger plants have rounded leaves at the base which usually disappear by the time the flowers are out.

RANGE: Spotty occurrence on drier grounds at lower elevations throughout B.C.

ALPINE HAREBELL (*C. lasiocarpa*) is only a few inches high. The small toothed leaves are less than 1" long and are almost overwhelmed by the single, large flower. Rocky places at high elevations through Central and Northern B.C., Rockies.

MOUNTAIN BLUEBELL
(*Mertensia ciliata*)

Tall Lungwort

This tall leafy plant is recognized easily by the clusters of bell-shaped blue flowers. There are 4 or 5 different species of these bluebells, all in eastern B.C., but the characteristic group of flowers is the same. Because of their lushness, porcupines and rock rabbits or pikas often eat this plant.

M. ciliata has a stout stem, usually unbranched and with a graceful droop at the top. Loose clusters of blue flowers each about ¾" long hang gracefully from short side stems. A long style in the center of each flower shows up very noticeably when the blossoms have dropped. The blooming period is from June to August.

RANGE: Shady streams. Rockies.

BLUE SAILORS
(*Cichorium intybus*)

Chicory, Batchelor's Buttons

Blue sailors is included as a wildflower although it could be more properly classed as an escape from cultivation. The bright blue flowers have taken their name from an old legend concerning a sailor's sweetheart who was deserted but nevertheless kept a faithful watch for him. The gods took pity on her and turned her into this plant which still haunts the roadsides from July to September.

The deep taproot has been used considerably in the past as a coffee substitute. The occurrence of blue sailors near the sites of early-day construction camps may be due to this use when coffee was extremely scarce. The tissuey blue flowers, from 1" - 1½" across, usually open in the morning but close in the afternoon.

RANGE: Sporadic occurrence along roadsides and in waste places near settlement throughout B.C.

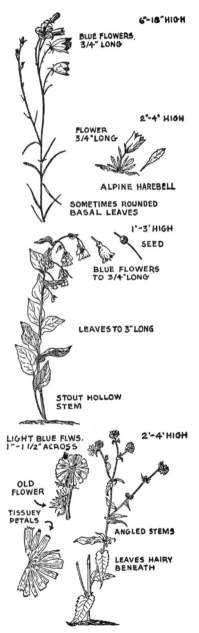

Image labels:
- 6"-18" HIGH
- BLUE FLOWERS. 3/4" LONG
- 2"-4" HIGH
- FLOWER 3/4" LONG
- ALPINE HAREBELL
- SOMETIMES ROUNDED BASAL LEAVES
- 1'-3' HIGH
- SEED
- BLUE FLOWERS TO 3/4" LONG
- LEAVES TO 3" LONG
- STOUT HOLLOW STEM
- LIGHT BLUE FLWS. 1"-1 1/2" ACROSS
- 2'-4' HIGH
- OLD FLOWER
- TISSUEY PETALS
- ANGLED STEMS
- LEAVES HAIRY BENEATH

FLOWERS (BLUE)

AMERICAN BROOKLIME
(*Veronica americana*)

The dainty blue garden forget-me-not is closely related to brooklime. A four-parted flower, about ¼″ across, with two spreading stamens will serve to distinguish the group of nearly a dozen species in B.C. The ribbed stem may vary from 4″ - 30″ high but usually carries 3 - 5 pairs of oval leaves. Those at the bottom are oval-shaped and scarcely toothed while the upper ones have distinct teeth and are more sharply pointed.

Flowers are carried in airy clusters and may be seen from May to July. The plant was once considered of high medicinal value in Europe.

RANGE: Wide range across North America in wet places. From low to fair altitudes.

NARROW-LEAFED SKULLCAP
(*Scutellaria angustifolia*)

The skullcaps take their name from a curious little projection or crest on the calyx. They are plants of moist ground with long funnel-like flowers of a dull bluish color. This species has the largest flowers of the group and blooms from early to mid-summer.

RANGE: Very limited in dry places of southern V.I. Sporadic in Dry Interior Zone.

MARSH SKULLCAP (*S. galericulata*) occurs in marshy ground and grows from 1′ - 3′ high. The flowers form in pairs and bloom from July and August. Across B.C. and into far north.

MAD-DOG SKULLCAP (*S. lateriflora*) has clusters of pairs of blue flowers so tiny as to easily pass notice. A late summer flower it is found in damp ground west of the Cascades. Alberni, Harrison Lake.

LOW LARKSPUR
(*Delphinium bicolor*)

From the names we see this plant is low in height and the flowers have 2 colors in them— blue and white. Generally low larkspur is about a foot high with many cleft alternate leaves to 3″ across. The blue flowers are carried on long stems, and form wide loose heads of bright hue. The flower with its wings and spurs has several shades of blue or purples. Two small petals that are bent back into the spur are whitish or yellowish making recognition quite easy.

RANGE: East of Cascades, Seton Lake, Okanagan, Chilcotin.

PALE LARKSPUR (*D. glaucum*) is a tall larkspur of rich meadows often at higher elevation. Leaves and stems usually have a waxy bloom. Flowers are short stemmed, about 1″ long and range from pale blue to dark purple. Central B.C., Vanderhoof, Smithers, Ootsa Lake.

(152)

DELPHINIUM
(*Delphinium menziesii*)

Larkspur

Delphiniums or larkspurs, as they are commonly called, range over most of North America and at least 6 species grow in the Province. Although they may be from 6" - 6' in height they are immediately recognized by the peculiar dark blue or purple flower with its long spur. The leaves too are featured by being deeply cleft into 3 - 5 main fingers and these usually cut again. A number of the delphiniums are considered very poisonous to grazing stock.

RANGE: Grows about 12" high and is almost lost in the grasses of the Dry Interior Zone. Spences Bridge, Kamloops, Princeton, Grand Forks, Cranbrook.

MONKSHOOD
(*Aconitum columbianum*)

Monkshood will be found as an individual or in a small patch and then not seen again in the entire vicinity. Moist open woods up to 4,500' elevation are preferred. Monkshood raises a stout stem 3' - 5' in the air, and tipped with a long loose cluster of large dark blue flowers.

The palmately veined leaves are deeply lobed and grow alternately from the main stem. Lower leaves have long stems but these decrease in length the higher they are up. One petal forms a large "monkshood" which lends such distinction to each bloom. The flowers are about 1" long and either hang from the tip of the main stem or short side branches. The seeds and roots are poisonous.

Monkshood is a late bloomer.

RANGE: Mountains of the Dry Interior Zone. North Central B.C., Manning Park, Nelson.

MOUNTAIN FORGET-ME-NOT
(*Myosotis sylvatica var. alpestris*)

The small pale flowers with their yellow centers gather importance by clustering together near the top of the stems. Like the garden forget-me-not, the blue flowers are less than ½" across. As with most alpine flowers, it blooms in middle and late summer. A fuzzy appearance is given the plant by reason of the small soft hairy leaves.

RANGE: High elevations east of the Cascades in Southern B.C. Across B.C. in the north.

FALSE FORGET-ME-NOT (*Lappula floribunda*) is similar to the above in habitat and flowers but is often over a foot high. The spiny seed catches in clothing leading to the name stickseed. The above has a smooth seed. Across B.C.

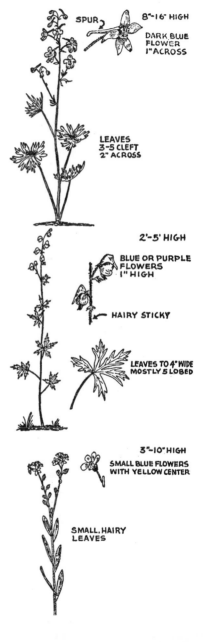

SPUR

8"-16" HIGH

DARK BLUE FLOWER 1" ACROSS

LEAVES 3-5 CLEFT 2" ACROSS

2'-5' HIGH

BLUE OR PURPLE FLOWERS 1" HIGH

HAIRY STICKY

LEAVES TO 4" WIDE MOSTLY 5 LOBED

3"-10" HIGH

SMALL BLUE FLOWERS WITH YELLOW CENTER

SMALL HAIRY LEAVES

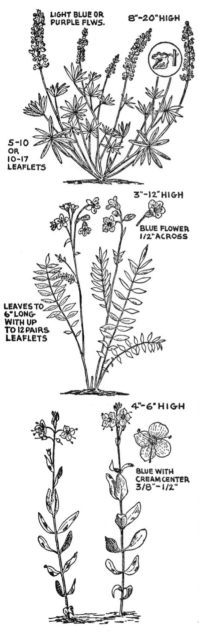

LIGHT BLUE OR PURPLE FLWS.

8"-20"HIGH

5-10 OR 10-17 LEAFLETS

3"-12"HIGH

BLUE FLOWER 1/2"ACROSS

LEAVES TO 6"LONG WITH UP TO 12 PAIRS LEAFLETS

4"-6"HIGH

BLUE WITH CREAM CENTER 3/8"-1/2"

LUPINES
(*Lupinus spp.*)

Lupines are one of the more common widespread flowers in B.C. Over 20 species give a range from sea level to alpine heights and an adaptability to a wide variety of soils. They are a common roadside plant at the Coast, a range plant on better soils in the Interior, and particularly abundant above middle mountain elevations.

The leaflets radiate from the leaf stem like a number of thin fingers. Some species have 5 - 10 leaflets, others 10 - 17. The leaflets "sleep" at night by folding down like a closed umbrella. During the daytime the whole head rotates as the sun moves.

The flowers, which cluster in long spikes, are generally from light blue to purple in color but several species are white to cream.

RANGE: Widespread through B.C. except in shade or most arid regions.

BLUE JACOB'S LADDER
(*Polemonium humile*)

Blue Skunkleaf, Polemonium

The various names for this plant result from the ladder-like arrangement of the small leaves and their rather rank odor. Its tufted form with cheerful bright blue flowers looks like an escape from a rock garden. The flowers in clusters at the ends of the stem are in bloom during June and July.

RANGE: To 4000' in open forests east of the Cascades. Also in dry places along Kootenay Lake and vicinity of Cranbrook.

There are several different polemoniums in B.C. One has white flowers and another is from 1' - 2' high with erect, unbranched stems and showy blue flowers.

VERONICA
(*Veronica wormskjoldii*)
(*Veronica alpina*)

Alpine Speedwell

Although small in stature, the orderliness and brightness of this little flower draws one's attention to it. The small ovalish leaves are neatly arranged in several opposite pairs along the thin stem while the flowers and buds cluster at the very top. Often it will be found near blue Jacob's ladder and blooming at the same time.

The four blue symmetrical petals surround a round cream center. The flower is made quite distinctive by the anthers and style protruding beyond the petals.

RANGE: Vancouver Island and Coastal Zone; edges of Dry Interior and into North Central B.C.

SELF-HEAL
(Prunella vulgaris)
Heal-all

Self-heal may be found on dry soil along road edges or in moist shady places. The long heads of flowers vary in color from a light blue to a dark purple. Each flower is about ½″ long and quite attractive if examined as an individual. Watch for self-heal in bloom during the entire summer. Here is another plant with square stems. Leaves are thin, alternate and from 1″ - 2½″ long.
RANGE: West of Cascades and also through Okanagan Valley to Central B.C.

GENTIANS
(Gentiana spp.)

Gentians prefer shady glades or the most moist alplands for their shy appearance. There are a dozen or more species in B.C. all with opposite or whorled leaves and erect blue flowers balanced in an artistic symmetrical fashion.
LARGE GENTIAN (*G. affinis*) is from 5″ - 12″ high with inch-long flowers clustered along the tip. Cranbrook to the Rockies.
FOUR-PARTED GENTIAN (*G. propinqua*) has several flowers rising from the leaf axils. It is often branched from near the base. Distinguished by flower being divided into four notches at tip. Spotty occurrence on Vancouver Island and Coastal regions. Central and Northern B.C.
NORTHERN GENTIAN (*G. acuta*) has flowers in threes or more. The flower is divided into five notches at the tip. East of Cascades and northward through Central B.C.

BLUE VIOLET
(Viola adunca)

Violets, be they yellow, white or blue are recognized almost instantly by all. Unfortunately the wild violets do not have the fragrance of their cultivated relations. Being early bloomers of April and May they are discovered with the main display of spring flowers. In this species the long-stemmed leaves are roundish and heart shaped with shallow teeth. The color of the flowers ranges from pale to dark blue. Two of the petals which stick out from either side of the flower have fine hairs on them.
RANGE: Common throughout the Province.

BLUE SWAMP VIOLET (*V. palustris*) is one of the half dozen native species with bluish flowers. The flowers range from blue to almost white. They have little or no stem. The range is in mountain swamps throughout B.C.

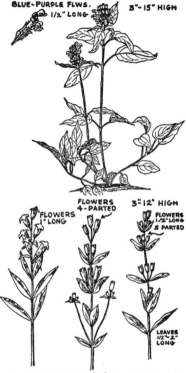

BLUE-PURPLE FLWS. ½″ LONG   3″-15″ HIGH

FLOWERS 4-PARTED   3″-12″ HIGH

FLOWERS 1″ LONG

FLOWERS ½″ LONG 5 PARTED

LEAVES ½″-2″ LONG

Large G.   Four-parted G.   Northern G.

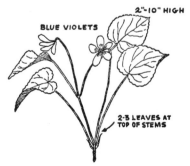

BLUE VIOLETS   2″-10″ HIGH

2-3 LEAVES AT TOP OF STEMS

(155)

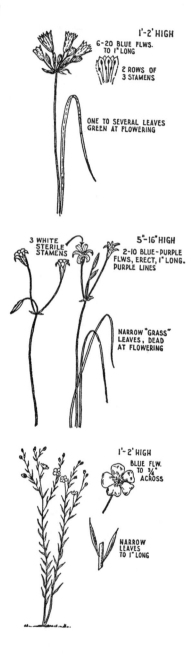

1'-2' HIGH
6-20 BLUE FLWS. TO 1" LONG

2 ROWS OF 3 STAMENS

ONE TO SEVERAL LEAVES GREEN AT FLOWERING

3 WHITE STERILE STAMENS

5"-16" HIGH
2-10 BLUE-PURPLE FLWS, ERECT, 1" LONG. PURPLE LINES

NARROW "GRASS" LEAVES, DEAD AT FLOWERING

1'-2' HIGH
BLUE FLW. TO ¾" ACROSS

NARROW LEAVES TO 1" LONG

LARGE-FLOWERED BRODIAEA
(Brodiaea grandiflora)

Other generic names used for the *Brodiaea* are *Hookera*, *Triteleia*, and *Hesperscordum*. Two common names are cluster lily and wild hyacinth. All brodiaea grow from small bulbs and most are an excellent food. Unbranched stems are topped by a radiating cluster of trumpet-like flowers with a line down each petal. Leaves are one to several, grass-like, and often withered away by the time the plant is in bloom.

Large-flowered brodiaea grows to 2' high and has green leaves in June at the same time as the flowers. The bright blue trumpets to 1" long form a cluster of from 6 - 20 flowers. The stamens are in 2 rows. Many species only have three stamens with the other three being reduced to white sterile filaments resembling petals.

RANGE: On V.I. southward from Cowichan Lake and usually under garry oak. Armstrong and Columbia River Valley south of Trail.

HARVEST BRODIAEA
(Brodiaea coronaria)

This beautiful flower is an indescribable color with vivid tones of blue, purple, and violet. The open trumpet is 1" long. The graceful petals are curved back and they and the long buds are veined with a distinctive purple line down the center. The three sterile stamens resemble three small white petals.

Often this plant is under a foot high and the very narrow leaves have withered by the time the flowers appear. The small bulbs, deeply buried, are very nutritious and were dug by the Indians.

RANGE: On dry exposed situations along the seacoast. V.I. and the Mainland.

WILD FLAX
(Linum lewisii)

A person may encounter this plant over a rather large range and never see it elsewhere.

Its saucer-like flowers of brightest blue are bound to arouse a desire to know more about it. These are carried on thin stems near the top of a single slender plant to 2' high or one branched near ground level. Each sky-blue bloom is about ¾" across and has its flower parts in fives. June to August is blooming time. Seed heads form brownish balls almost ¼" across.

The leaves are neatly staggered in alternate fashion and seldom are over 1" long. Linen thread has been made from the fibrous stems of the flax family since time immemorial.

RANGE: East of Cascades. Spotty occurrence in Dry Interior. More common in Cariboo, Chilcotin, Windermere Valley and Rockies.

MOUNTAIN PHACELIA
(Phacelia sericea)

Silky Phacelia

Mountain phacelia with its beautiful spikes of fuzzy violet flowers is in sharp contrast to the pure bright colors of most alpine blooms. The fuzzy appearance comes from long protruding stamens with a yellow dot at their tip. The long stamens are a characteristic of the phacelias as is the disagreeable odor or absence of smell.

Mountain phacelia forms a profusion of flower stems. Its leaves are so silky with fine hair as to appear silvery on occasion. The blooming time is late summer.

RANGE: Dry rocky places above timberline across B.C.

ONE-FLOWERED CANCER ROOT
(Orobanche uniflora)

Naked Broom-rape

Plant parasitics have no green leaves for nourishment is obtained by feeding on the roots of other plants. Flowers range in color from yellowish-brown to purplish tints and scales on the lower stem are general.

This oddity has thin stems, naked except for several scales, and a purplish flower resembling a penstemon with two upper flower lobes and three lower ones. The flower is about ¾" long and has a faint fragrance. On occasion the bloom may be yellowish. Watch for it in April and May in open forests at low elevations.

RANGE: Moist grassy places from V.I. to the Rockies. Not in dry regions.

CLUSTERED BROOM-RAPE (*O. fasciculata*) is often parasitic on such dry land species as sagebrush and eriogonums. The short visible section of stem is very scaly as well as coarsely hairy and glandular. The typical flower from ½" - ¾" long has two broad upper lobes and is 3-lobed below. Although usually purple-tinged it may be yellowish in color. May and June are the months it blooms. Dry sandy soils mostly east of the Cascades. Savary Island, Dry Interior Zone, Chase, Chilcotin, Pouce Coupe.

BUNCHED BROOM-RAPE (*O. grayana*) has a dense cluster of purple flowers each about ¾" long and with long, thin sepals. Blooming time is from June to September. Exposed bluffs from Cowichan Bay south and Gulf Islands.

GROUND-CONE (*Boschniakia strobiliacea*) is parasitic on salal. Flowers ½" - ¾" long poke out between the upper leaves. The upper lip is undivided but the lower is broken into three hairy lobes. Indians ate this plant. Lower elevations west of the Cascades.

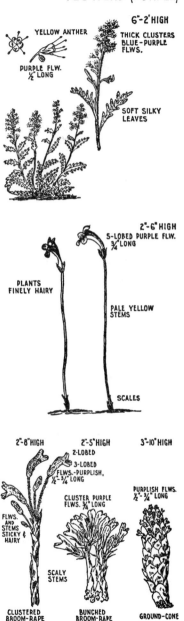

6"-2' HIGH

YELLOW ANTHER

THICK CLUSTERS BLUE-PURPLE FLWS.

PURPLE FLW. ½" LONG

SOFT SILKY LEAVES

2"-6" HIGH
S-LOBED PURPLE FLW.
¾" LONG

PLANTS FINELY HAIRY

PALE YELLOW STEMS

SCALES

2"-8" HIGH

2"-5" HIGH
2-LOBED
3-LOBED
FLWS.-PURPLISH,
½"-¾" LONG

3"-10" HIGH
PURPLISH FLWS.
½"-¾" LONG

CLUSTER PURPLE FLWS. ¾" LONG

FLWS. AND STEMS STICKY & HAIRY

SCALY STEMS

CLUSTERED BROOM-RAPE

BUNCHED BROOM-RAPE

GROUND-CONE

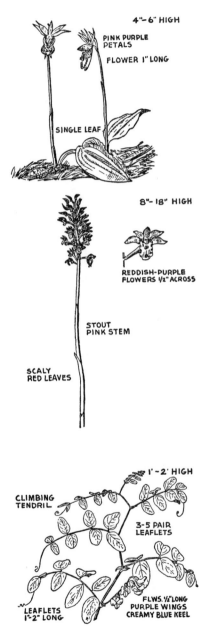

4"- 6" HIGH

PINK PURPLE PETALS

FLOWER 1" LONG

SINGLE LEAF

8"- 18" HIGH

REDDISH-PURPLE FLOWERS ½" ACROSS

STOUT PINK STEM

SCALY RED LEAVES

1' - 2' HIGH

CLIMBING TENDRIL

3-5 PAIR LEAFLETS

LEAFLETS 1"-2" LONG

FLWS. ½" LONG PURPLE WINGS CREAMY BLUE KEEL

FALSE LADY'S SLIPPER
(Calypso bulbosa)

Calypso - Lady's Slipper

Once the delicately tinted jewel has been found in the quiet seclusion of the mossy forest floor its beauty can hardly be forgotten for here is one of Nature's treasures in miniature. The little white bulb is deeply cradled in a protective layer of moss and needles. Only one shiny green leaf grows at the base of the reddish stem.

The colorful little orchid blooms during April to June.

RANGE: Throughout B.C. in shady coniferous forests up to elevations of 4500'.

CORAL ROOT
(Corallorhiza spp.)

Coral root is named from its mass of gnarled, knobby roots which resemble a piece of coral. The plant is parasitic and therefore can do without leaves except for small scales. There are several species in B.C. all having single stout stems clustered with small orchid-like flowers. Several have a white lip and others are colored either purple or brown. One has its blossoms handsomely striped while yet another produces pure yellow flowers.

Coral roots usually are found in fairly open and dry forests. They bloom during May and June but often the dead stalks are noticeable for months.

RANGE: Different species in various parts of B.C.

PURPLE PEA
(Lathyrus nevadensis)

The peas and vetches *(Vicia spp.)* are similar in appearance and mixed with many introduced species. Both have thin weak stems which are held up by twining tendrils. The leaves are formed of from 3 - 5 pairs of opposite leaflets. The "sweet pea" flowers provide the most easily recognized feature. Most of the vetches have smaller flowers and leaves than the peas.

Purple pea is a common plant particularly in moist Coast forests. Its string of purple blossoms with their bluish keels are almost hidden in the salal or other supporting shrubs. They are in bloom May and June.

RANGE: Damp shady woods of the Coastal regions also the Central Interior.

YELLOW PEA (*L. ochroleucus*) is recognized by its creamy yellow flowers about ½" long. There are 3 or 4 pairs of leaflets, 1" - 2" long. The range is in brushy places at low elevations from the Dry Interior through Central B.C.

COLTSFOOT
(Petasites speciosa)

Butterbur

Coltsfoot is among the earliest of the spring flowers and may be seen from March onwards. The first flowers are often in advance of the leaves thus leading to some confusion in linking the two at a later date. The purplish-white, sweet-scented flowers are in a soft loose head at the top of a thick stem 8" - 16" high. These turn into seeds without visible change in color or shape.

The leaves are up to a foot across and white woolly beneath. Each leaf has from 7 - 9 toothed lobes which are often split again.

RANGE: Damp ground on Vancouver Island and Coastal Forests; edges of the Dry Interior and in the Selkirks.

ALPINE COLTSFOOT (*P. frigida*) grows to 1' high and has kidney-shaped leaves to 4" long. Alpine meadows, Coast to the Rockies.

HEDGE NETTLE
(Stachys cooleyae) (S. ciliata)

This is a coarse weedy plant forming extensive masses of green until the red-purple flowers dress it in gay color. The flowers are trumpet-like with a protruding lower lip and form in whorls of about 6 at the top of the stems. During June hedge nettle is in bloom. The leaves suggest wild mint but they have a rank smell and are finely hairy. Main stems are square which may come as a shock to most people who believe all flower stems are round.

RANGE: At lower elevations in damp ground west of the Cascade Mountains. Prince Rupert.
S. palustris is less than 2' high and has light purple flowers. Wet ground east of the Cascade Mountains and north to Fort St. John.

CANADA MINT
(Mentha arvensis)

Wild Mint

There is only one native mint in B.C. but several escapes have established themselves around Vancouver and Victoria. Mint will be found around the edges of damp places and might often pass unnoticed except for the clean, spicy smell when it is stepped on. The flowers are an unobtrusive purple to pink color and form in balls between the opposite leaves. They are in bloom from July to August. The leafy plant grows erect with stout squarish stems which may be quite hairy on the upper sections.

RANGE: Throughout B.C.

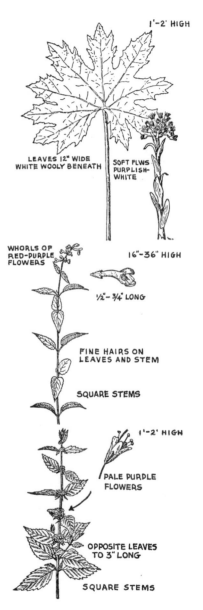

FLOWERS (PURPLE)

1'-2' HIGH

LEAVES 12" WIDE
WHITE WOOLY BENEATH

SOFT FLWS
PURPLISH-
WHITE

WHORLS OF
RED-PURPLE
FLOWERS

16"-36" HIGH

½"-¾" LONG

FINE HAIRS ON
LEAVES AND STEM

SQUARE STEMS

1'-2' HIGH

PALE PURPLE
FLOWERS

OPPOSITE LEAVES
TO 3" LONG

SQUARE STEMS

FLOWERS (PURPLE)

3"-16" HIGH

PURPLE FLOWERS 1 1/2" LONG

EVERGREEN

LEAVES 1/2"-2" LONG

LEAVES 1/4"-3/4" SOMETIMES TOOTHED

P. scouleri　　*P. menziesii*

BLUE-PURPLE TRUMPETS

8"-12" HIGH

FLWS. 1/2"-3/4" LONG

PENSTEMON
(Penstemon spp.)

Beard Tongue

At the Coast this beautiful plant chooses rocky bluffs and slides but in the higher mountains it is fairly common on gravel or sandy soils.

Of the dozen or more species in B.C. less than half that number are commonly recognized. Two forms, *P. scouleri* and *P. menziesii* often are classed as shrubs · because of their woody stems and evergreen leaves. All have a 5-lobed calyx, a funnel-like flower with two lips, the upper having 2 lobes and the lower 3. There are 5 stamens but only 4 anthers leaving one sterile. In some species the throat or tongue is very hairy.

MENZIES PENSTEMON (*P. davidsonii var. menziesii*) is a shrubby plant with thick, evergreen, ovalish leaves less than 1" in length. The throat or tongue of the flower is bristly with hairs. Open places in the high slopes of Coast and Cascade Mountains. Blooming during July and August.

SCOULERS PENSTEMON (*P. fruticosis var. scouleri*) is very similar to the above except for its narrow, serrated leaves. The range is east of the Cascades to the Rockies. Masses of bloom on rocky cliffs during May are likely to be this penstemon.

LITTLE FLOWER PENSTEMON (*P. procerus*) hasn't the mat-like effect of the above two species but grows upright to 12" high. The flowers are a dark blue and about 1/2" long. They grow in thick clusters from the topmost leaf axils and are out in early and mid-summer depending on the elevation. The range is east of the Cascades and north to North Central B.C.
(P. tolmie) is often given for this species or one very similar. For other penstemons see page 162.

SILKY WHITE HEAD　**8"-18" HIGH**

LAVENDER FLWS 1 1/2" ACROSS

YELLOW CENTER

SILKY, GREY LEAVES

PASQUE FLOWER
(Anemone patens)

This bright showy anemone is a stranger to people at the Coast but a popular harbinger of spring in the Kootenays and Cranbrook area. Here in April and May it grows abundantly and brings blushes of violet or lavender-white to the nooks and hollows. Six or seven large sepals radiating from a golden center form a cup-shaped blossom often 2" across. The short stems are covered with long silky hairs. Stems and leaves eventually push up to 1 1/2' in height. A silky seed head is produced to be blown away by fall winds.
RANGE: Creston-Cranbrook region also Windermere Valley, Fernie to Crowsnest Pass.

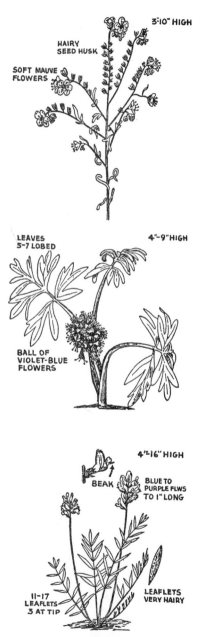

PHACELIA
(*Phacelia linearis*)

This pretty little wildflower is fairly common in arid waste places such as road edges. Sometimes there is a single main stem but more often a few short branches. As the branchlets extend, new flowers grow at the tip and the seeds of former blooms stand as husks along the twigs. The soft mauve or lavender color is one not often duplicated. A few thin twisting leaves adorn the higher stems but 3-lobed leaves are general on the lower branches... The blooming period is from May 15 - June 15.

RANGE: Dry Interior at lower elevations. Fraser Canyon to Yale. Vernon, Penticton, Cariboo and Gulf Island Zone, Kootenay Lake, Creston.

BALLHEAD WATERLEAF
(*Hydrophyllum capitatum*)

Like other wild flowers such as peacocks, yellow bells and buttercups, it blooms in early spring while the ground is still moist. The leaves are divided into 5 - 7 lobes, each of which may be further lobed. When young, these succulent "waterleaves" make excellent greens. The flowers mass in an appealing ball of violet blue made misty by a large number of protruding stamens.

RANGE: Dry Interior Zone, Princeton, Kamloops, Kootenays, and at high elevations between Grand Forks and Rossland. Mountains of Manning Park.

LOCOWEED
(*Oxytropis campestris*)

Crazyweed

The locoweeds are very similar to the milk vetches (*Astragalus spp.*) but the flowers have a sharp beak. There are at least 6 in B.C. and all range east of the Cascades. Some are poisonous and cause locism in grazing animals. The poison acts like a narcotic and once the animals get a craving for the weed they will search it out.

The plants form a tuft or clump and all have fine silky hairs on the leaflets. These may number from 11 - 29 depending on the species. The roots are heavy and penetrate deep in the soil in order that the locoweed can exist in the most exposed places. One variety is silvery white in color from the mat of hairs on the leaves. The purple flowers are carried in a spike. There are from 5 - 8 pairs of leaflets with an odd one at the top.

RANGE: Dry places at lower elevations from east of the Cascades to the Rockies.

One variety has 17 - 29 leaflets and yellow flowers. It is common on dry open places east of the Cascades.

FLOWERS (PURPLE)

3"-10" HIGH

HAIRY SEED HUSK

SOFT MAUVE FLOWERS

LEAVES 5-7 LOBED

4"-9" HIGH

BALL OF VIOLET-BLUE FLOWERS

4"-16" HIGH

BEAK

BLUE TO PURPLE FLWS TO 1" LONG

11-17 LEAFLETS 3 AT TIP

LEAFLETS VERY HAIRY

FLOWERS (PURPLE)

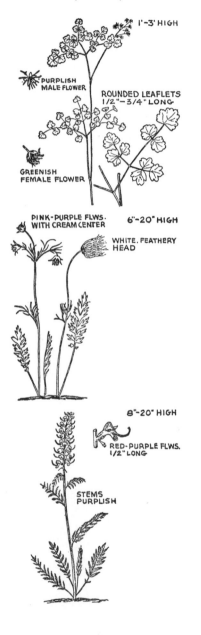

1'-3' HIGH

PURPLISH MALE FLOWER

ROUNDED LEAFLETS 1/2"-3/4" LONG

GREENISH FEMALE FLOWER

PINK-PURPLE FLWS. WITH CREAM CENTER

6"-20" HIGH

WHITE, FEATHERY HEAD

8"-20" HIGH

RED-PURPLE FLWS. 1/2" LONG

STEMS PURPLISH

MEADOW RUE
(Thalictrum occidentale)

The very delicacy of meadow rue will catch the attention for in shape it is a graceful airy mass of small, 3-lobed leaves each with a thread-like stem. Look closely and you may see tiny upright purple flowers on one plant and drooping green and purple filmy clusters on another. This results from there being female and male flowers on different plants. The male flowers are particularly delicate and attractive with their tassel of silky purple stamens.

Almost everywhere one finds Indian paintbrush growing there will be meadow rue. Shady, fairly moist places at middle elevations are preferred.
RANGE: Throughout B.C.

LONG-PLUMED PURPLE AVENS
(Geum triflorum)

Although not a particularly common wildflower the long-plumed purple avens is distinctive enough to command attention. It is a plant of open slopes at low and middle elevations where it may be found with such companions as lupine and sticky geranium.

The purplish stems bear three peculiar flowers. These appear purple from the long conspicuous sepals which flank the cream-colored petals. After blooming in late May or June the flower turns into a white-plumed seed head very like that of the western anemone and pasque flower.

The leaves grow in a tuft from the base of the stem and are deeply and finely lobed.
RANGE: Scattered throughout the Dry Interior regions across the Province. Also in the Cariboo and Peace River regions.

ELEPHANT HEAD
(Pedicularis groenlandica)

This plant will be recognized as one of the louseworts or *Pedicularis spp.* which have tightly packed flowers clustered on a spike and a curved bill to each flower. See page 141.

It grows in moist mountain meadows where it may reach 2' in height. The little elephant head flowers with upthrown trunk won't be forgotten once seen or mistaken for anything else. Their color is purple to red and, like most mountain flowers, they will be in bloom during July or August. The fringed leaves mostly occur near the base of the plant.
RANGE: Moist places near timberline on Vancouver Island, Coastal Mountains and through Central Interior and northward.

(162)

MILKWEED
(*Asclepias speciosa*)

These heavy looking plants form stout clusters 2' - 4' high along roadsides and fields. The thick fleshy leaves may be to 6" long. The smallest nick in the finely hairy leaves or stem releases a thick milky fluid which protects the nectar of the flowers from climbing insects with sharp claws.

The purplish flowers bunch together in a knobby head several inches across. Each flower is a complicated structure with 5 purple petals and 5 curved horns protruding from the central stamen tube. July and August are the usual blooming months. In the fall, long seed pods split open to release thousands of silky parachutes.

RANGE: Throughout the driest parts of the Province. Oliver, Ashcroft.

STICKY GERANIUM
(*Geranium viscosissimum*)

Cranesbill

Sticky geranium's coarse appearance comes from a branching of stout stems and lobed leaves all covered with sticky hairs. The most attractive feature is the rose-purple flowers from 1" - 1½" across. Each petal is finely veined. The blooming period is from late May to July.

RANGE: Open forests and aspen glades throughout the Dry Interior Zone including the Cranbrook region. Cariboo Parkland Zone.

WHITE GERANIUM (*G. richardsonii*) has thinner leaves and white flowers with pink veins. Moist locations. Rockies, Queen Charlotte Islands, Cariboo Parklands and Central B.C.

FIREWEED
(*Epilobium angustifolium*)

Its usual height, of from 3' - 5' raises it above most of the ground vegetation. The long, lance-shaped leaves are up to 8" long. Large, pink-purple flowers are strewn abundantly along the slight branchlets and keep fireweed in the picture for several summer months. The flowers develop seed pods which split open and disgorge hundreds of fluffy, white seeds. Fireweed is especially abundant on old burns and clearings as pioneer growth. Fireweed honey rates high with bee keepers.

RANGE: Throughout B.C.

ALPINE FIREWEED (*E. alpinum*) is a low shrubby plant to 16" high growing along mountain streams. The flowers are a beautiful mauve color. It ranges across B.C. and into the far north.

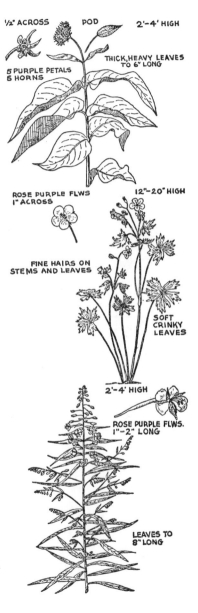

½" ACROSS   POD   2'-4' HIGH

THICK, HEAVY LEAVES TO 6" LONG

5 PURPLE PETALS
5 HORNS

ROSE PURPLE FLWS
1" ACROSS   12"-20" HIGH

FINE HAIRS ON
STEMS AND LEAVES

SOFT
CRINKY
LEAVES

2'-4' HIGH

ROSE PURPLE FLWS.
1"-2" LONG

LEAVES TO
8" LONG

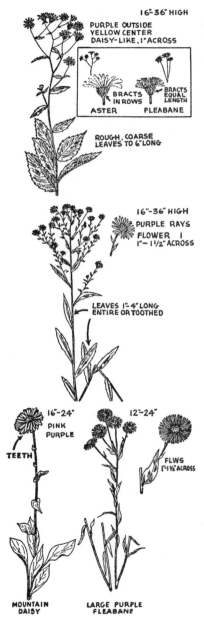

16"-36" HIGH

PURPLE OUTSIDE
YELLOW CENTER
DAISY-LIKE, 1" ACROSS

BRACTS
IN ROWS

BRACTS
EQUAL
LENGTH

ASTER

FLEABANE

ROUGH, COARSE
LEAVES TO 6" LONG

16"-36" HIGH

PURPLE RAYS
FLOWER 1
1"-1½" ACROSS

LEAVES 1"-4" LONG
ENTIRE OR TOOTHED

16"-24"
PINK
PURPLE

TEETH

12"-24"

FLWS
1"-1½" ACROSS

MOUNTAIN
DAISY

LARGE PURPLE
FLEABANE

LARGE PURPLE ASTER
(Aster conspicuus)

This aster is only one of about 30 in B.C. which, as a group, may be confused with fleabanes. Very widespread from valley bottom to middle mountain elevations. It grows to 2' high on gravelly soils in fairly open forests. Often it is quite ragged in shape. The flowers in the wide-spreading head are exceptionally colorful with their golden centers and purple petals. Since spring and early summer flowers are over by July, this plant captures its share of attention for the remainder of the summer.
RANGE: East of Cascade Mountains in drier areas to North Central B.C.

DOUGLAS ASTER
(Aster subspicatus)
(Aster douglasii)

There are over two dozen species of asters in the Province and few people will profess to tell many apart. The Douglas aster is representative of several widespread species on the Coast and in the Interior which have showy heads of many bright purple flowers. Usually the stout stems are branched a number of times leading to a rounded outline. The coarse leaves haven't stems and may or may not be toothed. This aster or similar species grows on a well drained soil such as found under open fir forests or along roadsides. It blooms during August and September.
RANGE: West of Cascades and Central B.C.

LARGE PURPLE FLEABANE
(Erigeron speciosus)

The difference between fleabanes and asters is shown above. The unusual name fleabane comes about from the belief that these plants would repel fleas.

During the summer months this showy "Michaelmas daisy" often reaches 2' in height and is rather bushy from long thin leaves reaching almost to the top. Lower leaves have stems but the upper have not. The flowers are massed in loose clusters with each yellow center surrounded by nearly a hundred thin purple ray-petals. Under favourable conditions the flower may be 2" across but more often it is slightly over 1". The blooming season is rather prolonged from late May to September.
RANGE: Common east of Cascades.

MOUNTAIN DAISY (*E. peregrinus*) is a handsome plant common in high mountains and alpine meadows. Its pink-purple petals are wide like an aster and are toothed at the tip. Generally one flower to the stem. Across B.C. and into northern regions. Peace River.

COMMON THISTLE
(Cirsium lanceolatum)

Pasture Thistle - Bull Thistle

There are over a half-dozen species, about half of them being introduced from Europe. Most have reddish or purplish flowers except the white thistle *(C. hookerianum)*. The single purple blossoms on their bristly green bur may be 2" across. Blooming time is July and August.

RANGE: Vancouver Island and Coastal region, spreading into the Interior.

CANADA THISTLE *(C. arvensis)* doesn't have the stiff spiny leaves of the above nor as bright a flower. The pale purple flowers grow in flat-topped clusters. This is an introduced plant now found at the Coast and in the Interior.

INDIAN THISTLE
(Cirsium edule)

Edible Thistle

The "ball" part of the flowers is a white woolly mass with many spines thus forming attractive pedestals for the several rose-purple blooms.

The thick stem 2'-5' high carries leaves to 10" long. These are very ragged and often those near the top are twice-lobed. Thin spines provide armament. The plump roots are about 1' long and can be boiled and eaten. The blooming period is from late spring to late summer.

RANGE: Low to high elevation mostly west of the Cascades. An attractive plant of alpine meadows. Garibaldi and Manning Parks. Okanagan.

WOOLLY THISTLE *(C. undulatum)* has an overall silvery white color of leaves and stems and a beautiful display of rose to lavender flower heads. Older plants branch freely and carry single flowers at the tip of each branch. Leaves are to 8" long, deeply cut, and protected by long yellowish spines. Poor dry soils east of Cascades, Similkameen and Okanagan Valleys.

BURDOCK
(Arctium spp.)

Dock

Its exceptionally large leaves and spiny burs arouse one's curiosity. The thick stem is much branched and the leaves are about the size of rhubarb but woolly on the underside. Purplish-tinged flowers are covered with rough, hooked bristles. By fall the sturdy plant is well covered near its top by hard round burs which cling tenaciously to clothing or animal hair.

Common burdock *(A. minus)* is most likely to be found at the Coast while Great burdock *(A. lappa)* is less plentiful and more characteristic east of the Cascades.

RANGE: Lower elevations throughout B.C.

FLOWERS (PURPLE)

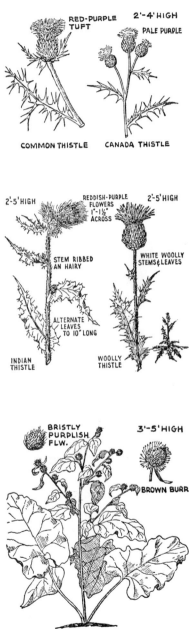

RED-PURPLE TUFT

2'-4' HIGH

PALE PURPLE

COMMON THISTLE   CANADA THISTLE

2'-5' HIGH

REDDISH-PURPLE FLOWERS 1"-1½" ACROSS

2'-5' HIGH

STEM RIBBED AN HAIRY

WHITE WOOLLY STEMS & LEAVES

ALTERNATE LEAVES TO 10" LONG

INDIAN THISTLE

WOOLLY THISTLE

BRISTLY PURPLISH FLW.

3'-5' HIGH

BROWN BURR

FLOWERS (PURPLE)

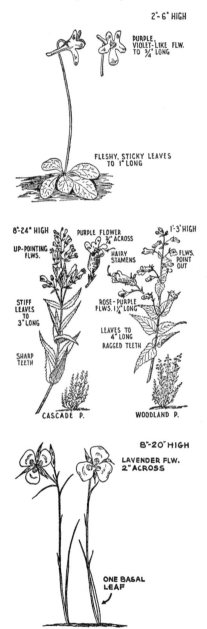

2"-6" HIGH

PURPLE, VIOLET-LIKE FLW. TO ¾" LONG

FLESHY, STICKY LEAVES TO 1" LONG

8"-24" HIGH

PURPLE FLOWER ¾" ACROSS

UP-POINTING FLWS.

HAIRY STAMENS

1'-3' HIGH

FLWS. POINT OUT

STIFF LEAVES TO 3" LONG

ROSE-PURPLE FLWS. 1¼" LONG

LEAVES TO 4" LONG RAGGED TEETH

SHARP TEETH

CASCADE P.

WOODLAND P.

8"-20" HIGH

LAVENDER FLW. 2" ACROSS

ONE BASAL LEAF

COMMON BUTTERWORT
(*Pinguicula vulgaris*)

This charming little flower 2"-6" high might pass for a violet by reason of its single rich purple, violet-like flower. The leaves to 1" long are yellowish green and form a low rosette around the stem. They are fleshy and sticky and flies caught on them are digested to help feed this most unusual plant. Like another insect-feeding flower, the sundew, the edges of bogs or wet rocky places are preferred.

The pretty bloom is strongly 2-lipped, the 3-lobed lower one much exceeding the 2-lobed upper. A bold spur provides suitable balance.

RANGE: Relatively high elevations on V.I. and Coastal mountains. Valleys in Northern B.C.

CASCADE PENSTEMON
(*Penstemon serrulatus*)
(*Penstemon diffusus*)

Spreading Penstemon

This is a showy plant with its bright head of purplish-blue trumpets. Often it forms a cluster of erect stems but sometimes it is branching and almost mat-like. The leaves are stiff, sharp-toothed, and quite attractive.

The typical penstemon flower with its 2-lobed upper lip and 3-lobed lower, is a lovely purplish-blue and over an inch long. It is particularly full-throated giving a wide face and blooms all summer.

RANGE: Generally west of the Cascade Mountains at low to medium elevations.

WOODLAND PENSTEMON (*P. nemorosus*) has one or several erect stems. Leaves are large and coarsely toothed. Flowers are ridged and rose-purple with hairy stamens. Blooms June to August on some mountains of V.I. Port Alberni.

GREEN-BANDED MARIPOSA LILY
(*Calochortus macrocarpus*)

The simplicity of this beautiful flower imparts an air of rarity that is further enhanced by its random appearance in drab range land. The stout stem carries one or more pale purple or lavender blooms often 2" across. The three large petals are marked on the inside with dark blotches near their base and a green band down their centre. One thin leaf grows from the base of the stem. The mariposa lily is seldom found in any quantity and often escapes notice because of its delicate shading. It will be found in bloom during late May and into June.

RANGE: Lower slopes of the Dry Interior Zone. Penticton to Kamloops, Clinton, Phoenix.

YOUTH-ON-AGE
(Tolmiea menziesii)

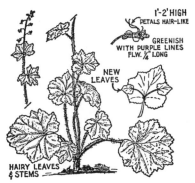

1'-2' HIGH
PETALS HAIR-LIKE
GREENISH WITH PURPLE LINES
FLW. ¼" LONG
NEW LEAVES
HAIRY LEAVES & STEMS

Despite the intriguing name most persons pass up this plant because of its inconspicuous flowers. But examine the leaves in the late summer and you will see that the reason for the odd name is because small leave are growing from the base of the old leaf blades. As the old leaves wither they slowly drop to the ground, giving the new leaves a chance to root.

Youth-on-age may reach 2' in height and from April to June carry a flower stem adorned by small yet odd-looking flowers. These are greenish streaked with purple and with petals reduced to 4 thread-like projections. Leaves are lobed and round-toothed with a fine covering of white hairs.

RANGE: Common plant of Douglas fir forests west of Cascades.

WESTERN STENANTHIUM
(Stenanthium occidentale)

Bronze Bells

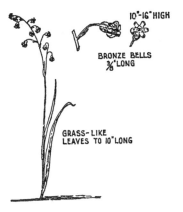

10"-16" HIGH
BRONZE BELLS ⅜" LONG
GRASS-LIKE LEAVES TO 10" LONG

Fortunately this shy plant is easily distinguished in the lush growth along shady mountain creeks. Its lily family characteristics are shown by a root bulb and the grass-like leaves. These arise from near the stem and are up to 10" long.

The drooping flowers are aptly called bronze bells for they take their unusual color from a greenish background streaked through with purple. Notice that the flower parts are in sixes and how the stamens form a cluster of tiny golden dots in the throat. The flowers have an elusive tangy perfume. The blooming time is from April to August depending on exposure and elevation.

RANGE: Middle mountain to alpine heights. East slopes of Cascade Mountains to Rockies.

WILD GINGER
(Asarum caudatum)

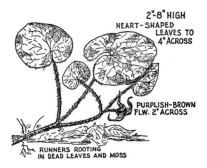

2"-8" HIGH
HEART-SHAPED LEAVES TO 4" ACROSS
PURPLISH-BROWN FLW. 2" ACROSS
RUNNERS ROOTING IN DEAD LEAVES AND MOSS

Because this plant has very inconspicuous flowers and low leaves, the beginner seldom notices it.

The large heart-shaped leaves generally occur in extensive patches from the creeping habit. Two leaves arise from every node and may be to 6" long and 3" across. Fine hairs cover the stem and veins and lower margin of the leaf.

The curious flower, purplish-brown, and growing singly, hugs the ground closely and remains unseen unless searched out. It is bell-like with 3 wide-spreading lobes. The whole plant has a faint ginger smell most pronounced when a root is crushed.

RANGE: In Coastal regions from rich bottom-lands to 3,500' elevation. Eastward it is found in damp places and beside creeks. Southern portion of B.C. from V.I. to Kootenays.

FLOWERS (BROWN-GREEN)

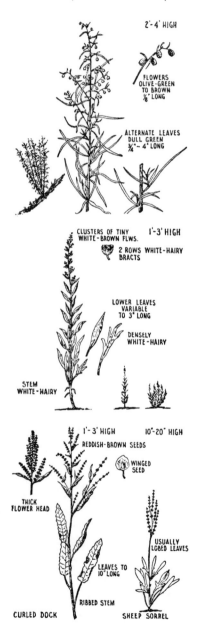

2'-4' HIGH

FLOWERS
OLIVE-GREEN
TO BROWN
⅛" LONG

ALTERNATE LEAVES
DULL GREEN
¾"- 4" LONG

CLUSTERS OF TINY
WHITE-BROWN FLWS.   1'-3' HIGH

2 ROWS WHITE-HAIRY
BRACTS

LOWER LEAVES
VARIABLE
TO 3" LONG

DENSELY
WHITE-HAIRY

STEM
WHITE-HAIRY

1'-3' HIGH   10"-20" HIGH
REDDISH-BROWN SEEDS

WINGED
SEED

THICK
FLOWER HEAD

USUALLY
LOBED LEAVES

LEAVES TO
10" LONG

RIBBED STEM

CURLED DOCK   SHEEP SORREL

DRAGON SAGEWORT
(*Artemisia dracunculus*)

False Tarragon

This coarse weedy plant has a wide occurrence in the Dry Interior.

Dry gravelly banks or road slopes are favored localities. A dozen or so thick woody stems form a 3' high spray of narrow dull-green leaves. These are alternate and up to 3" long. Occasionally some of the lower leaves are deeply 3-lobed.

The tiny olive-green or brownish flowers are less than ⅛" long and carried during late summer months on thin stems near the top.

RANGE: Common in the Dry Interior Region. Similkameen, Okanagan and Thompson River Valleys. Cranbrook, Fairmont, Chilcotin.

CUDWEED SAGEWORT
(*Artemisia ludoviciana*)

Mugwort

Two characteristics of this range plant warrant its inclusion. One is the slight resemblance to sagebrush through the shape of the leaves and their aromatic sage smell and the other is the overall silvery color. Cudweed sagewort is found on dry soils usually fully exposed to the sun.

Unlike sagebrush with its twisted stems, this plant grows erect from 1'-3' high. Often it consists of one stem but on occasion it branches freely.

Leaves are up to 3" long and have a silvery sheen from a dense mat of soft white hairs on both sides. Most are entire but lower ones may be lobed. Flowers form in August in dense clusters.

RANGE: Dry regions east of Cascade Mountains. Nicola and Okanagan Valley. Cranbrook.

CURLED DOCK
(*Rumex crispus*)

The numerous docks or sorrels have a weedy appearance and are recognized by their coarse-ribbed stems, and particularly by the spaced clusters of small russet flowers or winged seeds, which in some species measure ¼" across. Foliage and seeds have a sharp acid taste.

Curled dock grows to 3' high and is named from the tendency of the leaves to curl along the edges. Some leaves are without teeth and others have a finely waved margin. The flower head may be open or in a dense cluster. Blooming time is from June to August.

RANGE: Low to middle elevations mostly west of the Cascades.

SHEEP SORREL (*R. acetosella*) usually less than a foot high, carries very small reddish flowers and seeds. 'Long-stemmed leaves to 3" long may be entire or lobed. Poor, exposed soils V.I. to Okanagan.

STINGING NETTLE
(Urtica lyallii)

The chances are that a person will first discover stinging nettle the hard way for there is little to tell of its presence in the thickets. After a few encounters one watches for the rather ragged opposite leaves and the inconspicuous drooping clusters of greenish or whitish flowers. The coarsely toothed leaves are covered with fine stinging hairs which cause a severe irritation lasting for several days. Often great masses of it grow together making it almost impossible to pass through. Young nettle makes excellent greens and Indians used it in weaving cord. Some European species produce an excellent fibre equal to the best linen.

RANGE: Across the Province and into North Central B.C. in shady places.

SARSAPARILLA
(Aralia nudicaulis)

Sarsaparilla shows little variety in form being a short stem branching into three arms each carrying from 3 - 5 oval leaflets 2" - 4" long. The flower stalk is shorter than the leaf stem and so the umbrella cluster of tiny white-green flowers is generally hidden from sight. Plump, ribbed, green or brown unedible seeds are formed later.

The root has medicinal properties similar to the true sarsaparilla which is a tropical plant.

RANGE: Semi open and open forests in medium climates. Edges of Dry Interior Zone. North Central B.C. Fraser Canyon, Quesnel, Nelson.

CHOCOLATE LILY
(Fritillaria lanceolata)

Rice Root

This peculiar dark brown and green flower hardly seems real when compared with the usual bright-colored flowers of springtime. Because of its dull tones it can be missed among the grass or low brush where it grows. The cup-like flower, about 1" across, hangs down and has 6 mottled petals. The narrow-pointed leaves form whorls about the stem. The alternate name rice root comes from the appearance of the large white bulb covered with nodules resembling rice. The bulbs are edible and taste somewhat like rice when cooked.

RANGE: Vancouver Island, lower elevations of Coastal Mountains, edges of Dry Interior.

F. kamtschatcensis is a sturdier species with broader leaves than the above. The flower is not so mottled and a cluster of them is not common. Its range is west of the Cascade Mountains and in Central B.C.

FLOWERS (BROWN-GREEN)

2'-4' HIGH

SMALL GREENISH FLOWERS

LEAVES TO 4" LONG

RIBBED STEMS WITH FINE SPINES

8"-16" HIGH

GREENISH-WHITE FLOWERS

3-5 LEAFLETS ON EACH OF 3 STEMS

MOTTLED BROWN, GREEN FLOWERS

1'-2' HIGH

WHORLS OF LEAVES

F. lanceolata *F. kam--*

RICE LIKE GRAINS

(169)

FLOWERS (GREEN)

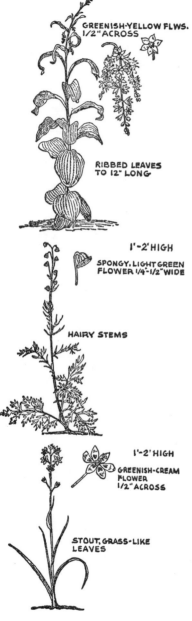

GREENISH-YELLOW FLWS. 1/2" ACROSS

RIBBED LEAVES TO 12" LONG

1'-2' HIGH

SPONGY, LIGHT GREEN FLOWER 1/4"-1/2" WIDE

HAIRY STEMS

1'-2' HIGH

GREENISH-CREAM FLOWER 1/2" ACROSS

STOUT, GRASS-LIKE LEAVES

INDIAN HELLEBORE
(*Veratrum eschocholtzii*)
(*Veratrum viride*)

Green Hellebore - False Hellebore

This is a tall rank plant with large plaited and heavily ribbed leaves. The exotic appearance would be more in place in the tropics than the mountain swales and meadows it prefers. The large size of from 3' - 5' brings it to attention sooner or later. Having a wide tolerance, Indian hellebore is found in shady moist forests near sea level and from there up to alpine meadows. This gives it a varied blooming period from May to August.

The flowers are an unusual inconspicuous color and size for so dramatic a plant. They form in thin branching spikes and are small and yellowish-green, a color that gives little or no contrast with their surroundings.

The roots contain a powerful poison which is used in medicine as well as for an insect poison.

RANGE: Moist mountains throughout B.C.

LONGSTEM GREENCAPS
(*Artemisia norvegica*)

For lack of a common name the above has been given. Like most of the *Artemisias* (sagebrushes) it hasn't a bright or large flower but there is little else to connect it with this plant group.

However in its range it is a common plant and not unattractive in late summer with the fringed leaves and hanging caps formed of minute spongy green flowers. Each round cap is from 1/4" - 1/2" wide and carried on a long stem.

RANGE: Sub-alpine slopes from Coast to Rockies. Abundant in central and northern Rockies.

GREEN LILY
(*Zigadenus elegans*)

Mountain Deathcamas - Wand Lily

The green lily produces such fascinating greenish-white flowers that it may be sure of receiving notice. These are carried on a spike and present a charming sight with their symmetrical arrangement of 6 waxy petals each decorated with a green or yellow spot near its base.

The plant grows from large bulbs and puts up a cluster of heavy grassy leaves. Most leaves spring from the base but a few small ones may be found on the stem. There is a suspicion that the plant is poisonous. Late June to August is the blooming time.

RANGE: Fairly abundant at higher elevations in the Rockies and north to Alaska. Also found in high places east of the Cascades.

CAT-TAIL
(*Typha latifolia*)
Bulrush - Tule

Cat-tail because of its wide distribution throughout North America and characteristic form is known to almost everyone. There is only the one species. The spongy dark brown spikes, 4" - 8" long and one inch thick, contain the pollen grains. Leaves are long, flat and about an inch wide. Indians in the Interior used the thin leaves to weave mats for use inside their summer shelters and also to make the walls of the shelter.

Cat-tails are always found in mud or shallow water where they form a dense jungle beloved by red-wing blackbirds and muskrats.

RANGE: Throughout B.C. but most plentiful around ponds and swamps of the Interior. Usually at low and middle elevations.

SCOURING RUSH
(*Equisetum hyemale*)

The scouring rush is recognized easily by its ridged green stem marked into definite sections by narrow ash-colored and black bands.

The hollow stems will pull apart into short sections. The finely ridged stems are gritty to the touch thus leading to the name. Several species with various slight differences to the above are to be found in certain localities.

RANGE: Common along the edge of Interior lakes and ponds. Also sporadic occurrence at Coast and on Vancouver Island.

COMMON HORSETAIL
(*Equisetum arvense*)

The name horsetail comes from the sterile green stems with their whorls of wire-like branches. These are the stems most commonly seen for they last all summer whereas the pale unbranched stalks occur early in the season. Horsetails have hollow jointed stems and no leaves as they are commonly thought of but the fringed scales around the stem joints actually are reduced leaves. The green sterile stems help out by performing the function of leaves. The pale brown stems bear a small cone at their tips which holds the spores or seeds. Small particles of silica give them their scouring quality.

Horsetail usually grows in a mass rather than as a stray individual. Moist sandy soils as often found in wet places along road edges are chosen. There are a half dozen or more species in B.C., but all will be recognized as horsetails.

RANGE: Damp sandy places throughout B.C. at low and middle elevations.

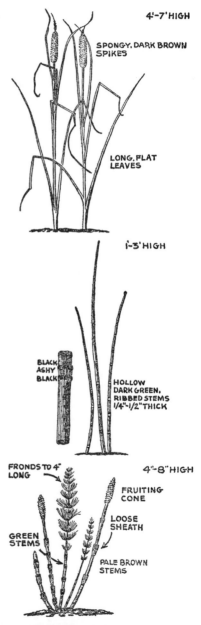

4'-7' HIGH

SPONGY, DARK BROWN SPIKES

LONG, FLAT LEAVES

1-3' HIGH

BLACK
ASHY
BLACK

HOLLOW DARK GREEN, RIBBED STEMS 1/4"-1/2" THICK

FRONDS TO 4" LONG

4"-8" HIGH

FRUITING CONE

LOOSE SHEATH

GREEN STEMS

PALE BROWN STEMS

(171)

APPENDIX

•

COMMON FERNS
NATURE'S CALENDAR
EDIBLE PLANTS
GLOSSARY

COMMON FERNS

WOODSIA (*Woodsia spp.*) is found on dry rocky places. *W. oregana* is quite abundant in the Dry Interior Zones where it is the common fern on the numerous rock slides. Its bunchy tuft of fronds are from 4" - 12" high. The fronds are smooth beneath.

RANGE: On Vancouver Island but most abundant east of Cascades. *W. scopulina* has hairy fronds and ranges across B.C. at middle and sub-alpine elevations.

PARSLEY FERN - ROCK BRAKE (*Cryptogramma acrostichoides*): A densely tufted little fern 6" - 12" high growing in rocky places at higher elevations. There are two distinct types of frond, the fertile being the taller and having its margins rolled under to enclose the spores. Ranges from Coast to Rockies but most abundant in eastern mountains.

POLYPODY - LICORICE FERN (*Polypody spp.*): The thickish roots have a licorice flavor which accounts for one common name. Often found on mossy cliffs, logs or tree trunks. A sparse fern with fronds to 12" long and 1" - 3" wide. Spores are large and round. Frond leaves are lobed to the midrib—a partial identifying feature. Species differ in the shape of the pinnae (small frond leaves). The Coastal species tends to be sharp pointed and the one east of the Cascades to be rounded.

LADY FERN (*Athyrium filix-femina*): A large graceful fern, common in damp shady woods to 4,000'. Fronds to 4' long and 10" wide arch outward. They are widest below their centre and taper in both directions. Coast and wetter regions of Interior. Alpine Lady Fern (*A. alpestre americanum*) is more stiffish in appearance with fronds rarely over 2' long and 3" wide. Ranges on rocky places at sub-alpine and alpine elevations throughout-out B.C.

MAIDENHAIR (*Adiantum pedatum aleuticum*) is the most delicate of our ferns with each tiny leaf frond fringed along the upper edge. Shiny black stems and not usually over 2' high. Often massed in damp, shady places.

RANGE: Vancouver Island and Coastal Forest Zone to elevations of 3,000', sporadic in Wet Interior.

DEER FERN (*Struthiopteris spicant*): A common fern in shady Coastal forests. Easily recognized from its two distinct types of fronds. The fertile or spore-bearing fronds shooting from the centre of the plant are often 3' high. Non-fertile or vegetative fronds are ever-green and form a low rosette. They taper toward both ends and have pinnules or leaves almost to the base.

RANGE: Vancouver Island and Coastal Forest Zone.

SWORD FERN (*Polystichum munitum*) forms dark green, symmetrical sprays of fronds to 3' long. Pinnules or side leaves are sharp-pointed and sharp-toothed. The underside is almost orange in color from twin rows of spore cases. Fronds are shipped east in large quantities for florists' decorations.

RANGE: Vancouver Island and Coastal Forest Zone.

BRACKEN (*Pteridium aquilinum pubescens*) is the most widespread and luxuriant fern in the Province. Coarse in growth and often to 6' high. Stems do not cluster from a compact base as with most ferns. A line of spore cases follow around the margins of the leaves. Found at lower elevations in coniferous forests from Vancouver Island to Rockies except in drier regions.

COMMON FERNS

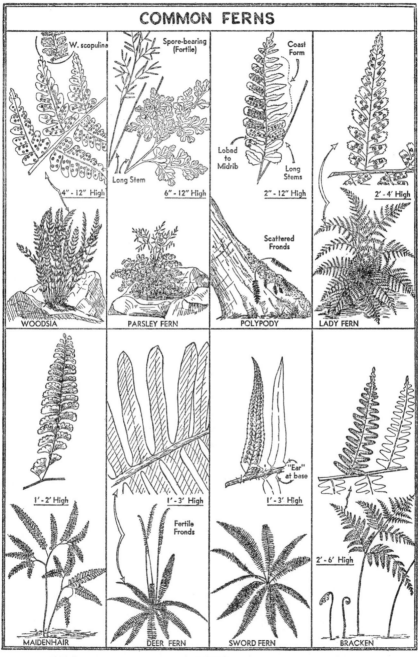

W. scopulina

Spore-bearing (Fertile)

Coast Form

Long Stem

4" - 12" High

6" - 12" High

Lobed to Midrib

Long Stems

2" - 12" High

2' - 4' High

Scattered Fronds

WOODSIA

PARSLEY FERN

POLYPODY

LADY FERN

1' - 2' High

1' - 3' High

Fertile Fronds

"Ear" at base

1' - 3' High

2' - 6' High

MAIDENHAIR

DEER FERN

SWORD FERN

BRACKEN

NATURE'S CALENDAR
FOR SOME
TREES AND SHRUBS

IN BLOOM ▇   **IN FRUIT** ▢

ADD ONE WEEK FOR EVERY 1000 FT. OF ELEVATION. ADD TWO WEEKS IF NORTH OF PRINCE GEORGE

TREES	MARCH	APRIL	MAY	JUNE	JULY	AUG.	SEPT.	OCT.	REMARKS
ARBUTUS									RED BERRIES
BLACK HAWTHORN									NO SMELL TO FLOWERS
BITTER CHERRY									RED BERRIES
W. CHOKE CHERRY									PURPLISH-BLACK BERRIES
BROADLEAF MAPLE									
DOGWOOD									MAY BLOOM TWICE A YEAR
PACIFIC CRABAPPLE									APPLE BLOSSOM FRAGRANCE

SHRUBS	MARCH	APRIL	MAY	JUNE	JULY	AUG.	SEPT.	OCT.	REMARKS
BLACKBERRY, TRAILING									
BLACK TWINBERRY									
BROOM									
CLEMATIS, WHITE									WHITE FLOWERS AND SEEDS
CURRANT, RED-FLOWER									
DEVIL'S CLUB									BRIGHT RED BERRIES
ELDER, BLUE-BERRY									
ELDER, RED-BERRY									
GOAT'S BEARD									
HARDHACK									
HAZEL									YELLOW CATKINS
HONEYSUCKLE, ORANGE									
INDIAN-PLUM									
KINNIKINNICK									SHINY RED BERRIES
LABRADOR TEA									
MAHONIA, TALL									
MOCK ORANGE									
NINEBARK									
OCEAN SPRAY									
RED-OSIER DOGWOOD									WHITE BERRIES
SALAL									
SALMONBERRY									
SASKATOON BERRY									
SILVERBERRY									
SNOWBRUSH									
SOOPOLALLIE									
THIMBLEBERRY									
TWINBERRY, RED									
TWIN-FLOWER									SWEET PERFUME
WAXBERRY									WHITE BERRIES TO MIDWINTER
WILD ROSE									HIPS LAST ALL WINTER

(176)

NATURE'S CALENDAR
FOR SOME
COASTAL FLOWERS

* ALSO FOUND EAST OF CASCADES (Coast Range) ADD ONE WEEK FOR EVERY 1000 FT. OF ELEVATION

ALL BLOOMING PERIODS ▬▬▬ SOLID LINES

FLOWERS	MARCH	APRIL	MAY	JUNE	JULY	AUGUST	SEPT.	REMARKS
* ALUMROOT			■	■				SEVERAL SPECIES
ASTER, DOUGLAS					■	■	■	
AVENS, LARGE-LEAVED				■				
* BLEEDING HEART		■	■	■				MINOR OCCURRENCE IN INTERIOR
* BLUEBELLS				■	■			MOST COMMON IN INTERIOR
* BLUE-EYED GRASS			■					PEACE RIVER DISTRICT
* BLUE-EYED MARY		■	■					
* BLUE SAILORS				■	■			
* BUNCHBERRY				■	■			MAY BLOOM AGAIN IN LATE SUMMER
* BUTTERCUP		■	■					
CAMAS		■	■					TWO SPECIES
* CAMAS, DEATH			■	■				
* CANADA MINT					■	■		
* CHOCOLATE LILY		■	■					
* COLTS FOOT	■	■						
* COLUMBINE			■	■				
* CORAL ROOT				■				MANY DIFFERENT SPECIES
* COTTON GRASS			■	■				FLUFFY COTTON BALL
* COW PARSNIP			■	■				
* DELPHINIUM		■	■					DRY, EXPOSED PLACES
EASTER LILY		■	■					
FAIRY BELLS, OREGON			■	■				SIMILAR SPECIES FOUND IN INTERIOR
* FALSE LADY'S SLIPPER			■	■				
FALSE BUGBANE			■	■				FOLLOWED BY RED BERRIES
* FALSE SOLOMON'S SEAL			■	■				
FIELD CHAMOMILE				■	■			
FIELD CHICKWEED		■	■	■				
* FIREWEED				■	■			
* FOAM FLOWER			■	■	■			
FRINGE CUPS		■	■	■				
* GOLDENROD					■	■		
GROUNDSEL, COMMON			■	■	■	■		
* GUMWEED						■		
* HEDGE NETTLE				■	■			ONE SPECIES IN INTERIOR
* HELLEBORE, INDIAN				■	■			
* INDIAN PAINTBRUSH			■	■	■			SPECIES FOUND AT LOWER LEVELS
INDIAN PIPE				■	■			
* LUPINE		■	■	■				
* MINER'S LETTUCE		■	■	■				

(177)

COASTAL FLOWERS (Continued)

FLOWERS	MARCH	APRIL	MAY	JUNE	JULY	AUGUST	SEPT.	REMARKS
*MINER'S LETTUCE, SIBERIAN								
*MONKEY FLOWER, RED					■	■		HIGH MOUNTAINS
*MONKEY FLOWER, YELLOW				■	■	■		GREAT ALTITUDINAL RANGE
*MONTIA			■	■				
*NETTLE, STINGING			■	■				
*ONION, HOOKER'S				■				
*OXEYE DAISY				■	■			LIMITED EAST OF CASCADES
*PEACOCK	■							
*PEARLY EVERLASTING					■	■		
*PIPSISSEWA				■				
*PURPLE PEA			■	■				
*PUSSY TOES, ROSY & WHITE		■	■					
*PYROLA				■	■			
*RATTLESNAKE PLANTAIN					■	■		MANY PLANTS DON'T BLOOM
*SATIN FLOWER		■						
*SAXIFRAGE		■						
*SKUNK CABBAGE		■						
*SEA BLUSH			■					SOME SPECIES IN INTERIOR
*SELF HEAL				■	■			
*SILVER-GREEN			■	■	■			
*SILVERWEED				■	■			FLOWERS INCONSPICUOUS
*SPRING GOLD			■	■				
*STAR FLOWER			■	■				
*STAR-FLOWERED SOL. SEAL			■	■				
*STONECROP				■				
*TANSY						■		
*THISTLE, COMMON					■	■		
THRIFT				■				SEA COAST PLANT
*WILD TIGER LILY				■	■			
*TRILLIUM, WESTERN		■	■					
*TWISTED STALK			■	■				
*WATER PARSNIP				■				
WILD LILY-OF-THE-VALLEY				■				RUBY BERRIES AFTER FLOWERS
WOOLY SUNFLOWER				■				POSSIBLY IN CENTRAL B.C. ALSO
*VANILLA LEAF			■					
*VIOLET, BLUE		■						
*VIOLET, YELLOW				■	■			
*YARROW				■	■	■		
*QUEEN'S CUP				■	■			BLUE BERRY AFTER FLOWER

(178)

NATURE'S CALENDAR
FOR
INTERIOR FLOWERS

FLOWERS	REMARKS
ALUMROOT, OVAL-LEAF	
ARNICA, HEART-LEAF	
ASTER, LARGE PURPLE	
AVENS, LONG-PLUMED, PURPLE	COMMON ROADSIDE FLOWER
BEARD TONGUE, SCOULER'S	
BEARD TONGUE, LITTLE FLW.	
BITTERROOT	VERY DRY PLACES
BROWN-EYED SUSAN	
CACTUS	
CINQUE FOILS	
ERIOGONUM, TALL WHITE	OTHER SIMILAR SPECIES
FLEABANE, LARGE PURPLE	
FLEABANE, WHITE	
GERANIUM, STICKY	
JACOB'S LADDER, BLUE	FROM LOW TO HIGH ELEVATIONS
LADIES TRESSES	
LOCOWEED	SEVERAL SPECIES
LILY, MARIPOSA	PALE PURPLE FLOWER
LILY, MOUNTAIN	ORANGE RED
LILY, SNOW	YELLOW
ONION, NODDING	
MEADOW RUE	DEPENDING ON ELEVATION
MILKWEED	
MOCCASIN FLOWER	
MONKSHOOD	IN MOIST MOUNTAINS
OYSTER PLANT	LIMITED OCCURRENCE ON V.I.
PASQUE FLOWER	EASTERN B.C.
PHACELIA	
PHLOX	SOUTH OKANAGAN
PHLOX, DOUGLAS	WINDERMERE
RAGWORT, GIANT	
SCARLET GILIA	RED TRUMPETS
SPRING SUNFLOWERS	
VERONICA	
WATER KNOTWEED	PINK CONES
WATERLEAF, BALLHEAD	LOW TO HIGH ELEVATIONS
WATER PLANTAIN	SWAMPY PLACES
YELLOW BELL	OKANAGAN
YELLOW POND LILY	

Months across the chart: MARCH, APRIL, MAY, JUNE, JULY, AUGUST, SEPT.

EDIBLE PLANTS

Other than well known berries.

NAME	EDIBLE PARTS	PREPARATION	SEASON
Bitterroot	Thick roots	Peeled and boiled	May
Bracken	Young shoots and roots	Shoots boiled—roots roasted	April - August
Bunchberry	Red berry	Eaten raw	August - September
Camas	Bulb	Boiled or roasted	April - May
Cow Parsnip	Young flower stems	Peel and use raw in salad or cook as greens	May - June
Fireweed	Stem centers	Split stalk and eat raw	June - August
Kinnikinnick	Red berry	Eaten raw	September - December
Mahonia (Oregon Grape)	Blue berries	Raw after first frosts	September - November
Milkweed	Young leaves or seed pods	Boiled	June or August
Miner's Lettuce	Leaves and stems	Raw in salads	April - May
Mountain Lily	Bulb	Boiled	June-July
Rice Root	Bulb	Boiled	April - May
Oyster Plant	Root or young shoots	Boiled	Spring or Fall
Salmonberry	Young stem shoots	Eaten raw	April - May
Siberian Miner's Lettuce	Leaves and stems	Raw in salads	April - May
Spring Sunflower	Root or seeds	Root boiled—seeds raw	May
Thimbleberry	Young stem shoots	Eaten raw	April - May
Wild Onions	Bulb	Boiled	May - July
Wild Roses	Outer part of fruit or hips	Eaten raw	September - December
Wild Tiger Lily	Bulb	Boiled	May - July

NOTE — When leaves or stems are boiled one or two waters should be thrown away to eliminate any bitterness.

The berries of the following plants are edible although not generally favored: crowberry, salal, silverberry, blue- and black-berry elder, soopolallie, wild cherries, gooseberries, currants, cloudberry, teaberry, Pacific crab-apple, hawthorne, Indian plum, thimble-berry, salmonberry, mountain ash.

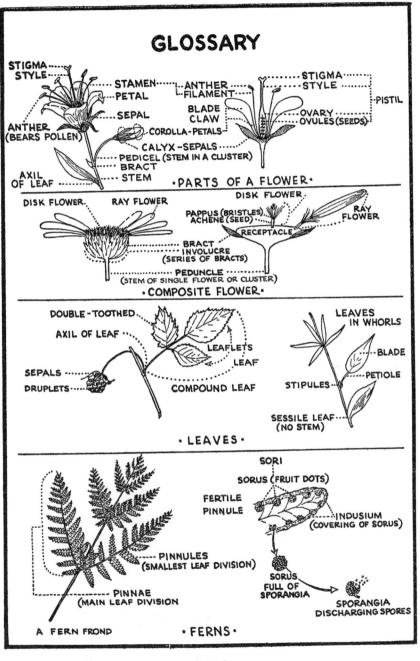

GLOSSARY

·PARTS OF A FLOWER·

STIGMA
STYLE
STAMEN
PETAL
SEPAL
ANTHER
(BEARS POLLEN)

ANTHER
FILAMENT
BLADE
CLAW
COROLLA-PETALS
CALYX-SEPALS
PEDICEL (STEM IN A CLUSTER)
BRACT
STEM

AXIL
OF LEAF

STIGMA
STYLE
PISTIL
OVARY
OVULES (SEEDS)

·COMPOSITE FLOWER·

DISK FLOWER
RAY FLOWER
DISK FLOWER
PAPPUS (BRISTLES)
ACHENE (SEED)
RAY
FLOWER
RECEPTACLE
BRACT
INVOLUCRE
(SERIES OF BRACTS)
PEDUNCLE
(STEM OF SINGLE FLOWER OR CLUSTER)

·LEAVES·

DOUBLE-TOOTHED
AXIL OF LEAF
LEAFLETS
LEAF
SEPALS
DRUPLETS
COMPOUND LEAF

LEAVES
IN WHORLS
BLADE
PETIOLE
STIPULES
SESSILE LEAF
(NO STEM)

·FERNS·

SORI
SORUS (FRUIT DOTS)
FERTILE
PINNULE
INDUSIUM
(COVERING OF SORUS)
PINNULES
(SMALLEST LEAF DIVISION)
SORUS
FULL OF
SPORANGIA
SPORANGIA
DISCHARGING SPORES
PINNAE
(MAIN LEAF DIVISION
A FERN FROND

INDEX